An Assessment Model to Foster the Adoption of Agile Software Product Lines in the Automotive Domain

Von der Fakultät für Elektrotechnik und Informatik
der Gottfried Wilhelm Leibniz Universität Hannover
zur Erlangung des Grades

Doktor der Ingenieurwissenschaften

Dr.-Ing.

genehmigte Dissertation von

M.ENG.

PHILIPP NIKOLAUS HOHL

GEBOREN AM 28.03.1988

IN RAVENSBURG

2019

Referent: Prof. Dr. Kurt Schneider
1. Korreferent: Prof. Dr. Jürgen Münch
2. Korreferentin: Prof. Dr.-Ing. Astrid Nieße

Tag der Promotion: 11.02.2019

Bibliografische Information der Deutschen Nationalbibliothek

Die Deutsche Nationalbibliothek verzeichnet diese Publikation in der
Deutschen Nationalbibliografie; detaillierte bibliografische Daten sind
im Internet über http://dnb.d-nb.de abrufbar.

ISBN 978-3-8325-4879-7

Logos Verlag Berlin GmbH
Comeniushof, Gubener Str. 47,
10243 Berlin
Tel.: +49 (0)30 42 85 10 90
Fax: +49 (0)30 42 85 10 92
INTERNET: https://www.logos-verlag.de

Acknowledgments

This dissertation was supervised by Prof. Dr. Kurt Schneider from Leibniz Universität Hannover and Prof. Dr. Jürgen Münch from the Hermann Hollerith Zentrum (Reutlingen University). In addition, this thesis would not have been possible without the people who encouraged and supported me in my work for the last three years. I thank ...

- my supervisor Prof. Dr. Kurt Schneider for giving me the opportunity to write this thesis in the context of the software engineering group at Leibniz Universität Hannover. Although there was a large physical distance he always supported me comprehensively with good advice and guidance. I really appreciate the fact that he and his team fully integrated me even though I was the external doctoral candidate from the south of Germany.

- my supervisor Prof. Dr. Jürgen Münch. On account of the physical distance to the Leibniz Universität Hannover it would not have been possible without the close cooperation with Reutlingen University, the Herman Hollerith Zentrum and in particular with Jürgen. The cooperation between both supervisors and universities led to optimal working conditions. Jürgen had an open ear for my problems at anytime and from wherever I was calling. He further introduced me to the agile community of Finland and thereby helped kick starting my research in the beginning. Thanks for the valuable guidance, advice, and encouragements throughout the last three years.

- my colleague Michael Stupperich for his endless patience with me. The fact that we were sitting face-to-face in one room opened up the possibility for discussing numerous questions. Thanks for the great support, guidance, feedback, and jokes which all helped to improve this thesis significantly.

- my direct supervisor Thomas Gantner, for giving me the chance to fill the vacant doctoral student position within his department. With his extensive knowledge regarding ASPICE and assessment procedures he was the perfect discussion partner for issues in conducting and setting up the assessment model. His review on the initial model improved the quality of the ASPLA Model in an early development stage.

- my colleagues at Daimler AG, in particular Ralf Neumann, Dr. Hannes Omasreiter, Heike Frank, Claudia Schlumpberger, Carsten König and Elke Baar. I really enjoyed

iv *ACKNOWLEDGMENTS*

the time with each of them and felt being in good hands. We had good constructive talks with technical or informal background and I have learned a lot.

- the Daimler AG for funding my research.

- the PhD students from Leibniz Universität Hannover, in particular Daniel Gritzner, Fabian Kortum, Oliver Karras, Tobias Baum and Carolin Unger-Windeler,

- the PhD students from Reutlingen University, in particular Matthias Gutbrod,

- the PhD students conducting their research in neighbor departments at Daimler AG, in particular Andreas Freymann, Alexander Nikic and Katharina Juhnke. Thank you guys for the discussions on how to produce valuable scientific work.

- Jil Klünder, who started her doctoral studies at the same time. She was an excellent co-author, manuscript reviewer and discussion partner throughout the years of my research. Thanks for endless hours of Skype™ sessions.

- Arie van Bennekum for his ability to inspire other people with the agile mindset. His profitable workshop really helped me a lot to stay on the right track with regard to agile.

- all the study participants, co-authors, students and reviewers who delivered valuable input which contributed my research and finally ended up in this thesis. Special thanks go to Ryan Lockard and James Gifford from the global agile practitioner coalition, Joachim Pfeffer from the Agile Automotive Team, and Martin Becker, Sven Theobald and Philipp Diebold from the Fraunhofer Institute for Experimental Software Engineering IESE.

- my friend Tobias Fleischer and his wife Julia for proof-reading this thesis several times.

- my family for their support and understanding. And the most important thank goes to my wife Daniela and my daughter Pia for their endless patience, and encouragement in times of heavy workload.

Abstract

The automotive industry is changing rapidly. E-Mobility, self-driving and other trends revolutionize the automotive industry. These trends have to be addressed when developing new car generations and future mobility solutions. This is challenging for the automotive domain with its special peculiarities such as rigid quality and safety requirements, deep integration between hardware and software, strong focus on development processes, and strong supplier involvement. Traditionally, software product lines have been used to cope with the large amount of software in cars by means of software reuse. Anyhow, there is a lack of knowledge about how to react flexibly on rapid changes with software product line development. The use of agile software development methods promises a flexible development with the possibility to react fast to changes. This raises the question, whether a combination of agile software development with software product lines is appropriate for the automotive domain.

One major goal of this thesis was to identify the factors that hinder or support the adoption of agile practices in the automotive domain. For this purpose, an interview study with 16 industrial participants was conducted. The results revealed two important insights: First, the structured software reuse approach, which is often implemented via software product line engineering is too inflexible to address rapid changes of requirements. The development processes currently used are seen as one of the most hindering factors to introduce agile software development. Second, there is a lack of experience on how to combine agile software development with software product lines. These results were also supported by a literature study that was conducted in addition to the interview study. Both, the literature and the interview study revealed the necessity to combine agile practices with software product lines for automotive software development. The general research question was: How to establish an agile software product line in the automotive domain.

Therefore, another essential goal of this thesis was to develop an approach for supporting organizations with the establishment of agile software product lines. In order to fulfill this goal, an assessment and improvement model, the so-called Agile Software Product Lines in Automotive Model (ASPLA Model), was developed to foster the adoption of agile software product lines in the automotive domain. The ASPLA Model identifies improvement potential for a change towards agile software product lines and provides a prioritized list of recommendations on how to combine agile software development with software product lines within the assessed development process. Main characteristics of the ASPLA Model are the compatibility with the widely-used

ASPICE model, the integration of a new product-focused category and empirically-based recommendations.

The evaluation of the ASPLA Model included its integration into the technical infrastructure of the business environment. In order to evaluate the ASPLA Model, the validation strategy was divided into two consecutive phases: an iterative learning phase and a case study. The case study compared the results from the ASPLA Model with the assessment results from experts. The evaluation of the ASPLA Model indicated that the assessment can help to foster the combination of agile software development with software product lines in the automotive domain. In comparison with experts' assessments and recommendations, the model produced similar or even better results.

Key Words: agile software development, software product line, assessment models, ASPLA model, software process improvement, software engineering, hybrid software development, automotive domain, embedded software development

Zusammenfassung

Die Automobilindustrie durchläuft derzeit einen rapiden Wandel. E-Mobilität, selbstfahrende Autos und andere Trends revolutionieren die Automobilindustrie. Diese Trends müssen bei der Entwicklung neuer Fahrzeuggenerationen und zukünftiger Mobilitätslösungen berücksichtigt werden. Für die Automobilbranche mit ihren Besonderheiten wie z. B. strikten Qualitäts- und Sicherheitsanforderungen, dem engen Zusammenspiel von Hard- und Software, der Vorgabe von definierten Entwicklungsprozessen sowie einer hohen Lieferantenbeteiligung stellt dies eine Herausforderung dar. Üblicherweise dient die Wiederverwendung von Software innerhalb einer Software-Produktlinie dazu, die Fülle an Software im Auto zu bewältigen. Dennoch mangelt es an Erfahrung, wie innerhalb der Software-Produktlinien-Entwicklung flexibel auf schnelle Änderungen reagiert werden kann. Der Einsatz von agilen Entwicklungsmethoden verspricht eine flexible Entwicklung und die Möglichkeit, schnell auf Änderungen reagieren zu können. Daher stellt sich die Frage, ob eine Kombination von agiler Softwareentwicklung und Software-Produktlinien für die Automobilbranche geeignet ist.

Ein wichtiges Ziel dieser Dissertation war es, Einflussfaktoren zu identifizieren, die eine Einführung von agilen Methoden in der Automobilbranche verhindern oder unterstützen. Für diesen Zweck wurde eine Interview-Studie mit 16 Teilnehmern aus der Industrie durchgeführt. Daraus resultieren zwei wichtige Erkenntnisse: Erstens ist die strukturierte Softwarewiederverwendung innerhalb von Software-Produktlinien zu unflexibel, um die schnellen Änderungen der Anforderungen zu berücksichtigen. Die existierenden Entwicklungsprozesse werden als eines der größten Hemmnisse für die Einführung von agiler Softwareentwicklung angesehen. Zweitens mangelt es an Erfahrung, wie agile Softwareentwicklung und Software-Produktlinien im Automobilbereich kombiniert werden können. Diese Erkenntnisse werden durch eine Literaturstudie unterstützt, welche zusätzlich zur Interview-Studie durchgeführt wurde. Beide Studien offenbarten die Notwendigkeit, agile Praktiken und Software-Produktlinien für die Softwareentwicklung im Automobilbereich zu kombinieren. Die allgemeine Forschungsfrage war, wie agile Software-Produktlinien im Automobilbereich eingeführt werden können.

Daher war ein weiteres wichtiges Ziel dieser Dissertation, einen Ansatz zu entwickeln, der Unternehmen bei der Einführung von agilen Software-Produktlinien unterstützt. Für dieses Ziel wurde ein Assessment- und Verbesserungsmodell – das sogenannte „Agile Software Product Lines in Automotive Model" (ASPLA Modell) – entwickelt, das die Einführung unterstützt. Das ASPLA Modell identifiziert Verbesserungspotentiale für einen Wandel hin zu agilen Software-Produktlinien und bietet eine priorisierte Liste von

Vorschlägen, wie beide Ansätze im Kontext des assessierten Entwicklungsprozesses kombiniert werden können. Hauptmerkmale des ASPLA Modells sind die Kompatibilität mit dem weit verbreiteten ASPICE Modell, die Einführung einer neuen produktorientierten Kategorie und empirisch gestützte Empfehlungen.

Die Evaluierung des ASPLA Modells beinhaltete seine Integration in die technische Infrastruktur des Unternehmens. Zudem wurde die Evaluierungsstrategie in zwei aufeinanderfolgende Phasen unterteilt: Eine iterative Lernphase und eine Fallstudie. Die Fallstudie verglich die Ergebnisse des ASPLA Modells mit den Ergebnissen von Experten. Die Evaluation des ASPLA Modells zeigte, dass das Assessment eine Kombination von agiler Softwareentwicklung und Software-Produktlinien in der Automobilbranche unterstützen kann. Im Vergleich mit den Assessments und den Vorschlägen der Experten lieferte das Model vergleichbare oder sogar bessere Ergebnisse.

Schlagwörter: agile Softwareentwicklung, Software Produktlinien, Assessmentmodelle, ASPLA Modell, Prozessverbesserung, Softwareentwicklung, hybride Entwicklungsmethoden, Automobilbranche, Embedded Software

Contents

List of Figures

List of Tables

Acronyms

AHAA	Agile, Hybrid Assessment Method for the Automotive Industry
APLE	Agile Product Line Engineering
ASD	Agile Software Development
ASIL	Automotive Safety Integrity Level
ASPICE	Automotive SPICE®
ASPL	Agile Software Product Line
ASPLA	Agile Software Product Line in Automotive
CI	Continuous Integration
CMMI	Capability Maturity Model Integration
D3	Design Driven Development
DoD	Definition of Done
DSDM	Dynamic Systems Development Method
ECU	Electronic Control Unit
FDD	Feature Driven Development
FEF	Family Evaluation Framework
HC	Honeycomb
HIL	Hardware in the Loop
HIS	Herstellerinitiative Software
IATM	Integrated Agile Transformation Model®
IP	Intellectual Property
LSEF	Legacy Software Evaluation Framework

MS-SPLE Mega Scale - Software Product Line Engineering

NATO North Atlantic Treaty Organization

OEM Original Equipment Manufacturer

PO Product Owner

PROFES International Conference on Product-Focused Software Process Improvement

RCMM Reuse Capability Maturity Model

RUG Rapid application development User Group

SAFe Scaled Agile Framework

SCAMPI Standard CMMI Appraisal Method for Process Improvement

ScrumPL Software Product Line Engineering with Scrum

SIG Special Interest Group

SME Small and Medium-sized Enterprise

SPICE Software Process Improvement and Capability Determination

SPLC International Systems and Software Product Line Conference

SoS Scrum of Scrum

SPI Software Process Improvement

SPL Software Product Line

SPLE Software Product Line Engineering

SSPL Software and Systems Product Line

TDD Test Driven Development

UML Unified Modeling Language™

VDA Verband der Automobilindustrie

WebApp Web Application

XP Extreme Programming

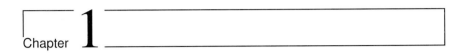

Chapter **1**

Introduction

This chapter describes the main challenges addressed by this thesis. It defines the research questions, as well as the goals and hypotheses. Furthermore, it presents the research contribution. Finally, the thesis structure is outlined.

1.1 Background and Motivation

Within the last decades, the amount of software and systems that rely on software has increased significantly. This rise is still an ongoing trend. Software surrounds us and is present in all areas of our daily life. According to Thomas [246], about 86% of the world's population own a smartphone. He mentions that there are more than 6 billion cellphone subscriptions. Nowadays, every smartphone can remotely control things. We use it to control our smart homes from all around the world. Furthermore, we are driving cars which are getting smarter and are connected to the environment. All over the world, people are craving for new technological enhancements and electronic devices. This desire can be observed in all industry sectors.

The automotive domain is recently in a disruptive change. E-Mobility, self-driving, and community owned cars are new technologies and upcoming market trends in the automotive domain [185]. Vehicles are no longer isolated but connected to the environment [241]. Upcoming challenges and market trends need to be addressed in the development of new car generations in order to cope with new ways of mobility. A lot of innovation for automobiles' functionalities is nowadays addressed in software.

According to Oliveira [196], 85% of the automobiles' functionalities are realized with software running on Electronic Control Units (ECUs). The amount of software has evolved from zero to tens of millions of lines of code [210], distributed on up to 70 ECUs [39, 184]. Broy [25] identified the increasing amount of software already in 2006. He stated that the amount of software in the car has increased exponentially in the last decades [25]. McCaffery et al. [176] expect that the quantity of software grows continuously. They further emphasize that software must be developed faster and in a more cost effective way, but still in high quality [176].

1.1.1 Quality Aspects and the Need for Software Reuse

The reuse of software parts is necessary to develop the large amount of different software variants, while simultaneously maintaining the quality of the software. Software product lines are a software paradigm for systematic software reuse [157]. This paradigm is particularly important for the automotive domain to meet different requirements across multiple markets [245]. Software product lines help to manage changes, coordinate the worldwide software development, and increase the software quality by the reuse strategy. Furthermore, the software variants enable a customization and individualization to meet customers' requirements and generate more value for the core business [109].

According to Wozniak et al. [267], the automotive domain is the most challenging environment for systems and software product line engineering. They identify a "very large number of individually complex products with incomparably rich feature variation" [267, p.336]. The variability in the software is made explicit through variation points which introduce the possibility to delay the design decision during the development [24]. Automotive software platforms can easily incorporate thousands of variation points and configuration parameters [245, 73]. The final decision, whether a feature is part of a specific product or not, is known as the binding time [259]. One can distinguish between four different binding times: during programming, at the integration, in the assembly, and during runtime [157]. All of them are used in the automotive domain. The consistency and the reliability of systems has to be ensured at all times [157]. Therefore, it is necessary to link and manage the variation points throughout all phases of the full product life cycle, such as requirements elicitation, implementation, test processes, and at the client's premises.

1.1.2 The Demand for Faster Software Development

Traditional working structures make it difficult to deliver the large amount of software fast enough [25], because the development processes are too slow to keep pace with the fast changing market [23]. Future challenges will likely be addressed in software and need flexible development processes to react on changing market demands. Furthermore, it is important to keep the development time short [221], in order to achieve business goals and release the software faster to the market to generate profit. However, currently used development processes have shown to be insufficient for handling such an exponential growth of software [63].

The development processes need to be redesigned in a way that allows to learn and adapt continuously at a fast pace. Agile methods are promising approaches to address these new challenges. Since 2001, agile software development methods promise an improved software development with a faster time to market and an increasing speed of learning. In addition, agile development practice offer the possibility to react on changing requirements and to refine the final software during the development process. The adaption of agile practices within the automotive domain is therefore a possible way to keep pace with fast changing market demands [140].

1.1.3 Development Process and Agile Transformation

The combination of agile software development and software product lines in the automotive domain is assumed to be difficult [140]. Agile methods are not tailored to the specific characteristics of the automotive domain. Although there have been efforts to apply agile methods in the automotive domain, widespread adoptions have not yet taken place.

Agile methods and practices are primarily designed for short development cycles in small development teams. One benefit of agile software development is that the used methods emphasize collaboration and communication between development teams as well as between the customer and developers [10]. Product Owners (POs) define requirements in terms of business value and collaborate with the development teams. For larger teams, agile methods are scaled up to approaches for large organizations, such as the Scaled Agile Framework (SAFe) or Scrum of Scrum (SoS). The scaled frameworks aim to maintain an open communication culture within the development team and between development teams. This is challenging whenever the software development is distributed all over the world [213]. In the automotive domain, software product lines are used to manage the global software development [245]. This leads to communication overhead for worldwide coordination, with several included POs. The POs are responsible for different markets and different model ranges. It is important for a global software development that Product Owners are consistent regarding the requirements to maintain the software product line. However, the worldwide scoping process and the need to find common solutions hinders short iterations [108].

Therefore, it is necessary to combine agile software development with software product line engineering to shorten the time to market and to meet customer and market demands even better. Furthermore, this combination promises an improved long-term productivity, efficiency, and profit [173].

1.2 Research Scope

The research scope of this thesis can be described along the three areas *Automotive Domain, Agile Software Development* and *Software Product Lines* as follows (cf. Figure 1.1):

1.2.1 Automotive Domain

In 2007, Pretschner et al. [209] characterized the automotive domain and presented five salient features of the automotive software domain. They mention the (1) "heterogeneous nature of the software, [(2)] the organization of labor, [(3)] the distributed nature of automotive software, [(4)] the huge number of variants and configurations, [(5)] and the predominance of unit-based cost models" [209, p. 4]. The research presented in this thesis is limited to automotive embedded software development with its special peculiarities, such as rigid quality and safety requirements [245]. Furthermore, the software development must consider deep integration between hardware and software, strong focus on development processes and strong supplier involvement [108].

This thesis focuses on improvements in the development of embedded software by the use of automotive specific assessment models. In the automotive domain, existing Software Process Improvement (SPI) approaches utilize well-established assessment models such as ASPICE [260] or Capability Maturity Model Integration (CMMI) [243] to push software process improvement [196]. The assessment and improvement model described in this thesis may be applicable to domains other than automotive software engineering. However, this is not its intended purpose. Other domains generally have different peculiarities, so the model might not be applicable or must be tailored to the context specific characteristics.

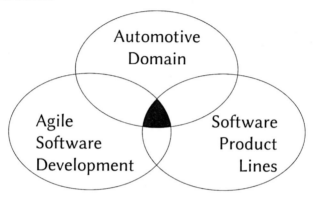

Figure 1.1: Overview of thesis scope

1.2.2 Agile Software Development

The definition of agility used in this study is the definition presented by Conboy and Fitzgerald [38, p. 110]: "the continual readiness of an entity to rapidly or inherently, proactively or reactively, embrace change, through high quality, simplistic, economical components and relationships with its environment." The research presented in this thesis is not limited to a specific agile method, such as Scrum [225] or Extreme Programming (XP) [12]. By identifying the software development demands of an organization and by complementing this knowledge with existing development processes, context specific agile practices such as pair programming or Continuous Integration (CI) are selected.

However, the gained knowledge about the applicability of agile practices and the identified benefits detected in the design of the assessment and improvement model can also be used by other organizations in the regulated domain.

1.2.3 Software Product Lines

This research maintains the benefits of software reuse introduced by the use of a software product line. The maintained benefits include large-scale productivity gains, increased product quality, and improved ability to apply mass customization [91]. This thesis uses the terminology from software product line development to derive an assessment and improvement model to combine agile software development with software product lines in the automotive domain.

1.3 Research Approach

This section describes the research approach of this thesis. In order to address the problem scientifically and to validate the solution, the research presented in this thesis follows the Design-Science Research guidelines proposed by Hevner and Chatterjee [99]. The decision to select this approach is based on the comparison performed by Peffers et al. [201]. They compared influential literature on Design-Science Research [201]. Peffers et al. [201] introduce a methodology that serves as a commonly accepted framework for carrying out research. This framework is based on Design-Science Research principles [99, 100]. The structure of the thesis, containing research activities and corresponding publications, is structured along the three areas represented by the Information Systems Research Framework [100].

The Design-Science Research Framework by Hevner and Chatterjee [99] is based on the general design cycle, which they have adopted from Vaishnavi and Kuechler [256]. The general design cycle consists of five process steps, the *awareness of the problem*, the *suggestion*, the *development*, an *evaluation*, and the *conclusion*. Figure 1.2 summarizes the process steps. As mentioned by Vaishnavi and Kuechler [257], the evaluation phase gains additional information in the construction and running of the artifact. Therefore, the evaluation phase is mentioned twice in Figure 1.2 to emphasize this incremental evaluation process to feed back the information to another round of suggestion. In addition, Figure 1.2 sets the Information Systems Research Framework by Hevner et al. [100] into correlation with the Design-Science Research Process by Vaishnavi and Kuechler [257].

The Information Systems Research Framework by Hevner et al. [100] is a conceptual framework for understanding, executing, and evaluating research combining behavioral-science and design-science paradigms. This research process is separated into the areas of *Environment, Artifact*, and *Knowledge Base*. The areas are connected by the relevance cycle, the rigor cycle, and the design cycle.

In the environment, existing technology infrastructure, applications, communication architectures, and development capabilities are assessed to define the needs or "problems" as perceived by the researcher [100]. The relevance cycle assures the needs of the environment and, consequently, the research relevance. The rigor cycle investigates if published solutions exist for the identified needs of the environment in the literature. It further identifies literature that might solve or help in solving the problem. Resulting from both cycles, the rigor and the relevance cycle, the artifact is designed. This step is also referred to as the design cycle. This cycle verifies that the artifact behaves as expected. Feedback is included and as the last step, the results are reported. The following outlines the five steps according to Vaishnavi and Kuechler [257]:

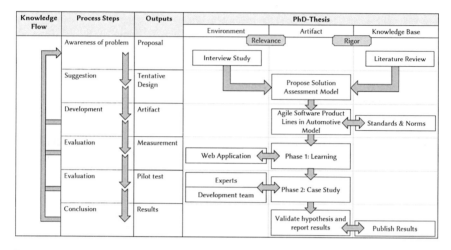

Figure 1.2: Research activities and their relationship to the Information Systems Research Framework by Hevner et al. [100]

Step 1: Awareness of problem. A case study within the automotive domain leads to the awareness of a research problem. The identified problem results from the idea to combine agile software development with development processes using software product lines to manage the reuse of software. An analysis of current state of the art and state of the practice is performed to get an overview of already existing solutions and further challenges that need to be overcome to solve the issue. The result of this process step indicates that there is a need for research in this field.

Step 2: Suggestion. This process step proposes a tentative solution. Ideas on how to solve the challenges identified in the previous process step are combined to a first solution. The need for an assessment model and improvement model to evaluate the current status and to support the combination of agile elements and software product lines within the automotive domain is identified.

Step 3: Development. The tentative solution is further developed and implemented in this phase. The assessment model is further specified in detail. It is important to select the relevant process area to improve the development with agile practices or product line approaches, while maintaining the existing development benefits. This initial assessment to combine agile software development and software product lines in the automotive domain is supported by the developed ASPLA Assessment Model. The main contribution of this step is the development of the ASPLA Model, which can be used as an assessment and improvement model to identify the maturity of agile software product lines in the automotive domain.

Step 4: Evaluation. The evaluation phase is an iterative process step to evaluate the artifact. This phase often results in additional information for the construction of the artifact. The artifact is therefore adjusted and reevaluated. A review with domain and assessment experts is conducted in order to validate the assessment model. The validity is further extended by the construction of the model including currently valid standards and norms for software development in the automotive domain. To validate the research hypotheses, a case study is performed. Therefore, an assessment is conducted with development teams. The results are compared against ad-hoc assessments by experienced assessors.

Step 5: Conclusion. The conclusion is the final step of the research process and ends in a result which is satisficing. In this phase, the results are published and conclusions are drawn. Hevner et al. [100] stated that the communication is very important in research. With the publication of the results, the environment and knowledge base benefit from the research.

1.4 Goals

The objective for solving the identified problems is to come up with an integrated approach for improving and transforming an automotive organization towards agile software product lines.
According to the presented objective and considering the aforementioned limitations, the main goal of this thesis is to foster software process improvement by the use of an assessment model to assess development processes to identify the applicability of agile methods in combination with software product lines. Combining agile approaches and their respective activities with software product lines in the automotive domain could lead to higher quality of software at an earlier stage in the development process and a faster learning cycle. An assessment model could help to identify potential improvement areas and gives recommendations to introduce agile software product lines in a structured way. To answer the main goal, three sub goals are identified to increase the knowledge in particular areas.

G1.1: Analyze and compare different approaches to establish an agile software product line in the automotive domain.
In order to provide a context specific approach that fosters the establishment of agile software product lines in the automotive domain, it is not sufficient to know already existing agile transformation frameworks. Different approaches provide different benefits and have different drawbacks when agile software development and software product lines need to be combined.

G1.2: Analyze problems with existing assessment model for introducing agile software product lines in the automotive domain.
Currently, process assessments are used in the automotive domain to evaluate the processes of an organizational unit against a predefined process assessment model. Assessing the current status of the development is a prerequisite for a successful combination of agile methods and software product lines in the automotive domain. However, it is necessary to analyze existing assessment models to identify problems regarding the introduction of agile software product lines in the automotive domain. Furthermore, this goal aims at identifying which parts of existing assessments can and need to be included in the specific approach and which parts can be omitted.

G1.3: Develop a domain specific assessment model for the combination of agile development and software product lines.
Currently, existing assessments in the automotive domain depend on expert knowledge and the experience of the assessor. For the combination of agile software development and software product lines, an assessor must be capable to assess both topics. With the domain specific assessment, a structured method to identify the most important fields for improvement is provided. Therefore, the approach provides a ranking on the fields for improvement to schedule tasks in order to establish agile software product lines in the automotive domain as optimal as possible.

1.5   Research Questions

As outlined in Section 1.1, a combination of agile software development and software product lines is desired and necessary to keep pace with market demands. The results of a case study [110, 107] reveals that there is currently no structured approach to combine agile development practices with software product lines in the automotive domain. In addition, a literature review [104] revealed that there exists no specific approach tailored to the automotive domain handling the combination of agile software development and software product lines. The general research question that emerges is:

RQ1: How to establish an agile software product line in the automotive domain?

Schloßer et al. [221] state that embedded software development benefits significantly from the introduction of agile methods. However, an agile transformation of software development in the automotive domain while still preserving software product lines have not yet taken place [146]. The general question evinces how an agile transformation of software development in the automotive domain can be established. Based on the general question, the following specific sub-questions have been identified:

RQ1.1: What are appropriate methods to establish an agile software product line? This research question examines three possible strategies to establish an agile software product line. For each strategy, appropriate methods are identified. The first strategy is to enrich a working software product line development with agile methods and practices. The second strategy is to extend agile development processes with a software reuse strategy. Finally, the agile software product line can introduce both at the same time. Depending on the initial situation and the context, the appropriate method and strategy to establish an agile software product line varies.

RQ1.2: Which tasks are relevant for improvement and transformation towards agile software product lines? Sharp and Hall [229] identify that the adoption of agile practices often starts in an uncoordinated way. The combination of agile software methods and software product lines in the automotive domain often fails due to the lack of a structured improvement approach. This research question aims at identifying the relevant tasks for a structured transformation towards an agile software product line.

RQ1.3: What are problems with using assessment models for introducing agile software product lines? Current software development in the automotive domain is heavily structured by standardized processes. Process assessments are used to evaluate the processes of an organizational unit against a predefined process assessment model. The most popular standards in the automotive domain are the Capability Maturity Model Integration (CMMI) [243] and the Automotive SPICE® (ASPICE) [260]. Both define methods to evaluate complete process models and organizations [98]. However, neither CMMI [243] nor ASPICE [260] focus explicitly on the combination of agile development practices and software product lines. The accuracy of assessments to determine the current status regarding the combination of agile development and software product lines is not precise enough to start a structured improvement initiative. This research question highlights problems with existing assessment models for introducing agile software product lines.

RQ1.4: What are the automotive specific aspects that need to be addressed in an assessment of agile software product lines? Katumba and Knaus [140] mention that the introduction of agile methods into the automotive software development is hindered by special peculiarities of the automotive domain. Specifically, the automotive context is restricted by rigid quality and safety requirements [245]. Moreover, complex relationships between hardware and software development must be considered. The development process involves a lot of suppliers which are closely linked and integrated in the development. It is essential to consider all aspects introduced by the need for functional safety, security, robustness, legal compliance, and modularity [59]. This research question identifies the demands on an assessment model for the combination of agile development and software product lines with respect to the peculiarities of the automotive domain.

RQ1.5: How do existing assessment models need to be modified to introduce and improve agile software product lines? Existing assessment models aim at introducing agile and software reuse strategies into organizations. Campanelli et al. [31] introduce the agile transformation success factors assessment to assess an organizational environment. This includes the company's goals and the perception of the team members. Furthermore, recommendations are given to provide awareness of how an organization should prepare for the next steps in the agile transformation [31]. However, the presented assessment approach is not considering a reuse strategy by the use of a software product line. Jasmine and Vasantha [134] present a capability maturity model for reuse that is based on the software development process. They focus on a systematic reuse strategy to increase software quality, productivity, and customer satisfaction. Therefore, they introduce the Reuse Capability Maturity Model (RCMM) as an adoption of CMMI [243]. However, the RCMM is not considering agile software development approaches. An assessment model to combine agile development practices and software product line development is not available. This research question evaluates existing assessment models and extracts working methods to check their suitability with regard to agile software product lines.

1.5.1   Mapping Research Questions to Goals

The research questions stated in Section 1.5 relate to the goals introduced in Section 1.4 as follows. Goal G1.1 maps to RQ1.1, G1.2 maps to RQ1.3 and G1.3 maps to RQ1.2, RQ1.4 and RQ1.5. Table 1.1 displays the mapping.

Table 1.1: Mapping research questions to goals.

	Goal 1.1	Goal 1.2	Goal 1.3
RQ1.1: What are appropriate methods to establish an agile software product line?	X		
RQ1.2: Which tasks are relevant for improvement and transformation towards agile software product lines?			X
RQ1.3: What are problems with using assessment models for introducing agile software product lines?		X	
RQ1.4: What are the automotive specific aspects that need to be addressed in an assessment of agile software product lines?			X
RQ1.5: How do existing assessment models need to be modified to introduce and improve agile software product lines?			X

1.6 Hypotheses

All hypotheses are based on a comparison between experts and the assessment model. First, it was intended to select several experts who are familiar with agile development practices and software product lines. However, there exists a certain ambiguity of the term "agile" among agile experts. Therefore, the selected experts were internal consultants of the Daimler AG. The selection criteria was based on the fact that they are familiar with automotive software development, software product lines and share the same idea of agile as fostered by senior management. Detailed information about the expert selection can be found in Section 6.4.3. For evaluation purposes, the following hypotheses are defined.

Hypothesis 1: The results from applying the assessment model is in agreement with the recommendations of the experts that assess the current development process. One of the problems with any kind of assessment models is that they reflect the desired reality based on best practices as known at the design time of the model. For example, when Booch [22] introduced CI in 1991 to measure productivity in a better way, no one imagined that it will be as important as it is today, used as backbone for all continuous tasks such as DevOps. Therefore, the assessment model itself must be adjustable and in agreement with the recommendations given by experts who are familiar with the state of the art.

The solution described in this thesis is meaningful and in agreement with the recommendations given by experts that assess the current development process. The assessment model generates a list with important recommendations in order to establish an agile software product line. This list is in agreement with the recommendations given by experts. In total, the number of recommendations given by the model is deviating by less than 30 % when compared to the recommendations given by experts.

Hypothesis 2: The results from applying the assessment model are not missing important recommendations given by experts that assess the current development process. Similar to the possibility of proposing wrong or outdated recommendations, the assessment model can miss important parts which need to be considered and are necessary to establish an agile software product line.

The solution described in this thesis is complete and covers the recommendations of experts that assess the current development process. The number and the content of the recommendations given by experts is in agreement to the recommendations provided by the assessment model. As noted before, the number of missing recommendations given by the model is deviating by less than 10 % when compared to the recommendations given by experts.

Hypothesis 3: With the developed assessment model, the time for conducting an assessment could be reduced by a factor of 2 when compared to the assessments conducted by experts. Current assessments in the automotive domain such as ASPICE are designed to be conducted within a week. The Standard CMMI Appraisal Method for Process Improvement (SCAMPI) which is the assessment form to provide benchmark-quality ratings relative to CMMI [243] could even last longer. Wallmüller [262] mentions that a SCAMPI assessment is limited to a maximum duration of 90 days.

The solution described in this thesis promises to reduce the time for conducting an assessment by a factor of 2 when compared to the assessments conducted by experts.

1.6.1   Mapping Hypotheses to Goals

The hypotheses stated in Section 1.6 relate to the goals G1.1, G1.2 and G 1.3 introduced in Section 1.4 as follows. G1.1 and G1.2 are not covered by the hypotheses. These two goals are addressed in the literature reviews presented in Chapter 4. The Goal 1.3, which aims to develop a domain specific assessment model for the combination of agile software development and software product lines, is mapped to all three hypotheses. The developed domain specific assessment model is in agreement with the recommendations of experts (Hypothesis 1), is not missing important recommendations (Hypothesis 2), and is two times faster when compared with assessments conducted by experts (Hypothesis 3).

1.7   Contributions of Thesis

The contributions of the research in this thesis lie in the design, development, application and validation of an automotive specific assessment model for combining agile software development and software product lines. The contributions of this PhD can be categorized as follows: theoretical work, practical work and empirical work. Each category can be summarized as follows.

1.7.1   Theoretical Work

This category comprises the identification of constraints that hinder the combination of agile software development and software product lines in the automotive domain.

- A literature review on existing agile software product line approaches in the automotive domain which includes the identification of challenges that hinder a successful combination.

- A literature review on existing assessment models for agile software product lines in the automotive domain.

- The identification of recommendations to overcome the identified problems and possible proposals for a successful implementation of agile software product lines in the automotive domain.

1.7.2 Practical Work

The practical work in the context of this thesis is to develop an automotive specific assessment model to assess the combination of agile software development and software product lines.

- The ASPLA Model allows for a systematic and structured assessment of a software development that aims at combining software product lines with agile development practices in the automotive domain.

- The ASPLA Model provides recommendations to improve the development process.

- The implementation of a Web Application (WebApp) to conduct assessments, evaluate the results and provide recommendations to foster the combination.

1.7.3 Empirical Work

This category comprises two industrial case studies to verify the challenges in the automotive domain and validate the assessment model.

- The initial interview study confirms the relevance of the research project to address the question how to establish an agile software product line in the automotive domain.

- The interview study analyses the current state of the practice on agile adoption in the automotive domain. Forces and key challenges that hinder a successful combination of agile software development and software product lines in the automotive domain are identified.

- The validation of the developed assessment model. This confirms the relevance of the recommendations given by the assessment model for the industrial practice. This is shown by a comparison with an ad-hoc assessment conducted by experts and a case study in the automotive domain within development teams.

The contribution gained through this thesis are summarized as a monolithic work, however parts of the results have been published and shared with the scientific community. The publications are summarized in Appendix G.

1.8 Structure of Thesis

The structure and road map of this thesis is shown in Figure 1.3. It is based on Information Systems Research Framework by Hevner et al. [100] presented in Figure 1.2. Each chapter starts with a short introduction and provides a link to the corresponding phase of the research approach. Furthermore, a summary of the main results are provided at the end of each chapter. The remaining chapters of this thesis are structured as follows:

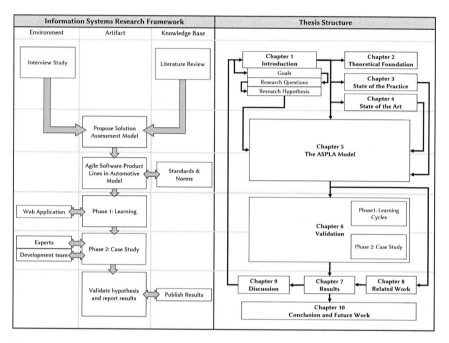

Figure 1.3: Assignment of chapters to corresponding research step according to the research activities by Hevner et al. [100]

Chapter 2. This chapter presents the main concepts and principles of software product lines and agile software development. Furthermore, it outlines the peculiarities of the software development in regulated domains, focusing exclusively on the automotive domain. The chapter describes relevant background information that introduces the context of the research and gives information on concepts which are the basis for the proposed ASPLA Model.

Chapter 3. This chapter investigates whether and how a combination of agile software development and software product lines are used in practice for today's automotive software development. In addition, relevant challenges that have an impact on the combination of agile software development practices and software product lines in the automotive domain are identified.

Chapter 4. This chapter presents two literature reviews. The first literature review identifies existing literature on agile software product lines in the automotive domain. This review helps to identify existing challenges that deal with (1) the use of agile methods in the automotive domain, (2) the use of product line development in the automotive domain, and (3) the combination of agile methods and product line development. The review offers an intersection of all three topics and helps to identify already existing solutions for a successful combination in published literature.

The second literature review examines the use of assessment models to foster agile development in the context of automotive software development processes which are structured along a software product line.

Chapter 5. This chapter introduces the ASPLA Model. It serves as an assessment model to assess embedded software development processes in the automotive domain. The objective is to identify potential improvements with regards to the combination of agile software development practices and software product lines. According to the assessment result, the model provides recommendations to overcome the challenges in combining agile software development and software product lines and to improve the development process while maintaining the already achieved benefits in the development.

Chapter 6. This chapter presents the definition, planning, execution, and analysis of the case study that is used to validate the hypotheses for the ASPLA Model approach. It further shows the applicability of the recommendations given by the ASPLA Model in the context of embedded software development in the automotive domain.

Chapter 7. This chapter presents the findings of the research addressed by this thesis. The findings are presented by each research question.

Chapter 8. This chapter surveys previous work on related assessment models for agile software development and software product lines. It extends the findings from the literature review presented in Chapter 4.

Chapter 9. This chapter discusses the limitations and potentials of the ASPLA Model. Specifically, the research process is evaluated according to the Design-Science Research guidelines proposed by Hevner et al. [100]. Moreover, the ASPLA Model is compared to the guidelines for the development of assessment models proposed by Maier et al [169].

Chapter 10. This chapter summarizes the presented research, provides an outlook and identifies possible future work which is out of scope of this thesis.

Appendices. The appendices present detailed information on the ASPLA Model and study results. Appendix A provides the improvement potential and recommendation list for the conducted assessments by Developer 1 and Developer 2. Appendix B highlights the data collection and gives information about the workshops. Challenges that hinder a combination of agile software development and software product lines in the automotive domain are presented in Appendix C. The tables in Appendix D describe all recommendations given by the ASPLA Model. Appendix E presents the complete ASPLA Model, with Base Practices, Product Attributes and Work Products. It further specifies the relations between all components in the model. Furthermore, Appendix E comprises the complete collection of all assessment questions that are used for the Web Application. Finally, Appendix E includes a detailed overview of the mapping from ASPICE and ISO/IEC 26550 to the ASPLA Model. The results of the literature review presented in Chapter 4 can be found in Appendix F. Appendix G provides details on the results that have been published and shared with the scientific community.

1.9 Chapter Summary

This chapter provides an introduction for the understanding of the topic under research. It presents the motivation and identifies the main goal of this thesis. Furthermore, research direction and hypotheses are introduced that guide the research process. The research approach and the contribution of this thesis are defined. Lastly, the structure of the thesis is presented.

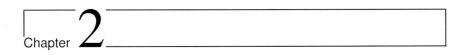

Chapter 2

Theoretical Foundation

This chapter presents the main concepts and principles of using assessment models, software product lines and agile software development. It provides information on concepts that form the basis for the proposed assessment model. First, the peculiarities of the software development in regulated domains and the use of assessment models is described. Second, the paradigm of software product lines is explained. In the third section, agile development practices and methodologies are presented. Finally, the combination of agile software development and software product lines in practice is discussed.

2.1 Automotive Assessment/Reference Models

2.1.1 The Need for High Quality and Faultless Software

The automotive domain is confronted with an increasing complexity of embedded software. Upcoming market demands and desired customer features are addressed in software. Therefore, it is important to ensure that the software is working as expected and is of high quality. All software development processes aim to ensure a high quality and faultless software. In the automotive domain, ISO 26262 [124] specifies software development tasks to realize and verify requirements introduced by safety-critical functions [221]. For this purpose, the software development process is organized in phases, comprising activities and tasks for a specific part of software development [237]. The phases are aligned to a V-shaped curve, the so-called V-Model, which is prevalent in the automotive domain and prescribed by ISO 26262 [122]. In 2005, the V-Model was replaced by the "V-Modell XT" [66] which is published by the German government and defines a standard software development process for IT-projects [66]. The V-Model combines design phases on the left descending path and testing phases on the ascending side of the V. Testing processes demonstrate that the software units fulfill the software unit design specifications. Furthermore, testing processes verify that the software does not contain undesired functionality and is of high quality [122].

2.1.2   Automotive Software Process Improvement

Improvements can be made in many areas within the development process. For example, one possible improvement is the development process itself. Different standards for software process improvement have evolved over the past. Process maturity models provide a technique to assess existing processes, determine process compliance levels and improve the development process. The possibility of using a process assessment model and the improvement resulting from an assessment always depends on the development context. Relevant standards for different contexts are considered. Process assessments are used to evaluate the processes of an organizational unit against a predefined process assessment model. The most popular standards in the automotive domain are CMMI [243] and ASPICE [260]. Both define methods to evaluate complete process models and organizations [98].

These process models define how software shall be developed and tested. Furthermore, they represent best industry practice. Following standardized processes have the advantage that outcomes are reproducible and comparable. This is important for the automotive domain, especially in collaboration with suppliers in order to make outcomes comparable.

2.1.3   ASPICE Process/Reference Model

The ASPICE Process/Reference Model [260] is a model to evaluate the process capability of the development of embedded automotive systems. Automotive Original Equipment Manufacturers (OEMs) use this assessment model to assess the software capability of their suppliers. The ASPICE Process/Reference Model defines the processes and introduces two process-specific performance indicators: Base Practices and Work Products. The former is defined as an activity or task to achieve the process outcome. The latter focuses on the outcome of the process and is result oriented [260].

ASPICE is maintained by the German Association of the Automotive Industry, called Verband der Automobilindustrie (VDA). The VDA has more than 600 members[1]. Member companies are large OEMs, but also many renowned Small and Medium-sized Enterprises (SMEs). In addition, the membership is nowadays not limited to German companies only. The ASPICE standard itself was not newly developed by the VDA. It has been drafted in 2005 "under the Automotive SPICE initiative by consensus of the car manufacturers within the Automotive Special Interest Group (SIG), a joint special interest group of Automotive OEM, the Procurement Forum and the SPICE User Group" [260, p. 2], and evolved since that time to the latest release 3.1 in 2017.

The ASPICE Process/Reference Model groups the processes into process categories and process groups according to the type of activity they address [260]. Three categories are defined: (1) Primary life cycle processes, (2) Organizational life cycle processes, and (3) Supporting life cycle processes [260]. Figure 2.1 shows the three categories of life cycle processes and the processes which are assigned to them.

---

[1]https://www.vda.de/en/association/members

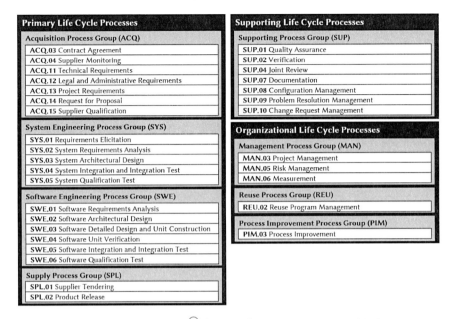

Figure 2.1: The Automotive SPICE® (ASPICE) process reference model. Processes are assigned to the three categories of life cycle processes [260].

The (1) primary life cycle processes category comprises processes that are used in the collaboration with customers and suppliers. The category provides processes that help to acquire and support a product or service [260]. Furthermore, the life cycle processes category includes engineering processes for elicitation and management of customer requirements, specifications, development of the corresponding software architecture and design, integration and testing of the software [260].

The (2) organizational life cycle processes category provides processes that support the organization in achieving its business goals. Specifically, processes are provided that help to manage the development process and improve the processes performed in an organizational unit. Furthermore, reuse opportunities are exploited to manage a systematic reuse [260].

The (3) supporting life cycle processes category may be applied by any of the other processes. The use of these processes is not restricted to a specific point in the life cycle. In fact, supporting life cycle processes, such as documentation and quality assurance, need to be considered continuously [260].

The process reference model contains the unique functional objectives of each process and provides a list of specific and expected results of the process [260]. An overview of the ASPICE Process/Reference Model is provided in Figure 2.1. For each category, a set of processes is provided.

ASPICE and its dependencies to other standards is presented in Figure 2.2. ASPICE is based on existing standards and reproduces relevant material from ISO/IEC 15504-5:2006 [126] and ISO/IEC 33020:2015 [130]. The SPICE standard ISO/IEC 15504-5:2006 [126] has been revised by ISO/IEC 15504-5:2012 [127] in 2017. ISO/IEC 15504-5:2012 [127] provides a process assessment model with a detailed description of important components and processes to conduct an assessment. ISO/IEC 15504 is a standard that aims to ensures a high-quality software development and software products [98]. Since 2006, it is an international standard [98].

ISO/IEC 15504-5:2012 [127] is based on the common framework for software life cycle processes for the software industry established by ISO/IEC 12207:2008 [125]. The process reference model and the process assessment model in ISO/IEC 15504-5:2012 [127] are used as a basis for ASPICE [260]. The process performance indicators Base Practices and Work Products, as well as the definition of the processes have their origin in the SPICE standard ISO/IEC 15504-5:2006 [126]. The Work Products and Base Practices can be used by assessors to evaluate the capability level of processes [127]. In 2017, the ISO/IEC 12207:2008 [125] was withdrawn and replaced by the ISO/IEC/IEEE 12207:2017 [131]. The interrelation between these processes is still present in the current version of the ASPICE standard [260]. It is mentioned that appropriate processes from other process reference models such as ISO/IEC 12207 or ISO/IEC 15288 [132] can be used to meet business needs [260].

Furthermore, ASPICE [260] is inspired by ISO/IEC 33020:2015 [130]. This standard defines a process measurement framework for assessment of process capability. The framework complies with the requirements of ISO/IEC 33004 [129] and can be used to assess the performance of the process capability. The process capability is a quality characteristic related to the ability of a process to meet business goals [130]. The process capability levels include a set of attributes that provide a major improvement in the process performance. The process capability levels of ASPICE are identical to those defined in ISO/IEC 33020 [130]:

Level 0: Incomplete process. The process is not implemented, or fails to achieve its process purpose.

Level 1: Performed process. The implemented process achieves its process purpose.

Level 2: Managed process. The previously described performed process is now implemented in a managed fashion (planned, monitored and adjusted) and its Work Products are appropriately established, controlled and maintained.

Level 3: Established process. The previously described managed process is now implemented using a defined process that is capable of achieving its process outcomes.

Level 4: Predictable process. The previously described established process now operates predictively within defined limits to achieve its process outcomes. Quantitative management needs are identified, measurement data are collected and analyzed to identify assignable causes of variation. If necessary, corrective action is taken to address assignable causes of variation.

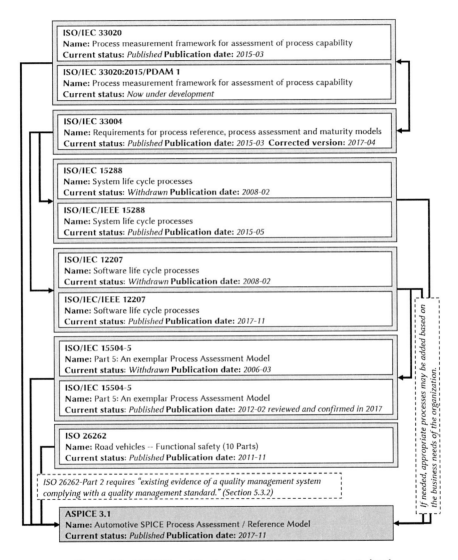

Figure 2.2: ASPICE and its dependencies to other standards [260]

Level 5: Innovating process. The previously described predictable process is now continually improved to respond to organizational change.

The capability of the process can be measured using process attributes, which are features of a process that can be evaluated on a scale of achievement. ASPICE [260] uses a two-dimensional framework to determine the process capability (cf. Figure 2.3).

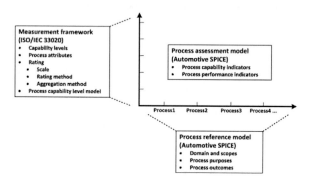

Figure 2.3: The process assessment model relationship as presented in [260]

The first dimension is denoted as the process dimension. It represents all processes defined in the ASPICE process reference model. The second dimension consists of capability levels and is therefore denoted as the capability dimension. Six capability levels are defined in ISO/IEC 33020 [130] starting with the process capability level 0, which identifies a non-implemented process or a process which fails to deliver its outcomes.

To measure the characteristics of the process capability, process attributes are selected that address a specific aspect of the capability level. The degree of achievement of a process attribute provides conclusions about the process capability. The relationship between process dimension and capability dimension is illustrated in Figure 2.3. The ISO/IEC 33020 [130] measurement framework is used to rate the process attributes in ASPICE [260].

2.1.4   The VDA-Scope (former HIS Scope)

The Herstellerinitiative Software (HIS) scope was established to make assessment results comparable. It is a reference scope used by automotive OEMs for assessing predefined processes of suppliers and departments within the software development [196].

The HIS scope defines a sub-scope of ASPICE [260] with a selection of Base Practices for the automotive industry to promote an easier adoption of the ASPICE standard [196]. In ASPICE 3.1 [260], the HIS Scope was renamed into the VDA-Scope.

ASPICE assessments help to assess software development processes within the automotive domain. Capability levels define the achievement of the capability of the development process. Processes which need further improvements could therefore be identified and the maturity of the development process gets confirmed. Even if ASPICE assessments are helpful, there are some conceptual gaps in ASPICE such as safety-critical software of product line development which need special awareness [196].

2.2 Systematic Software Reuse Strategies

In 1969, a conference on software engineering techniques, sponsored by the North Atlantic Treaty Organization (NATO) Science Committee, was held [30]. This conference was the natural continuation of the NATO conference on software engineering held one year before in Garmisch (Germany). At the conference on software engineering techniques, Lampson, a participant of the conference employed at the Department of Computer Science of the University of California, mentioned the need for a basic structure that allows extensions in order to meet changing requirements and keep the development flexible [30]. He recommended modularization to isolate modules and encouraged economical reuse of existing constructs [30]. The motivation to build independent and reusable modules is still valid. Münch et al. [184] point out that software-intensive systems can only be mastered with highly modular architectures enabling the reuse of verified and validated components. Furthermore, Habli et al. [87] mention that a systematic software reuse is an approach to reduce development cost of high-integrity software. They argue that it is more cost-effective to develop parts of the software once and reuse them in multiple other projects [87].

Hohl et al. [108] emphasize that a systematic reuse strategy is necessary to develop the large amount of different software variants, while simultaneously maintaining high software quality in the automotive domain [108]. The large amount of different software variants is the result of software customization and the need to satisfy demands of different markets [108]. In addition, Diaz et al. mention that the reuse strategy supports long term planning and helps to satisfy future customer needs [52].

Boehm [21] identifies eight critical success factors for software reuse. These factors are: (1) the adoption of a product line approach, (2) a business case analysis to determine the right scope and level of expectation for the product line, (3) black-box reuse, (4) empowered product line managers and stakeholders, (5) reuse-oriented processes and organizations, (6) carefully chosen pilot projects and real-world feedback, (7) metrics-based reuse operations management, and (8) a pro-active product-line evolution strategy [21].

Deelstra et al. [48] mention different levels of scope of reuse to identify the commonalities of related products. They identify the method of a standardized infrastructure, a platform-based development and the use of a software product line as possible methods to identify common parts [48]. Software product lines are particularly important and used in the automotive domain [245].

2.2.1   Software Product Lines

Blau and Hildenbrand [18] point out that software product lines include different software products that share a common set of functionalities. This set of functionalities should satisfy the different market demands [190]. It is therefore necessary to manage the development of features and to identify possible reusable software parts, so-called core assets, to avoid redundant development [18]. Buckle et al. [29] point out that products should be engineered in a way to obtain advantage of their commonalities while controlling their differences. Production economies can be achieved with this approach [190]. Furthermore, Santos and Lucena [219] mention that software product lines help to develop software products in a productive way.

The standard for product line engineering and management (ISO/IEC 26550) [128] summarizes the disadvantages of using single-system engineering compared to a software product line. The ISO/IEC 26550 [128] standard provides a reference model representing the key processes of software and system product line engineering. As denoted in the standard, "single-system engineering and management approaches may end up with highly complex and low-quality products, low productivity, high employee turnover, and less than expected customer satisfaction" [128, p. 13].

Definition of Software Product Lines

The international standard ISO/IEC 26550 [128] provides a definition for a software product line.

Definition 1. *"Product Line - Set of products and/or services sharing explicitly defined and managed common and variable features and relying on the same domain architecture to meet the common and variable needs of specific markets" [128, p. 10].*

In the same vain, Weiss and Lei [263] define the product line as a family of products, which are designed to take advantage of their common aspects and predicted variabilities [263]. Furthermore, Pohl et al. [208] provide another definition for software product line engineering that focuses mass customization aspects.

Definition 2. *"Software Product Line Engineering - Software product line engineering is a paradigm to develop software applications (software-intensive systems and software products) using platforms and mass customization." [208, p. 38]*

The idea of a software product line is to develop different products from one core asset base (also called a platform) [29]. Pohl et al. [208] mention the platforms used for mass-customization in their definition. For software customization, customer-specific product variants can be generated using some parts from the platform and customize it to fulfill customers' demands [18]. Platforms are used to plan anticipatively for parts that can be reused [208]. Furthermore, the development and the management of reusable parts is addressed by the platform solution [208]. Mass customization needs management of variability to address common parts in the application, such as shared requirements and software implementations [208]. In addition, Hanssen [89] emphasizes that the preparation and the support of variability is the main concept of a software product line.

Motivations for Product Line Engineering

Babar et al. [10] studied software product lines and identified that these paradigms are often promoted as means of reducing time to market, increasing productivity, improving quality and gaining cost effectiveness and efficiency. The benefits they are referring to are confirmed by Thiel et al. [245] for the automotive domain. They point out that for more than 30 years, reuse has been the longstanding notion to solve cost, quality, and time to market issues [245].

Reduced Costs. Software Product Lines are an efficient approach to develop software products [29]. The economic justification for introducing product line engineering is the reduction of costs [208]. The concept for software reuse is simple. The reuse of already implemented software parts saves the costs of designing, writing and testing new code [264]. However, budget steering is essential to balance the reuse of software parts on the one hand and the amount of customer-specific solutions on the other hand [18]. Wentzel [264] points out that the benefits of a reuse program must be considered from a long term perspective. He mentions that the benefits result in an earlier time to market and decreasing long term maintenance costs due to a strategic software reuse [264].

Increased Quality. The standard ISO/IEC 26550 [128] indicates that quality issues may result from the lack of a reuse culture. Reusing well-tested components results in less defect density [128] and increased software stability [79]. Ghanam and Maurer [79] note that the reused components can be better tested. They furthermore emphasize that with an increasing number of software variants, the effort for testing amortizes due to software reuse [79].

Shorter Time To Market. Tian [247] mentions that the reduction of time to market is a critical success factor for a product today. A fast pace in the development is necessary to satisfy market demands. He points out that product line engineering can shorten the time to market [247]. However, it is important to consider the long term. Furthermore, he points out that the time to market is initially higher for the first couple of products in a software product line [247]. This is based on the fact that it takes initial time to build the common artifacts. With a reuse strategy of these artifacts, the time to market is shortened [247].

Separated Development Processes

The international standard ISO/IEC 26550 [128] recommends to establish software product lines that consist of two separated development processes, denoted as domain engineering and application engineering [128]. Bosch et al. [24] emphasize the clear separation of these two development processes for the organization of the software development process within software product lines [24]. The separation of these two processes and the connection to the Asset Base is illustrated in Figure 2.4.

Reusable assets produced from both the domain and application engineering are stored in the Asset Base [128]. The standard ISO/IEC 26550 requires a good collaboration between domain engineering and application engineering teams when managing the Asset Base [128]. However, the standard does not prescribe the use of specific software engineering methods and practices. The selection of a suitable methodology is up to the company [128]. It is recommended to differentiate between the two separated development processes in order to facilitate the strategic creation, reuse, and configuration of software [128, 248].

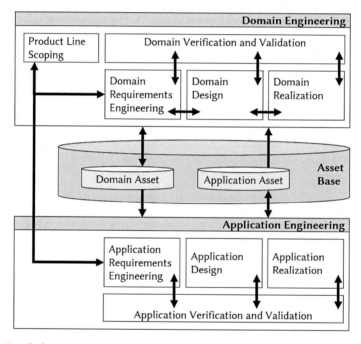

Figure 2.4: Reference model for Software and Systems Product Line (SSPL) engineering and management [128]

Domain Engineering. Pohl et al. [208] define domain engineering as a process "of software product line engineering in which the commonality and the variability of the product line are defined and realized" [208, p. 44]. Within the domain engineering, the reusable platform, commonality and the variability of the product line are established [208]. The ISO/IEC 26550 standard defines domain engineering as follows:

Definition 3. *Domain engineering - a life cycle consisting of a set of processes for specifying and managing the commonality and variability of a product line [128, p. 3].*

Domain engineering encompasses the implementation of a set of reusable assets. These domain assets are reused and can be assembled into customer-specific software systems [248]. The success of a product line is highly affected by a strategic reusability of domain assets [128]. The reusability of the domain assets requires strategic long-term planning to focus on the domain and to develop feasible domain assets [128]. For long-term planning, the domain engineering process includes the task of product line scoping [138] which defines the core assets and variable features that will be developed [138, 208]. Furthermore, it schedules and manages the development of the product line and its products [138]. According to Balbino et al. [11], scoping is the first activity to start a software product line. For a successful software product line, it is indispensable to conduct the scoping properly [11].

Application Engineering. Pohl et al. [208] define application engineering as a process "of software product line engineering in which the applications of the product line are built by reusing domain artifacts and exploiting the product line variability" [208, p. 44]. The ISO/IEC 26550 [128] mentions a traditional viewpoint, in which application engineering can be seen as the development of a single product. Strategic reuse and shared core assets across several products are not covered by application engineering [128]. Moreover, the ISO/IEC 26550 standard defines application engineering as follows:

Definition 4. *Application engineering – a life cycle consisting of a set of processes in which the application assets and member products of the product line are implemented and managed by reusing domain assets in conformance to the domain architecture and by binding the variability of the platform. [128, p. 44]*

The application engineering mainly focuses on the market and aims at satisfying market and customer demands [138]. Short development cycles are established to support a fast time to market. For this purpose, core assets are selected as part of the product line and tailored to the current field of application. The process of mass-customization in the application engineering leads to a high amount of different variants and therefore increases the development complexity [138].

2.3 Agile Software Development

In the context of this dissertation, a case study with the originators of the agile manifesto was conducted and accepted for publication in the Journal of Software Engineering Research and Development. The study provides detailed information on the origin of the agile movement and encompasses the view of the original contributors. The following section is based on the results presented in the Journal publication [106].

The agile uprising started in 2001 with the introduction of the manifesto for agile software development. Since that time, the four statements of the manifesto changed the way of developing software tremendously. However, the agile uprising continuous and all areas of organizations are now attempting to adopt the agile mindset. One disadvantage is that "agile" is often interpreted differently and the question arises: Is it "being agile" or "doing agile". Many agile adopters are not aware of the initial diversity of agile methods and the underlying principles. Scrum is often seen as the only agile practice [147]. Various publications [102, 54, 3] provide interpretations on the statements of the manifesto. These publications focus on the introduction of agile practices, principles, and methods. Whenever developers aim at conducting an agile development, the manifesto for agile software development is mentioned [15]:

We are uncovering better ways of developing software by doing it and helping others do it. Through this work we have come to value:

Individuals and interactions over processes and tools
Working software over comprehensive documentation
Customer collaboration over contract negotiation
Responding to change over following a plan

That is, while there is value in the items on the right, we value the items on the left more.

In 2001, 17 software practitioners "uncover better ways of developing software" [15] and defined the manifesto for agile software development in a meeting in Snowbird, near Salt Lake County, Utah. Cockburn [161] compares the meeting in Snowbird with the NATO Conference of Software Engineering in 1968 [186]. The success of the manifesto took off and the agile mindset was spread faster than all authors of the manifesto initially anticipated [167, 162, 166]. However, organizations nowadays have challenges in differentiating between "doing agile" and "being agile". Bennekum [206] defines "doing" as following rituals without significant change in the way of working [206]. Martin [163] points out that the misinterpretation and false implementation of agile is caused by politics, imagination, and economic interest. In addition, Beedle is disappointed because many people "maybe just have misunderstood [the concepts of agile] and doing [it] on the cheap" [162]. According to Marick [165], Agile and Scrum are a "brand rather than a mindset", and the craft of software development has been lost. In contrast, "being" agile means that the individual employee, the development team, and the whole organization has changed [206, 163].

2.3.1   Agile Methods and Practices

Dynamic Systems Development Method (DSDM).   DSDM was published in February 1995 and has its origin in the Rapid application development User Groups (RUGs). The Intellectual Property (IP) of DSDM is community owned. DSDM is an agile framework maintained by the DSDM Consortium for dynamic, non-predictable projects. It fosters a close customer collaboration and aims at delivering frequently in an iterative development process. A well adopted practice of DSDM is to slice projects into small, so-called "time-boxes". Requirements are prioritized per time-box [57].

Test Driven Development (TDD). Beck [14] presented this incremental method in detail in 2003. TDD was part of the XP practice of test-first, which was already presented in 1999 [154]. The development process in TDD starts by writing a test, which consequently fails in the first attempt due to missing code. After writing the tests, the developer implements as much code as necessary in order to fulfill the test criteria.

Adaptive Software Development. Highsmith [101] published his book "Adaptive Software Development" in 2000. Adaptive Software Development provides guidelines for speculating, collaborating and learning. With these guidelines, Adaptive Software Development defines a framework for managing complex systems by an adaptive culture in a collaborative way.

Design Driven Development (D3), Refactoring. The D3 approach assumes that the possibility to manage a randomly occurring event during the conception process is very important for success and key to innovation. In 1999, Fowler [71] published his book "Refactoring". In his book, he states that badly designed software can be transformed into better designed software by refactoring the code continuously.

Scrum. Scrum is one of the best known agile methods. It is not a software development technique, but a framework for managing various kinds of projects. Scrum separates the whole development process into small periods of time, so-called sprints [224]. Within a sprint, a given set of requirements is developed. Scrum consists of several core activities, artifacts and roles which need to be extended by suitable practices. The core activities consist of meetings during the sprints, like a daily Scrum or a retrospective [224]. The artifacts encompass a product backlog containing all requirements that have not been implemented so far, a sprint backlog that defines all tasks for the ongoing sprint, and a product increment that is the sum of all product-backlog elements that have been implemented already [224]. Three roles are defined: the Product Owner defining the requirements, the development team fulfilling the Product Owner's requests and the Scrum Master helping to create a good atmosphere for the team and to preserve agility [224].

Crystal. Cockburn developed a family of agile software development methods. For each "member of this family", he assigned a color. The basic variant is called "Crystal Clear". Crystal includes a couple of principles, such as passive knowledge transfer, continuous delivery, frequent releases and automated testing [37].

Extreme Programming (XP). Beck published the first edition of his book "Extreme Programming explained" [13] in 2000. The book marked the starting point for the success of XP. In XP, several practices are described. The most common practices from XP nowadays are pair programming and continuous integration.

Pragmatic Programming. In their book "The Pragmatic Programmer: From Journeyman to Master" [119], Thomas and Hunt defined software development as a craft. They outline a pragmatic way for the efficient, profitable development of high-quality products based on easily understandable tips [119]. The tips are based on their experience and can help other programmers to care about the craft of creating software.

Modeling languages. Mellor created a modeling language that was the forerunner to Unified Modeling Language™ (UML) [232]. He identified the "underlying reason why peoples say [that models are bad is] [...], because they think that models are just sketches" [168]. He provides a modeling language that seamlessly can translate the component models into code. As he points out, code components are compiled into an executable component which is then deployed [179].

Feature Driven Development (FDD). FDD was first described by De Luca, and afterwards influenced by Coad and Kern through their collaboration in writing the book "Java modeling in color with UML" [36]. The development process is separated in short iterations. The main idea of FDD is to decompose complex functions until each sub-problem is small enough to be called a feature.

2.4   Agile Software Product Lines

2.4.1   Presumed Benefits of Agile Software Product Lines

Agile software product line engineering is an approach to harness the benefits resulting from the use of agile development and software product lines. Dìaz et al. [51] mention that the aim of combining these two development paradigms is to reduce upfront planning while simultaneously making the development more flexible and adaptable to changes. Furthermore, they mention that the term Agile Product Line Engineering (APLE) is synonymous to the term Agile Software Product Line (ASPL) [50].

Hanssen and Fægri [91] specify benefits for the adoption of an ASPL, such as an improved productivity with a decreased time to market. They state that the product quality and customer satisfaction increases due to the use of an ASPL [91]. The benefits are confirmed by Noor et al. [188]. They also identify that a combination under certain conditions results in an increase of customer satisfaction and a decreased time to market [188].

Hanssen and Fægri [91] differentiate between proactive engineering and reactive engineering for the development that uses an ASPL [91]. In the first case, the reusable assets are developed upfront. The latter engineering approach implements application assets, defines the reusability of them and returns them to the asset base as domain assets if needed [91]. However, the introduction of ASPL is not addressed by Hanssen and Fægri [91]. Organizations must choose their own method that suits their needs regarding cost and software quality [91]. Tian and Cooper [248] identified two possibilities to set up an ASPL. They propose the introduction of agile elements into an existing software product line development as the first approach for combining. The second approach uses the existing agile development method and tailors it to software product lines [248]. In 2017, Hayashi et al. [94] propose an agile development and management method for multiple product lines of automotive software systems. Their combination approach aims at taming the variability in software product lines by the use of agile methods [94].

2.4.2 A Critical View on Agile Software Product Lines

Noor et al. [188] point out that the introduction of ASPL causes several challenges, such as the combination of complex planning to maintain the software product line in the long-term in contrast to the fostered short-term value-creation in agile methods [188]. Other authors such as McGregor [177] and Pohjalainen [207] take a critical stance on ASPL. McGregor [178] raises the question whether agile software development and software product line engineering can be effectively combined. Blau and Hildenbrand [18] identify the different realizations and focus on the architecture in agile methods and software product lines. They mention that software product lines contain managed core assets to generate customer-specific products. In contrast, the agile architecture is open for refactoring and more flexible than the architecture used in the software product line [18]. Münch et al. [184] identify the need for flexibility to handle an increasing rate of change as a major challenge for software product line development [184].

Pohjalainen [207] goes one step further and declares agile methods and software product lines to be incompatible at all. The incompatibility arises from different practices and methods fostered by development approaches [207].

2.5 Chapter Summary

This section presents the theoretical foundation of the thesis. The need of high quality and faultless software in the automotive domain is pointed out. To achieve this, the automotive assessment ASPICE is presented. Software reuse strategies are discussed and software product lines are introduced. Furthermore, agile basics are recalled and the methods which influence the agile manifesto are described. The last section of this chapter summarizes the motivation behind the combination of agile software development and software product lines and points out the presumed benefits.

Chapter 3

State of the Practice

This chapter investigates whether and how agile software development approaches are combined with software product lines in practice in today's software development in the automotive domain. It presents results from an interview study (cf. Section 3.2) conducted by the author of this thesis. The chapter further investigates challenges of the agile transformation and derives requirements for a solution approach addressing the problems found in practice. The identified challenges are clustered and assigned to the forces model introduced in Section 3.4. The forces model presents supporting and hindering factors for agile adoption in the automotive domain.

Furthermore, the results of the interview study were aligned to published literature. Development process descriptions, as given by Schäuffele and Zurawka [220], coincide with the statements found in the interview study. Some parts of the results have been published in [107, 110, 109] and [108], and presented at relevant international conferences.

3.1 Automotive Software Engineering

The automotive domain is one of the most challenging environments to develop software [267]. The characteristics for automotive software development are high quantities with high cost pressure, test and validation under real-time conditions and a large amount of software variants [107, 60]. The development of safety-critical applications and the regulations which are necessary to release the software require to follow strict development processes. Strict processes and a structured way of working are a fundamental prerequisite to manage the complexity in the development [220]. Wozniak and Clements [267] point out that each product itself is highly complex and there exist millions of different variants. Different variability techniques allow to manage the complexity. Variability is introduced in different development stages of the software. Specifically, variability may be introduced by branching development trees or using preprocessor statements. After implementation, different calibration datasets introduce further variants due to parameterization. Schäuffele and Zurawka [220] denote that a high number of parameters and characteristics are necessary to define the software functionality associated with different variants of engines, vehicle transmissions and car models [220].

Current development in the automotive domain is based on a large amount of software reuse in order to manage the complexity during development. Thereby, the software development paradigm of software product lines is used. Thiel et al. [245] denoted the software product lines to be particularly important to the automotive domain. They mention that car suppliers lean towards the integration of more and more software functionality [245]. Software product lines help to manage changes, coordinate the worldwide software development, and increase the software quality by reuse [111]. Furthermore, software variants enable a customization and individualization of customers' requirements and generate more value for the core business [111]. Grewe et al. [86] point out the necessity for a high reuse rate across different types of vehicles in order to keep software development for vehicles cost efficient.

The organization of the software product line is managed by a strict development process. The development for different markets and different model series uses one global software platform within a defined established process for all involved partners. The development process is usually based on the V-Model. The main development cycles and the corresponding main software releases are synchronized with the development cycle of the vehicle. In addition, the development needs to be synchronized with test phases, such as summer and winter test drives under real conditions. The synchronization of all development cycles is important because a final validation is only achieved by acceptance tests in real cars [220].

The introduction of a new functionality and changes in the software are only possible if a strict development process is followed. It has to be verified that the software product line does not fall apart due to the different needs for different markets all over the world. A desired new functionality is entered into a globally managed database. The global product management is primarily responsible for product line scoping [128]. In the scoping process, the common and variable features among the products are defined [128]. Market specific adjustments to the software are analyzed from an economic point of view. If the realization of the desired functionality is approved, different roles analyze the desired functionality, identify the affected related items and agree on the implementation. The implementation is either done in-house or it is outsourced to a supplier. In 2006, Broy [25] points out the large amount of outsourcing. The interview study conducted within this thesis revealed a desired increase of the in-house development in order to keep the development more flexible [109]. Especially for new features, flexibility in the software development is desired [109]. Nevertheless, a lot of software implementation, especially in the field of low level functionality, is still provided by suppliers. In regular meetings with the supplier, the implementation steps are defined and the features for the next software version are commissioned.

The development processes are well established and it is possible to manage the complexity of the development. However, the introduction of the software product line to coordinate the distributed development increases the development time. The time between the initial idea of a feature to be implemented until the feature is available for the end-customer in the car increases. Regular meetings around the globe on different hierarchy levels are hard to coordinate. The management of the global software platform results in an increased effort for the development.

The current software development in the automotive domain is heavily structured by standardized processes. Process assessments are used to evaluate the processes of an organizational unit against a predefined process assessment model. The most popular standards in the automotive domain are ASPICE [260] and CMMI [243].

Both standards define methods to evaluate complete process models and organizations [98]. For automotive embedded software and systems, the ASPICE process assessment model is applied. ASPICE is maintained by the German Association of the Automotive Industry [260]. CMMI [243] is a collection of best practices that supports organizations to improve their processes. CMMI focuses on activities for developing products to meet customers' needs [243].

3.1.1 Need to Introduce Agile

The current development processes are seen as too inflexible in order to keep pace with fast changing market demands [23, 63]. Hence, the development processes need to be redesigned in a way that it allows to learn and adapt continuously at a fast pace [111]. The use of selected agile practices are promising approaches to address these new challenges [109]. Since 2001, agile software development methods promise an improved software development with a faster time to market and an increasing speed of learning. Furthermore, agile development practices offer the possibility to react on changing requirements and to refine the final software during the development process [109]. The adoption of agile practices within the automotive domain is therefore a possible way to keep pace with fast changing market demands [140].

3.2 Interview Study

This section describes the interview study conducted by the author of this thesis in order to identify challenges and recommendations with regard to agile software product lines in the automotive domain. Results of this interview study have been published in [107, 110, 109] and [108], and presented at relevant international conferences.

3.2.1 Research Design

The study is based on a qualitative survey and designed as an exploratory semi-structured interview. Bryman [28] recommends to implement an interview guide to conduct a semi-structured interview. The interview guide was structured along a funnel model [216]. For the funnel mode, each section in the interview begins with open, exploratory ground mapping questions [58]. These questions reveal all topics of interests [212]. In addition, dimension mapping questions are used to focus on interesting topics [212]. The interview guide was tested in a pilot interview and adjusted to the problems which have arisen. The approach provides insights into the examined topic and gives essential information to understand the phenomenon in its real context [55, 216].

3.2.2   Research Sites and Participants

The interview participants were selected from employees of an OEM and an automotive consultant. The interviewee selection was based on two criteria: First, the interviewee should have a work experience of several years. The length of employment varied from 3 to 20 years, with an average working experience of 16 years. Second, the interviewee should already use agile practices for software development in order To get different point of views on the examined topic. The following participants were selected: Two managers, five process owners, two system architects, six software developers and one automotive consultant for agile development processes. The interviews were conducted by the primary researcher at the interviewees' departments from May to June 2016.

3.2.3   Interviews

In the data collection process, 14 face-to-face interviews as well as a group interview with two participants were conducted. Every interview session took around one hour. The questions were initially defined in English and translated to the native language of the interviewees. In consent with the interviewee, the interview was recorded and transcribed verbatim for detailed analysis. All transcribed interview notes were managed using the reference management program Citavi and are documented in a company internal report [103].

3.2.4   Analysis

According to the classification of Stol et al. [239], the three coding phases of Straussian Grounded Theory were used. Open coding, axial coding, and selective coding were selected for data analysis [239, 42]. The interpretive process of open coding generates categories and concepts by breaking down the data analytically. The concepts were grouped together and related to their subcategories in the axial coding. In the selective coding the central categories were defined.

3.3   Benefits of Agile Software Product Lines

This section is based on the data collection presented in Section 3.2 and the results published in [108]. For a successful transformation towards agile development, it is necessary to identify the driving forces behind that movement. The interview study identifies benefits for a combination of agile software development and software product lines in the automotive domain. The study reveals two areas in which the participants identified a benefit.

Customer collaboration. All participants mentioned that it is necessary to react faster on customer expectations in order to have future success. This ensures that customer oriented products or features can be rapidly launched in the market with profit. One participant noted that with a rapid customer feedback the software development will be more effective. Not accepted solutions by the customer are identified in an early stage and could be dropped before they are further developed. The development capacity is better and more efficiently used. Trends in customers' behavior could be recognized and developed towards customer satisfaction.

Improvement of development. The main expected benefit is an improvement of the software development process. These benefits could be categorized as: (1) transparency, (2) collaboration within the development team, (3) efficiency in development, (4) flexibility, (5) software quality, (6) development speed, (7) reduced cost of delay, and (8) a better verification and reuse strategy.

With the introduction of agile development, an agile mindset is presumed to be introduced as well. Most interviewees mentioned that (1) transparency in work will result from the new way of (2) collaborative working. With the consequential distribution of knowledge within the software development team, it is expected to be (2) an open and genuine cooperation between employees. The developers mentioned that (3) work could be more effective by granting more responsibility to lower hierarchy levels. This results in less coordination for management approval. A possible solution is the resolving of too many levels in the hierarchy into flat hierarchies with self-organizing teams. However, some participants were still critical about this proposed way of working. They mentioned that some developers do not want to change their working behavior and it is not possible to force a mindset change. Furthermore, such a change needs time and is not always necessary. A mixture of employees specialized in a specific field and more general oriented employees are necessary. With the right mixture, the development could (4) benefit from in-depth knowledge and flexibility in the development. This flexibility is explicitly mentioned by the managers as a need to react on customer needs.

For developers, the (5) customer satisfaction is of secondary importance when compared to software quality. They assumed that with a combination of agile software development and software product lines, it will be possible to (5) deliver high quality software at the (6) required faster pace due to increased software reuse and shorter release cycles. They further emphasized that it is important to bundle the competence in-house in order to deliver software faster and react on changing requirements. With faster in-house communication channels, one participant mentioned that this will be beneficial considering (7) the cost of development and cost of delay. In addition, the developers mentioned that (8) a good reuse strategy and software product line is necessary to use parts of the software more often and save further money. All participants emphasized that an agile development speeds up the development to get a high quality software, whereas the existing software product line helps to ensure that already verified software is reused within a mature reuse strategy.

3.4 The Agile Adoption Forces Model

The interview study conducted as part of the thesis results in the creation of the Agile Adoption Forces Model. The Forces Model includes six categories of forces on agile adoption (cf. Figure 3.1). Each category aims to better understand the different aspects of the agile transformation process from traditional to agile development practices. The model includes two main directions for the forces: one from traditional towards agile approaches and one for the opposite direction. The forces that lead to agile adoption are distinguished between "trigger", "push" and "pull". In contrast, "inertia", "anxiety", and "context" are forces that prevent the agile adoption. The classification is inspired by the Customer Forces Diagram by Maurya [175] that itself is inspired by the Forces Diagram by Moesta and Spiek from the Jobs-to-be-done framework[1].

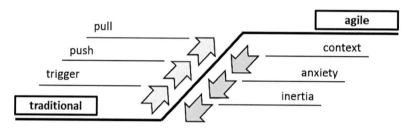

Figure 3.1: The Agile Adoption Forces Model [107, 109]

The "trigger" force initiates a change from current development practices towards the agile adoption. The initiation of change is often triggered from outside of the development teams based on demands from management or initiated by technological innovations [109]. The "push" force leads an individual or an organization towards adopting agile practices based on issues or demands. The "pull" force comes into effect when the agile adoption progresses based on the attractiveness of a future situation. The "inertia" force consists of habits which keep people from trying out something new and hence prevent agile adoption. The "anxiety" force includes uncertainties and new situations which lead to fears that influence and prevent the adoption of agile. The "context" force results from constraints and obstacles in the environment such as organizational structures or process barriers [107].

3.4.1 Forces that Support Agile Adoption in the Automotive Domain

This section is based on the data collection presented in Section 3.2 and the results published in [109]. The interview study (cf. Section 3.2) revealed several statements that foster the agile adoption in the automotive domain.

Trigger. Most interviewees are of the opinion that the market applies pressure on development time. There is an emerging demand to understand and react faster to customer needs. Agile software development is seen as a potential solution to keep pace.

---

[1]http://jobstobedone.org

The participants of the study note the necessity to shorten the development time at a reasonable price without losing quality.

Push. Forces that push agile adoption are primarily connected to software quality. The interviewed developers expect that an increase of internal releases and incremental builds will improve software quality. They mention that it is easier to detect and remove defects during development rather than later during integration. Another force that pushes agile adoption is the need to shorten release cycles for new features. Managers consider the current release cycles as too long. Features which are implemented in an agile way could be delivered faster to the customer and launched with profit. Furthermore, they point out the importance of customer involvement. For example, a fast feedback could prevent unprofitable development. Several participants consider that agile methods are applicable in situations where mechanical integration and tests are not heavily needed. This is the reason why interviewed participants employed in software development teams without mechanical integration have already introduced agile practices. They were able to integrate and test their software virtually without time consuming endurance tests. Nevertheless, there is a need for better system integration and simulation environments such as virtual verification environments.

Pull. An important pull force for software developer is the possibility to learn faster from internal and external customer feedback. This is seen as a means to increase the quality of specifications and code. Most of the developers expect that they will be able to implement more features in the same time with agile practices. The participated managers mention that top management considers agile practices as a necessary element of a future-proof organizational structure in order to meet customer and market demands.

3.4.2 Challenges with Increasing the Degree of Agility

Increasing the degree of agility leads to various challenges that hinder the agile adoption. These challenges result from different causes which classify each challenge into the presented forces model.

Forces that Prevent Agile Adoption in the Automotive Domain

This section elaborates the hindering factors that prevent an agile adoption in the automotive domain. It is based on the data collection presented in Section 3.2 and the results published in [107].

Inertia. Most of the interviewees point out that a major problem is the lack of understanding of the applicability of agile methods within their context. Some interviewees emphasize that it is not clear for the management how to manage agile development and how to integrate it into their departments. Managers point out that a change in the mindset is needed to adopt agile but it is currently unclear how to achieve this. All interviewees mention that applying agile methods might require more communication effort. 50% of the interviewees agree that communication effort is manageable in local, small teams but it is difficult to coordinate if the development is distributed.

Anxiety. The developers believe that it is necessary in agile development to give more responsibility to software developers. However, they also mention that management does not want to give up responsibilities. The managers emphasize that it is unclear how to provide correct estimations on development efforts when applying agile practices. They realize that it is difficult to prioritize features without correct estimations. In addition, the managers indicate that they do not want to displease software developers by changing roles and responsibilities. In fact, they fear that annoyed developers might leave the department. For the software developers, the biggest fear is that customer-relevant defects remain in the delivered software.

Context. All interviewees except of two point out that in the current structure of the company, too many responsible persons are involved in negotiations about feature implementation. The interviewees state that this slows down software development and prevents agile adoption. Most of the interviewees consider the large amount of process-dependencies for software development as an impediment for the transition towards agile development. One manager mentions the demand for more employees to maintain and manage the intersection between the agile department and the traditional organization. The processes of the higher system levels are seen as important. At the same time, however, they are considered to prevent and restrict agile development. The software developers emphasize the need to synchronize software and hardware development. However, they point out that synchronization meetings are slowing down the development process.

In addition, one interviewee attributes the longer development time to the increased communication effort during implementation. The interaction with the purchasing department and suppliers is highlighted by most interviewees as a challenging task. The communication with a supplier is identified to be a problem. Challenges with respect to communication are as well present in the context of globally distributed software development projects.

All interviewees point out the high effort to fulfill compliance and validation. Technical risks and challenges are mention by seven interviewees. It is important that the software is validated and of high quality. The developers mentioned that test and validation departments cannot increase speed due to the necessity of integration and validation in a real car. All interviewees refer to limited capacity in manpower and test systems when it comes to validation. Therefore, it is necessary to reuse software parts in order to reduce certification efforts. Other restrictions, which are seen as important for adopting agile, are long term field tests and endurance runs that are enforced by law, e.g. summer and winter tests. These tests must be kept at reasonable costs.

3.5 Automotive Challenges on Agile Software Product Lines

The identification of automotive specific challenges is following guideline 2 for design-science research by Hevner et al. [100]. The guideline helps to identify the problem relevance for the automotive domain. The interview study presented in Section 3.2 as well as the workshops (cf. Appendix B) help to identify challenges in the context of the automotive domain. Results presented in this section are partially published to the academic community and presented at international conferences [108, 112].

In the first instance, the automotive domain is confronted with the same challenges as other domains in the introduction of agility. The management of employees and the introduction of change processes must always be taken into consideration [206]. Sureshchandra and Shrinivasavadhani [240] point out that moving from traditional to agile cannot be done overnight. Bennekum [206] emphasizes that it is necessary to change the way people work and break down the silos [106]. He furthermore emphasizes that for an agile transformation, it is necessary that the team is putting the mindset before the technology [106]. However, it takes time for people to unlearn old traditional practices and to overcome the old paradigms [106, 240]. Campanelli et al. [31] state that a change in mindset is one of the hardest success factors to implement.

Compared to the three forces that prevent agile adoption the first two, "inertia" and "anxiety", are hard to change. These forces will mitigate over time with the strengthening of the supportive forces. However, they can only be affected by the employees themselves. The only force that can actively be influenced is the "context" force. According to Bennekum, "being agile means that the individual, the team and the organization have changed" [106].

Therefore, the context needs to change in order to mitigate the hindering factors. The interview study revealed that the automotive context includes peculiarities for the adoption of agile software development. Agile methods and practices are primarily designed for short development cycles in small development teams. Agile software development practices emphasize collaboration and communication between developers as well as between the customer and developers [213]. For larger teams, agile methods are adapted for large organizations, such as SAFe or SoS. The scaled frameworks aim at maintain an open communication culture in and between development teams.

However, they did not maintain the gained benefits by using the software product line. In the automotive domain, the software product line helps to manage the large number of software variations, coordinates the worldwide software development, and increases software quality by the reuse strategy [23]. Especially with regard to legal requirements and certification of software, it is necessary to reuse software parts. This is particularly important in the automotive sector, as legal requirements require lengthy certification processes. The aim is to maintain these benefits of the current development and enrich the development processes by agile practices.

Automotive specific challenges in the development process are considered, as the process must change and be adopted to verify a smooth development in an agile way. The challenges could be categorized into (1) organizational challenges, (2) worldwide development, (3) management, (4) dependencies, (5) synchronization processes, (6) validation, (7) release , and (8) the software development process itself.

Organization. All participants mention that coordination is a challenge when introducing agile elements to the existing software product line. The existing hierarchy is changing slowly towards an open minded agile development. However, the existing processes are not useless and still valid. Special milestones in the processes verify worldwide coordination and planning. Scoping processes decide which features are relevant for implementation.

By introducing agile development into the processes, it is seen that the coordination of the software development hinders a faster pace. The pace is influenced by coordination among the software product line. One challenge is to prevent a decomposition of the software product line. With many software variants and a faster development pace, there is the risk that the common software part becomes stunted. Therefore, it is important to consider synchronization points between software variants, several development processes like hardware and software, as well as supplier and in-house development.

Worldwide distribution of the development team. A major challenge is the collaboration with suppliers and a worldwide distribution of the development team. Different cultures and mindsets are likely hindering an agile development. In the current processes, the purchase department will often interfere the agile collaboration with suppliers. These challenges are important to consider when setting up the development process. New payment strategies need to be considered.

Furthermore, the worldwide distribution of the development team leads to challenges with regards to team communication. Different time zones, no face-to-face conversation and mistakes in translation constitute big dangers. In addition, the process to maintain and scope the common software parts requires a lot of communication between all participants. This is seen as slowing down the development because of slow communication channels. A lot of planning and coordination is needed to maintain the software product line. The communication is not only top-down but also bottom-up.

Management. Interviewees note that management does not want to give up any responsibility. With less responsibility on management level, scheduling the development and reporting will be challenging. It is unclear for managers how the agile software product line could be planned and features are scoped. However, planning is of high importance in an automotive development.

Dependencies and synchronization. The automotive software development is distributed with a lot of dependencies, like many included technical systems, test and verification steps and other developments domains like hardware and mechanical. A dynamic coordination is seen as a necessity to introduce agile development practices into software product line development.

The development process across several domains must be synchronized. Challenges could arise if only some parts of the organization work in an agile way and others do not. Interfaces between those departments must be well organized and set up.

Validation and Release. Compliance with standards while developing a lot of different software variants is seen as highly challenging. On the one hand, the development speed is increasing but on the other hand, it is necessary to validate the software to comply with standards like ISO 26262 and other legal restrictions. It is a challenge to scale the test framework in order to test all variants within the software product line. It is unclear how far the automation of test could help in the process. The testing strategy must be context-specific and scalable.

With the use of a software product line, already validated software parts could be reused. To keep pace with the market demands, composable certification could be one solution. However, composable certification is still far from being officially approved and not represented in valid regulations. New ways of certification and releasing software must be considered.

Software Development. One major challenge is the software development itself. The identified challenges in the software development are clustered as (1) technical issues, (2) costs, (3) requirements management, (4) software architecture, (5) software quality, (6) safety regulations and (7) the use of software product line and variants.

The automotive domain is a cost-driven business. Therefore, oftentimes the smallest possible hardware is selected to meet the requirements. However, this does not mean that there is a reduction of quality or functionality. Instead, it leads to the unpleasant effect that in some cases, different variants of software are compiled separately to fit on the hardware. To get such a high modularity, it is necessary that the architecture is well chosen. It is challenging to maintain a good shaped architecture while still having the possibility to integrate not foreseen features into the software. Furthermore, it is necessary that all adoptions are always related to the selected hardware target.

Another benefit of the agile development is to re-prioritize features. The downside of this is that it is challenging to freeze the functionality for different variants of the software product line due to late or incomplete requirements. However, in large and distributed developments, it is important to analyze and prioritize the features to prevent chaos. This is even more important when developing within a software product line. Scoping must always be considered to check for the affected variants. All variants must be validated in order to work as expected and defined by standards. The challenges in the software development are hard to tackle but worth to consider.

3.6   The Agile Software Product Line Portfolio

This section is based on the data collection presented in Section 3.2 and the results published in [110]. It categorizes the interview partners into the agile software product line portfolio. The distribution within the portfolio is verified by the workshop presented in Appendix B.2.

The interview study revealed that agile development methods are not used in many organizational units or only very rudimentary in the automotive domain. Furthermore, agile software development in the automotive domain is not or only partially coupled with software product lines. Figure 3.2 defines the portfolio to classify the development according to agile software development and the reuse of software. The first area represents organizations without a systematic software reuse strategy and no adoption of agile practices at all. Area 2 represents current automotive development, as seen in safety critical development fields such as powertrain. A systematic reuse strategy to manage the complexity is set up, however, agile practices are less distributed. Departments that use systematic reuse in the form of software product lines have so far used only a few agile elements. Conversely, it turned out that organizational units that already use many agile elements in the development have hardly any systematic reuse. Development for telematics functionality can be categorized into Area 3. The departments for telematics functionality are using a high amount of agile practices to satisfy the fast changing market demands in this field. However, they often follow the principle of "clone and own" and do not consider a systematic reuse.

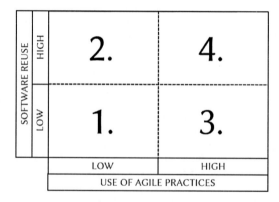

Figure 3.2: The portfolio of agile software product lines in the automotive domain

Area 4 is the desired way to develop software in the future. It represents a development that combines a strategic software reuse strategy, enriched with a high amount of agile methods. There are three basic paths to implement the combination of agile software development with software product lines. The first possibility is to set up a working software product line and enrich it with agile elements. The second one is that agile development processes are established and expanded with a software product line. The third possibility is to introduce agile elements and the software product line at the same time. Depending on the initial situation, different strategies are suitable.

3.7 Lack of Structured Combination Approach

This section is based on the data collection presented in Section 3.2 and the results presented in [111]. Furthermore, it contains the results of the workshops (cf. Appendix B).

The question arises how to combine agile software development and software product lines in the automotive domain. The current software development in the automotive domain is heavily structured by standardized processes. Process assessments are used to evaluate the processes of the organizational unit against a predefined process assessment model. Standards used to assess automotive development process are ASPICE [260] and CMMI [243]. However, neither CMMI [243] nor ASPICE [260] focus explicitly on the combination of agile development practices and software product lines.

Optimization is a journey that starts with the first step of determining where you are today [182]. Hence, Heidenberg et al. [96] emphasize the importance of defining the current state of the development practice [96]. This importance is also identified by Boehm and Turner [19] by encouraging developers to conduct a "hands-on evaluation" of their current organization to balance agility and discipline. They further point out that the current status is necessary to identify the next direction of change and develop strategies for "balancing [...] agility and discipline to meet future objectives and challenges" [19, p. 718]. Campanelli et al. [32] mention that assessing the current status can help to define the road-map for improvement.

Heidenberg et al. [96] mention that a combination of interviews, workshops, and external help can be helpful methods for defining the current status. According to the results of the interview study (cf. Section 3.2) and the insight from the workshops (cf. Appendix B), a lack of a structured combination approach is identified. The identified lack suggests to introduce an assessment and improvement model to foster the combination of agile software development and software product lines in the automotive domain. An assessment model to determine the current status is selected as these models (cf. [260, 127, 243, 262]) are widely accepted and adopted within the automotive domain. Furthermore, current assessors know how to use assessment models and also developers are familiar with assessments [111].

Boehm and Turner [19] point out to use the identified current status as the starting point to combine agile and discipline software development approaches. Thereby, the assessment shall provide a detailed overview about the current situation and foster the transformation due to recommendations given to the user.

3.8   Chapter Summary

This chapter identifies the automotive domain as one of the most challenging environments to develop software [267]. To manage the complexity and to keep the software development for vehicles cost efficient, current development in the automotive domain is based on a high amount of software reuse across different types of vehicles [86]. The development is heavily structured by standardized processes which are seen as too slow in order to keep pace with fast changing market demands [23, 63]. Agile practices are a promising approach to improve the software development with a faster time to market and an increasing speed of learning [109].

In addition, this chapter presents the results of an interview study, which identifies expected benefits for a combination of agile software development and software product lines in the automotive domain. In addition, the interview study revealed the agile adoption forces model [107]. The forces model contains two main directions for the forces: one from traditional towards agile development approaches and one into the opposite direction. The forces that lead to agile adoption are distinguished between "trigger", "push" and "pull". In contrast, "inertia", "anxiety", and "context" are forces that prevent the agile adoption.

Furthermore, the interview study revealed that agile software product lines are not used in many organizational units in the automotive domain. A strategic software reuse strategy enriched with a high amount of agile methods is the desired way to develop software in the future. Three basic paths to implement the combination of agile software development with software product lines are presented in this chapter. However, it is not clear how to introduce and start an agile transformation of existing software product lines in the automotive domain. As a conclusion, this means that there exists a need for an assessment model that deals with the current status of agile software product lines in the automotive domain. The assessment shall provide a detailed overview about the current situation and foster the implementation of agile software product lines based on recommendations given to the user.

Chapter 4

State of the Art

This chapter presents two literature reviews. The first literature review examines existing challenges which arise when agile development and software product lines are introduced in the automotive domain. The identified literature deals with challenges in (1) the use of agile methods in the automotive domain, (2) the use of product line development in the automotive domain, and (3) the combination of agile methods and product line development. This first part of this chapter offers an intersection of all three topics. The results of the literature study are published in [104].

The second literature review examines the distribution of assessment models for agile software product lines in the automotive domain. The data extraction aims at identifying already existing solutions in published literature and to derive recommendations from it. The different representation of the two literature reviews is due to the fact that results of the first literature review are already published [104].

4.1 Existing Literature on Automotive Agile Software Product Lines

This sections is mainly based on results presented in the publication [104]. However, the findings are extended by more recent resources that have been published after the literature review [104] conducted in 2016.

4.1.1 Research Design

The Design-Science Research approach includes a rigor cycle that extracts expertise from the literature into the research [100]. As part of the research presented in this thesis, a literature study [104] was conducted to identify challenges and recommendations for agile software product lines in the automotive domain. The results of this literature study are updated to cover the time from 2016 until 2018. For this purpose, the identical research string and databases are used as mentioned in the previous study [104]. However, the inclusion criteria are modified to include only publications published in the time between 2016 and 2018. In total, 19 publications are added to the original data collection presented in [104]. The updated literature study provides an overview of agile methods for embedded software development in the automotive domain, especially with respect to software product lines.

4.1.2   Searching for Common Ground

An overview of all identified publications can be found in Table F.1 in the Appendix. Several publications could be identified in the area of agile software product lines in the automotive domain since 2016. The questions that guide this mapping study are *What are appropriate methods to establish an agile software product line? (RQ1.1)* and *Which tasks are relevant for improvement and transformation towards agile software product lines? (RQ1.2)*. These questions are addressed by three sub-questions to provide different views on the topic. Figure 4.1 presents the three different ways to address the combination of agile software product lines.

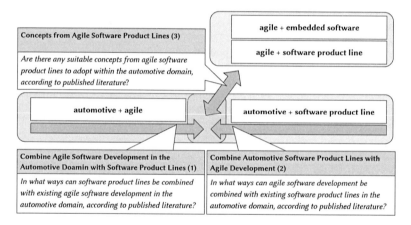

Figure 4.1: Three different ways to address the combination of agile software product lines

Combine Agile Software Development in the Automotive Domain with Software Product Lines (1)

In what ways can software product lines be combined with existing agile software development in the automotive domain, according to published literature?

Until 2016, the published literature does not provide significant information or approaches on how to adapt software product line development to existing agile software development approaches in the automotive domain. Several publications are identified that focus on the adaptation of agile software development approaches to the specifics of the automotive domain. However, none of these publications addresses the introduction of software product line development into existing agile software development processes.

The findings can be summarized as follows:

(1.) Adapting agile software development in the automotive typically concentrates only on selected agile elements such as CI. However, the published literature until 2016 does not show any recommendations to use a comprehensive set of agile elements and practices together in the automotive domain. Thiel et al. [245] suggest to introduce selected agile approaches to automotive systems engineering. This suggestion is also supported by the "Agile in Automotive Survey" from Kugler and Maag [150]. The survey highlights that many companies do only introduce single agile elements into existing and proven development cycles. After 2016, Hohl et al. [108, 112] point out challenges and give recommendations for a successful combination of agile software development and software product lines in the automotive domain.

(2.) The majority of the published literature suggests that agile models and processes should get customized to the specifics of the automotive domain before they are implemented in practice. The survey conducted by Kugler and Maag [150] recommends not to apply a purely Scrum approach in practice. Instead, they emphasize that pure Scrum is often not applicable due to the context factors and the development environment [150]. Therefore, agile methods must be adapted and customized to the field of application.

(3.) Several agile models and processes that are already customized to the specifics of the automotive domain are proposed in the published literature. The concurrent *Feedback Loop Model* introduces feedback loops for different organizations to enable cooperation [93]. The cooperation (including communication) between different organizations is managed by a new architect role that shortens the development time. The Agile, Hybrid Assessment Method for the Automotive Industry (AHAA) considers safety critical development [176]. Software quality is important for software critical companies like in the automotive domain to ensure high reliability and maturity of software. Plan-driven practices are assessed with respect to software process improvement like CMMI [243] and ASPICE [242]. Additionally, the assessment suggests agile based improvement solutions within the automotive domain.

Combine Automotive Software Product Lines with Agile Development (2)

In what ways can agile software development be combined with existing software product lines in the automotive domain, according to published literature?

The majority of the published literature is concerned with software product lines within the automotive domain without considering an adaptation to agile software development methods. In fact, there exists no ready-made solution to combine agile software development with software product lines in the automotive domain [104]. Several variant management approaches and appropriate methods and processes to handle variants are discussed. Some product line approaches are presented that might be helpful in understanding what to consider when combining with agile development. Four different binding times, programming, integration, assembly, and runtime lead to a "very large number of individually complex products with incomparably rich

feature variation among them" [267, p.336]. Wozniak and Clements [267] introduce
the Mega Scale - Software Product Line Engineering (MS-SPLE) approach. This
approach is applied for large product sets with complex products and complex feature
variations like the automotive domain. MS-SPLE is a possibility to manage, for
example, calibration parameters for the software variation mechanism and the complexity
management. However, agile software development aspects are not taken into account
within MS-SPLE [267].

In 2017, Hayashi et al. [94] propose an agile development management method for
multiple product lines of automotive software systems. They introduce an iterative
agile development method to manage the diversity of software variants. The presented
method reduces the complexity of the software product line and leads to a stable
development [94]. Therefore, they divided the application engineering into iterative
sprints. Furthermore, they introduce an iterative development process that consists of
application development processes in order to cover multiple projects [94]. The minor
iteration loops on a project-level and the major iteration loops across the projects help
to increase the manageability [94].

Concepts from Agile Software Product Lines (3)

*Are there any suitable concepts from agile software product lines to adopt within the
automotive domain, according to published literature?*

The literature provides concepts for the combination of agile software development and
software product lines. These concepts might reveal helpful insights for an adaptation
in the automotive domain. Concepts from agile product line development and agile
development in embedded domains are identified. In the embedded domain, safety aspects
are a prime goal to satisfy [136]. Therefore, the use of agile practices in regulated and
safety-critical domains is still limited [136]. The study of Kaisti et al. [137] finds no
reason why agile methods could not be used in the embedded domain. Eklund et al. [61]
point out the necessity to consider different development cycle-times for hardware and
mechanics. It is important to synchronize these cycles and freeze the design at a quality
gate and milestone. The published literature can be considered from a technical viewpoint
and a business viewpoint.

Within the business viewpoint, it is often mentioned that it is essential to deliver
high-quality software in time and within estimated cost and effort as time to market is
an increasingly important success factor for companies. It is therefore important to know
which parts of the software development process are able to become more agile and how to
apply the agile practices to speed up the development [160]. McGregor [178] emphasizes
that an entire customer satisfaction always requires a trade-off between flexibility and
software waste due to late rework of code and a late binding time of variability [156, 180].

The technical viewpoint can be divided into *agile methods and models* which are
already in use and *agile aspects* like documentation or scoping which should be considered
for a successful combination.

Agile Methods and Frameworks. Different agile methods are described to combine agile software development and a reuse strategy of software components. Well-known agile methods such as Scrum and XP are described in the literature. However, these methods are often tailored to the field of application. Lindvall et al. [160] describe a project which utilizes the XP approach that consists of auxiliary processes in order to define the scope and to adjust delivery time in advance. Diaz et al. [52] present a tailored Scrum approach. In this approach, domain engineering and application engineering processes are performed in an iterative way in different sprints [52]. Santos and Lucena [219] combine the Scrum life cycle phases and the Software Product Line Engineering (SPLE) sub-processes to form Software Product Line Engineering with Scrum (ScrumPL).

Another approach of combining software product lines and agile development is the *Feature Driven Approach* with the use of *Feature Models* [6, 211]. This hybrid method captures the initial view of the results of the commonality and variability analysis [178]. In this approach, both disciplines are merged. As a result, feature orientation blends the benefits of product line engineering with those of agility [142]. As an extension of the feature model, the composite feature model is described by Urli et al. [255]. Their solution relies on the definition of composite feature models and the use of a model-driven evolution process to support it on large real systems [255].

Neves and Vilain [187] present the idea of Test Driven Development (TDD) as the basis to combine agile software development and software product lines. Furthermore, they mention that the practice of refactoring introduces a reactive variability in agile software product line engineering [187]. Therefore, a Software Product Line (SPL) evolves and acquires variability points on demand [187]. Due to the speed up of the development, it is necessary to retest and certificate some parts repeatedly [8]. It is therefore essential to automate test procedures. It is a significant effort to set up tools and maintain the test environment [171]. Ghanam et al. [81] extend the idea of TDD and describe tests not only in form of regression tests. They rather describe the test approach as a way to determine commonalities in software systems of the same domain [81].

Agile Aspects. This section presents cross-cutting aspects like architecture, scoping, communication and safety regulations. These aspects should be considered in detail when combining Agile Software Development (ASD) and SPLs.

Architecture. Typically, agile development disregards a detailed consideration of the architecture. However, in product line development, architecture is an important aspect to consider [10]. It is necessary to find the right trade-off between the management of architecture evolution and refactoring without sacrificing the principles of agility [178]. Furthermore, architecture erosion should be avoided at any time [23]. The use of proprietary architectures could help to avoid this. In contrast, Chong [33] promotes the adoption of open standards, rather than closed proprietary architectures. He considers this as an essential economic driver for opening closed markets to competition [33, 17].

Scoping. Ghanam et al. [77] introduce a new lightweight variability analysis technique to determine commonalities and variations between the new requirements and the existing ones. The analysis is conducted iteratively in every agile iteration [77]. In addition,

Atherton and Collins [8] divide requirements into small pieces of functionality. These small parts are categorized and prioritized in a lightweight approach [8].

Communication. Gren [84] identify communication as a key factor for a successful combination of ASD and SPLs. Intra- and inter-organizational communication practices and the awareness for software reuse are essential [172]. Good communication is necessary within development teams, between teams, and the units they depend on, e.g. validation and business units [172]. It is important to keep the communication overhead low [142].

Safety regulations. Development organizations have to comply with legal regulations [142]. Regarding regulations and standards, process descriptions and development documentation are required. However, this may become inefficient if the overhead to organize document writing, signing, reading, reviewing, and revising increases. A production of waste such as functionality that potentially never gets shipped to a customer should be avoided [142].

4.2   Existing Literature on Assessment Models for Agile Software Product Lines in the Automotive Domain

Assessment models are a well used approach in the automotive domain to determine the capability and maturity of organizational processes to develop software and define improvement steps. Assessing and determine the current status compared to a well-defined standard enables organizations to organize the processes and keep projects manageable. Different norms and standards have evolved for assessments in the automotive domain, such as CMMI [243] and ASPICE [260]. Both define methods to evaluate complete process models and organizations [98]. The second literature review examines challenges of existing assessment models in introducing agile software product lines and identifies specific aspects that need to be addressed given the peculiarities of the automotive domain. Therefore, the essential process steps proposed by Petersen et al. [205] for a systematic mapping study are used.

4.2.1   Research Design and Definition of Research Questions

In order to identify relevant literature and to gain an overview of the research area, the research method of a mapping study was selected [143]. The research process follows the process described by Petersen et al. [205]. For the search of relevant literature, a search string was constructed and a search was conducted within suitable reference databases. The questions that guide this mapping study are *What are problems with using assessment models for introducing agile software product lines? (RQ1.3)* and *How do existing assessment models need to be modified to introduce and improve agile software product lines? (RQ1.5)*

4.2.2 Conducting the Search for Relevant Papers

The essential process steps are executed to conduct the research process as recommended by Petersen et al. [205].

Selection of databases. The selection of databases is essential to make the research outcome as comprehensive as possible. Six databases are selected: Science Direct, IEEE Xplore, Springer Link, Wiley Online Library, and Google Scholar.

Definition of the search string. The construction of the search string includes three different directions to examine assessment models for agile software product lines in the automotive domain. The first direction starts with existing assessment models in the automotive domain and searches for extensions with regard to agile software development or software product lines. The second direction addresses assessment models for agile software development and examines if they are conducted in the automotive domain or are combined with software product lines. The last direction starts with assessments for software product lines and searches for connections to agile software development or software development in the automotive domain.

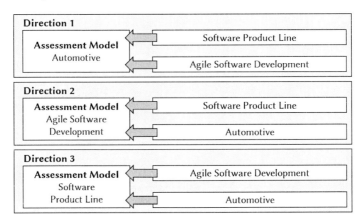

Figure 4.2: The three directions addressed by the literature review

The selected directions lead to three constructed search strings:

Direction 1: *(((("assessment(s)" OR "maturity model") AND "automotive") AND "software product line(s)") OR ((("assessment(s)" OR "maturity model") AND "automotive") AND "agile Software Development"))*

Direction 2: *(((("assessment(s)" OR "maturity model") AND "agile software development") AND "software product line(s)") OR ((("assessment(s)" OR "maturity model") AND "agile software development") AND "automotive"))*

Direction 3: *(((("assessment(s)" OR "maturity model") AND "software product line(s)") AND "agile software development") OR ((("assessment(s)" OR "maturity model") AND "software product line(s)") AND "automotive"))*

The scope of the search is limited to titles, abstracts and keywords. The shapes of the search strings are adjusted to the selected database.

4.2.3   Screening of Papers for Inclusion and Exclusion

The screening of papers is conducted by applying the defined inclusion and exclusion criteria to the set of all found publications. The relevant papers that answer the research questions are identified. Irrelevant findings are excluded by the exclusion criteria [205].

Inclusion criteria:

- The paper discusses process maturity approaches with at least two of the selected search keywords (agile software development, software product line, or automotive).
- The paper is written in English or German.

Exclusion criteria:

- The paper presents assessment models in general.
- The paper presents assessment models for partial aspects not directly connected to the selected search keywords.
- The paper is not in accordance with at least two of the search keywords.
- The paper is not accessible.
- The paper addresses agile manufacturing in the automotive domain.
- Duplicated papers.

The applied screening process is divided into several subsequent filtering steps to select the relevant papers. The search process within the databases resulted in 879 papers. Applying the exclusion criteria on the title and keywords resulted in 94 independent studies. In this filtering step, duplicates were excluded as well. Filtering by abstracts reduces the total number of relevant papers to 25. Reading the complete publication for the data extraction reduced the number of papers to 16.

4.2.4   Keywording of Abstracts, Data Extraction and Mapping

In this literature study, three main facets of assessments or maturity models are considered: (1) automotive assessments combined with software product lines or agile software development, (2) agile assessments in the automotive context or combined with software product lines and (3) software product line assessments combined with agile development or in the context of the automotive domain.

Table F.2 in the Appendix presents an overview about the identified publications and the categorization into one of the three identified directions to address the topic.

4.2.5 (1) Automotive Assessments combined with Software Product Lines or Agile Software Development

Different norms and standards have evolved for assessments over the past. CMMI [243] and ASPICE [260] define methods to evaluate complete process models and organizations [98]. The possibility of using process assessment models and the improvement resulting from an assessment is always dependent on the development context. Automotive OEMs use assessment models to assess their suppliers' software capability. For automotive embedded software and systems, the ASPICE [260] process assessment model is used. CMMI [243] is a collection of best practices that helps organizations to improve their processes. The model focuses on activities for developing quality products and services to meet the needs of customers and markets. The development of the models is closely linked with the industry and government. This collaboration provides a comprehensive and integrated set of guidelines for developing products and services [243].

CMMI provides little information on any particular software development approach [243]. Notes have been added to the process areas of *Configuration Management*, *Product Integration*, *Project Monitoring and Control*, *Project Planning*, *Process and Product Quality Assurance*, *Requirements Development*, *Requirements Management*, *Risk Management*, *Technical Solution*, and *Verification* in order to help the assessor in agile environments . As stated in CMMI [243], the notes for agile development and agile management are neither necessary nor sufficient for implementing the process area. The definition of agile adheres to the Manifesto for Agile Software Development [15]. However, CMMI limits the usage of the notes by recommending to be "cautious when using these notes" [243, p. 58]. Nevertheless, CMMI [243] proposes to establish the agile practice of CI as part of the product integration process. Furthermore, customer and potential end user involvement is recommended and identified for project success.

The AHAA by McCaffery et al. [176] considers safety-critical development. Software quality is important for software critical companies like in the automotive domain in order to ensure high reliability and maturity of software [176]. The AHAA aims to be a low-overhead assessment method, based on CMMI [243] and ASPICE [260], for small-to-medium sized organizations [176]. It aims at assessing organizations that wish to become automotive software suppliers [176].

Hantke [92] presents a development process that includes requirements both from Scrum [225] and Software Process Improvement and Capability Determination (SPICE) [127]. He introduces first results such as clearer and more transparent requirements, an improved team communication, and a better understanding of project goals within the team. Furthermore, he mentions that the coverage of the SPICE practices by the Scrum activities is relative large. He presents a method for implementing the combination in a pilot project. In contrast to our approach, Hantke [92] does not focus on software product lines. The potential benefits of the strategic software reuse are not considered in the comparison of SPICE and Scrum.

In 2015, Selleri Silva [227] conducted a systematic review of maturity levels that are combined with lightweight processes. They identified 81 publications that cover the topic of CMMI in combination with agile methodologies [227]. They conclude that agile methodologies can be used to reach the level two and three of CMMI and identify training, process visibility and automation of complex activities as the main success factors [227]. In addition, they point out that the number of published studies is growing and that research on this combination approaches are relevant [227].

In 2017, the VDA released guidelines for the assessment using ASPICE in the development of software-based systems [76]. Similar to CMMI [243], ASPICE [260] does not predefine any agile practice or method [76]. However, the used agile approach shall be compliant with required rules and standards [76]. Therefore, assessment recommendations for agile environments are provided [76]. These recommendations are based on practical experience and have no pretension of completeness [76]. They address the management of requirements, project planning, risk management, software architecture, software testing, and quality assurance. However, the recommendations do not support agile development or foster the introduction of agile elements into the development. Rather, it is recommended to down rate the assessment result if the applied agile approach is not sufficiently implemented.

Pelliccione et al. [203] present an architecture framework within a project at Volvo Carss which focuses on CI and deployment. Furthermore, they suggest to reduce the number of ECUs and to enable rapid communication with suppliers [203]. The presented framework is based on existing architecture frameworks in the automotive domain [203].

4.2.6   (2) Agile Assessments combined with Software Product Lines or the Automotive Domain

In 2015, Gren et al. [85] discuss the applicability and validity of the adoption framework. They identify items to measure agility, but at the same time question agile maturity models as a way to assess agility [85]. They point out the necessity to extend assessment measurements by categories such as organizational culture and innovation propensity [85].

Özcan-Top and Demirörs [198] identify nine assessment models for agility in a systematic literature review on keywords to agile maturity. Furthermore, they identify 37 assessment tools that partially automate the assessment process. Özcan-Top and Demirörs [197] show how sufficient the existing agile maturity models are and highlight the strengths and weaknesses of five selected agile maturity models. They introduce assessment criteria, such as "Fitness for Purpose", "Completeness", the "Definition of Agile Levels", "Objectivity", and "Correctness" to evaluate these models. All identified models had deficiencies at a certain level, according to six assessment criteria [197]. Furthermore, none of the identified models cover the peculiarities of the automotive domain.

4.2.7   (3) Software Product Line Assessments combined with Agile Development or the Automotive Domain.

Jasmine and Vasantha [134] define the Reuse Capability Maturity Model (RCMM) which focuses on reuse. This model helps to ensure a well planned and controlled reuse-oriented software development. The RCMM is inspired by CMMI and consists of five maturity levels. Each maturity level specifies an achieved level in the evolution to a mature reuse process [134]. Therefore, the RCMM model defines a basis for estimating the level of software reuse practice within an organization. However, Jasmine and Vasantha [134] do not evaluate the suggested model so far. They argue that it is too early to be certain that this model also fits for an automotive development. In contrast to Jasmine and Vasantha [134], ASPLA Model is tailored to the automotive domain. It retains the benefits resulting from the use of software product lines and enriches the processes by tailored agile practices.

There are various evaluating frameworks to assess the maturity and potential of product line engineering practices. For example, the Family Evaluation Framework (FEF) proposed by van der Linden [158, 259] which has been developed in the CAFÉ/Families EU projects. It provides a four dimensional evaluation scheme to assess the readiness or maturity of product line adoption within an organization. The Legacy Software Evaluation Framework (LSEF) proposed by Yoshimura et al. [270] is a framework to help an organization to assess and determine the degree of maturity of its legacy system from the view point of software product lines. They introduce software product line activities into several business divisions such as automotive systems [270].

In 2006, Yoshimura et al. [269] introduced an assessment approach to merge existing embedded software into a product line approach. This assessment approach focuses on the economical benefit of software product line engineering by identifying the return on investment expectations of the product line [269]. Furthermore, the effort for building reusable assets is identified [269].

4.2.8 Threats to Validity

The outcome of the literature studies are biased by different factors. The treats to validity are categorized according to Wohlin et al. [265] as *internal, external, construct* and *conclusion validity.*

Definition of the search string. The search string is defined to address the topic from three different directions. These three directions, as well as synonyms for keywords are used in order to find relevant publications. Synonyms are used for "assessment" and "maturity model" as these two words are often used as synonyms (*construct validity*).

Definition of inclusion and exclusion criteria. Inclusion and exclusion criteria are defined to retain a certain objectivity of the results. In order to reduce biases introduced due to subjective decisions (*internal validity*), inclusion and exclusion criteria are formulated. The exclusion criteria defined in the presented literature review narrowed the selection to get precise results for the automotive domain. However, it needs to be stated that there are various maturity models presented within the literature to address agility. A lot of information in the agile community is published in blogs, white papers and experience reports. However, these publications are categorized as grey literature and are therefore not included in the literature review of this thesis. Grey literature often misses peer reviews which assure validity and correctness within the academic context. The

perspective of the certification body Intacs[1] on "Clarifying Myths with Process Maturity Models vs. Agile" [16] was used as a basis for the extension of agile development in the VDA released guidelines for the assessment using ASPICE [76]. However, this whitepaper is also not included in the review and therefore not considered. Furthermore, Linders [159] offers a list with more than 70 agile self-assessment tools and frameworks on his homepage[2]. None of the presented agile assessment models are defined to be used in the automotive domain. Assessment models such as bootstrap [152] are not considered as they find no application in the automotive practice anymore and are therefore excluded.
Selection of databases. Many databases published papers in the area of software engineering. Therefore, it can happen that a publication is listed in more than one database (*construct validity*). The threat of missing publications is mitigated by using eight databases in the first literature review (cf. Section 4.1) and six in the second one (cf. Section F.2).
Execution. The literature reviews are mainly executed by the author of this thesis. This increases the amount of researcher bias *(internal validity)*. Therefore, the selection of publications is based on the authors opinion, however it is guided by inclusion or exclusion criteria. In case of doubts, the author decided to include the paper. The whole process was reviewed by the second researcher and the results are published to the academic community and presented at international conferences [104, 105].
Results. Due to the construction of the studies *(construct validity)*, it is not guaranteed that all relevant papers were found *(external validity)*.

4.3   Chapter Summary

The first literature review present that there exists no approach specifically tailored to the automotive domain handling the combination of agile software product lines. Similarly, searching for existing literature that deals with the introduction in the automotive domain also did not reveal significant results. However, by looking at related domains many insights were provided on how to combine agile software development and software product lines in the automotive domain. These insights are useful to identify the starting points to modify automotive software development processes in such a way that they can benefit from both agility and systematic reuse through product lines.

The second literature review focuses on assessment models to identify the current status of agile software product lines in the automotive domain. The interesting intersection of the keywords was addressed by approaching the topic from three different perspectives. The study reveals that there exists no assessment model that assesses the current status of agile software product lines in the automotive domain. Available assessments models are only covering some parts of the development cycle or just focusing on specific agile methods.

---

[1]http://www.intacs.info/
[2]http://www.benlinders.com/tools/agile-self-assessments/

Chapter 5

The ASPLA Model

Both, the literature (cf. Chapter 4) and the interview study (cf. Section 3.2) revealed the necessity to combine agile practices and software product lines for the automotive software development. Existing assessment models do not assess the current status of agile software product lines in the automotive domain. This gap is filled by the Agile Software Product Line in Automotive (ASPLA) Model. The model can be used to assess the current status and identify improvement areas for a successful combination of agile practices and software product lines in the automotive domain.

5.1 The Type of Research Artifact

Hevner et al. [100] set up seven guidelines for conducting Design-Science Research. They mention that the understanding of the problem and its solution is achieved in the implementation and application of an artifact [100]. Hevner et al. define artifacts as "constructs (vocabulary and symbols), models (abstractions and representations), methods (algorithms and practices), and instantiations (implemented and prototype systems)" [100, p. 77]. Furthermore, Hevner and Chatterjee mention that "artifacts are synthesized, may imitate appearances of natural things, can be characterized in terms of functions, goals, adaptation, and are often discussed in terms of both imperatives and descriptives" [99, p. 24].

The artifact described within this thesis is the so-called ASPLA Model, an assessment model to assess the current status of agile software product lines in the automotive domain. In Design-Science Research, the artifact must be a viable and technology-based solution to an existing and relevant problem [100]. The case study [107] revealed existing problems with regards to the implementation of agile software product lines in the automotive domain. The interviewees mentioned the problem of an insufficient definition of their current position regarding agile development in combination with existing software product line development. Furthermore, the study revealed that the high variety of different definitions of "agile" and the ignorance about existing agile methods and practices makes it difficult to set up agile software product lines in the automotive domain [107]. There are several publications presenting different approaches to transform a large company, which is working in a traditional way, into an agile one [146].

Boehm and Turner's work on "Balancing agility and discipline: evaluating and integrating agile and plan-driven methods" [19] in 2003 can be seen as one of the first attempts regarding agile transformation using a risk-based decision making. In 2017, Abidin et al. [2] conducted a literature review to identify the agile transformation models (ATMs). They categorized the identified ATMs into four categories: "People-oriented Model", "Instructive Model", "Maturity Model", and "Scalable Model" [2].

The so-called agile transformation of organizations is a frequently discussed topic [106]. However, developers often declare themselves "agile" when just using Scrum by the book [106]. In this case, the meaning of "agile" and the underlying basics are wrongly interpreted and not understood [106, 147]. To understand the basics of agile and identify the possibilities of agile transformation, a study with the original contributors of the manifesto for agile software development was conducted [106]. A workshop with Arie van Bennekum, one of the co-authors of the agile manifesto, was held in 2017 [206]. Details about the workshop can be found in Appendix B.1.

5.1.1   Agile Transformations

Agile transformation is seen as a necessity to be able to deal with upcoming challenges in the software development and to achieve business goals [31, 32]. There exist various different approaches to initiate an agile transformation [146]. Klünder et al. [146] classify the transformation approaches into bottom-up and top-down strategies as well as into step-by-step and big-bang transformations. They point out that it takes between one and two years to transform an organization to an organization that works in an agile way [146]. Gandomani et al. [135] mention that an agile transformation needs a lot of effort to change the organization and this process can last for a long time [135]. An impediment that hinders the agile transformation is that companies need to *"overcome old paradigms"* [206]. The old paradigms affect the way organizations work and restrict people from working in an efficient way [206]. Bennekum [206] point out that people tend to abide by the ancient rules, because they often belief that administrative actions within a company are mandatory and it has always been done in this way. Agile promotes a different way of approaching organizations, teamwork and leadership. It is important to realize that the behavior and changing capabilities of people make the difference [182].

Cilliers and Greyvenstein [35] identify how a "silo mentality" impacts employees and gets them to follow the orders they are told by senior management levels. Employees with no responsibility, who are not trusting in their self-determination, hinder an agile way of working [206]. Self-organized teams shall be established and the team spirit shall be improved. "The better the team spirit, the better their performance" [238, p. 254]. Agile encourage people to improve their interactions within the company [56]. Interaction techniques help to create a maximum of transparency throughout the organization, projects and operations [206]. However, working agile "involves a lot of informal communication and tacit knowledge" [238, p. 254]. Bennekum emphasizes that "transparency is the carrier of Agile, without transparency a transformation and a new way of working will not work" [206].

Furthermore, it is mandatory that the whole company is involved in the transformation process [146]. Bennekum [206] points out the necessity of the existence of a "vertical commitment through all levels of hierarchies which helps to initiate and implement the transformation" [206, 150]. It is therefore important to include all supporting entities of the organization such as human resources, marketing, and legal. With a missing commitment by the business, the transformation is bogged down after a while and the company will return to the traditional way of working [206]. Individuals as well as organizations tend to fall back into old patterns and continue using the old hierarchies, decision-making processes, and standards [206]. The inherent resistance to change is based on the feelings of employees who may feel threatened by the new way of working or may feel they lose power and status [96]. It is not possible to change individuals by telling them what to do [107].

In order to be able to work in an agile way and to undergo an agile transformation, it is necessary that the team is putting the "mindset before the technology" [206]. To define a road map for the agile transformation, Heidenberg et al. [96] point out the importance of defining the current state. Bennekum [206] fosters the Integrated Agile Transformation Model$^{\circledR}$ (IATM) to define the starting point and the aim of the transformation. The IATM assessment process is based on six organizational competencies: (1) Culture and style, (2) Foundations, content and process, (3) Participatory environment, (4) Appropriate solutions, (5) Knowledge management, and (6) Mindset and attitude. These competencies are aligned with the transformation objectives and are observed during the assessment. The selected competencies are refined on a regular basis. Starting with addressing developers' needs, an assessment is conducted within the development teams. The result of the assessment creates the transformation backlog. After defining the agile baseline for the company, the concept starts with a disruptive change of the environment. This is needed to create a breach with the old paradigms. The employees get agile training and focus on team rituals and team feedback [96]. New tooling is introduced and the agile coach hands over the coached and trained teams. People are first trained, then coached in team context and later in individual context to support a sustainable change.

Heidenberg et al. [96] consider interviews, workshops, and external help as helpful methods for defining the current state. The research artifact and the main contribution of this thesis is defined as an assessment model that defines the current state of combination of agile software development and software product lines. The model is called Agile Software Product Line in Automotive (ASPLA) Model. The purpose of the ASPLA Model and of assessments in general is to evaluate or estimate the nature, ability, and quality of the development and to improve the processes according to the assessment results. The ASPLA Model offers the methodology to combine agile software development and software product lines in a structured way. Such a methodology was neither found in the literature review [104] nor in practice [107, 109] but is identified to be desired for guiding the transformation process [108]. Optimization is a journey and starts with the first step of determining where you are today [182].

Reasons for the selection of an assessment model as part of the ASPLA Model and research artifact of this thesis are:

- Results of assessment models can identify the current status regarding the assessed topic. It is necessary to standardize the view, as everyone declares themselves as "agile" and is doing a reuse of software.

- Assessments are a standardized way to change organizational processes [64].

- The use of process oriented assessment models (cf. [260, 127, 34, 262]) is widely accepted and adopted within the automotive domain. The assessors know how to use assessment models.

- Currently, there is a lack of automotive assessment models regarding agile methods and practices in combination with software product lines [111] (cf. Section 4.2).

5.2   Setting up the ASPLA Model

Hevner et al. [100] propose seven guidelines for conducting Design-Science Research. To set up an artifact, the guidelines require the "creation of an innovative, purposeful artifact (Guideline 1) for a specified problem domain (Guideline 2)" [100, p. 82]. Douglass points out that "the best way [...]is to] identify the key pain points of your development organization or project and apply the practices that specifically address your greatest pain" [27, S. 765]. For a purposeful artifact, it is necessary to evaluate existing challenges within the domain [100].

5.2.1   Real-life Challenges that Need to be Addressed

The interview study [107] identified forces that prevent an agile adoption. The preventing forces (inertia, anxiety, context) are described in detail in Section 3.4.2. Agile adoption and an agile way of working call for a change in mindset [240]. The mindset change is related to the hindering forces "inertia" and "anxiety". These two forces affect each employee individually and are hard to address. A mindset change will be the result of a slow and stepwise integration of agile methods into the rigid and inflexible surrounding processes [107]. The attraction of the agile way of working will dissolve anxiety and break up inertia. Therefore, the focus of this thesis is the "context" forces such as the development process itself, in order to ensure a smooth development in an agile way.

Figure 5.1: The four challenge categories

Based on the results of the interview study [107], several challenges are identified [108, 112]. A list of all challenges can be found in Appendix C. These challenges are categorized into (1) organizational challenges for distributed development,

(2) challenges related to the coordination of the software product line, (3) challenges in adopting agile elements within the development process, and (4) challenges regarding automotive specific constraints. Figure 5.1 presents the four challenge categories.

(1) Organizational challenges result from the complex coordination of different departments and the distribution of development teams. To manage a distributed development, big companies in the automotive domain are often organized in a complex hierarchical structure. Several management levels are involved in the coordination of the development. A challenge is that managers within upper management levels do not want to lose any control [107]. They are often addicted to the old paradigms of top-down management and it is difficult to change their mindsets towards an open, agile way of developing software [206]. In addition, they consider it hard to plan and coordinate the development in an agile working environment [107]. Hence, the upper management levels stick to a stage-gated development process with milestones to coordinate distributed development and support planning of the software development process [61].

Table 5.1: Exemplary presentation of organizational challenges [108, 112].

ID	Text
135820	The distribution of the development team leads to challenges in the team communication.
135800	The existing hierarchy is addicted to the old paradigms and is changing slowly.
135867	It is challenging to manage the collaboration of agile and non-agile development teams within the organization.
135816	Purchase department is interfering an agile collaboration with suppliers.
135794	It is challenging to synchronize distributed development teams.
An exhaustive list of all organizational challenges can be found in Table C.2	

The synchronization of software development with other departments such as hardware or mechanical is challenging. In addition, challenges arise in the coordination of software development with supplier involvement and in-house development. Working with suppliers gets even harder if the development is distributed. The management of distributed teams across the borders of countries contradicts with the agile practice of co-located teams that need to work closely together. As it becomes apparent in the interviews, cross-cultural understanding is hard to achieve. Different cultures and different mindsets are likely hindering an agile development. A worldwide development leads to challenges in the communication within the team. Challenging is the communication between different time-zones without face-to-face conversation [223]. Table 5.1 shows organizational challenges that have been identified in the interview study [107]. A complete list of organizational challenges can be found in Table C.2.

For (2) software product lines, it is essential to consider the software baseline. Planning and coordination of the development is necessary to maintain the software product line and avoid an erosion of the common baseline. The software product line could decompose due to many branches in the software baseline and a high amount of variation points within the software. It is necessary that the common software part is maintained continuously. The process to maintain and scope the common software parts requires a lot of communication. Communication efforts slow down the development process. Hence, communication channels within teams and across the organizational hierarchy are hindering a flexible development of features [107].

Handling different variants and freezing the functionality for several variants of the software product line independently, is challenging. Developers complained about the process to evaluate the common functionality within the scoping process, because of independent freeze dates across different software variants [107]. To set up a reuse strategy that complements the principles of agile development and foster software reuse is a complex task. It is a challenge to maintain highly modular software components that remain compatible and exchangeable with the software basis [86]. Table 5.2 presents the identified challenges for software product lines [107]. A complete list of software product line challenges can be found in Table C.3.

Table 5.2: Exemplary presentation of software product line challenges [107, 108, 112].

ID	Text
135787	It is challenging to avoid the decomposition of the software product line during the development.
135924	It is challenging to freeze the functionality for different variants of the software product line while implementing in an agile environment.
135914	It is challenging to maintain a high modularity of the software components.
136238	It is challenging to set up a reuse strategy that complements the principles of agile development and foster software reuse.
135920	It is challenging to integrate not foreseen features into the software.
	An exhaustive list of all software product line challenges can be found in Table C.3

The interview revealed that the challenges for (3) agile software development are mainly based on the interaction with the customer. The customer is not closely integrated into the development process and the development is not enough focused on the specific customer needs. Furthermore, release cycles take several months and the cost of delay is not addressed. This is based on the circumstance that it is not possible to release software in a fast pace. Thorough testing and the creation of approval-relevant documentation is necessary to comply with all requirements given by the law.

Table 5.3: Exemplary presentation of agile software development challenges [108, 112].

ID	Text
135908	The cost of delay for software features is neglected.
138221	The development is not fully focused on the customer needs.

An exhaustive list of all agile software development challenges can be found in Table C.4

Several challenges are identified for the (4) automotive domain regarding the software development process and the related processes. The automotive domain is a highly cost-driven business and hardware is often designed to the minimum of acceptable performance and the minimum assembly of components on the circuit board.

This does not affect the quality or functionality but it leads to the unpleasant effect that different variants for specific markets are compiled separately to fit the hardware [108]. A modular architecture is a prerequisite for further progress but it is challenging to maintain a well-shaped architecture in order to integrate not foreseen features into the software at the same time. Changes in requirements at a later time in the development process are hard to address. All adoptions always depend on a selected hardware target and software variant and must be tested before released.

Table 5.4: Exemplary presentation of automotive specific challenges [108, 112].

ID	Text
135902	Hardware restrictions must be taken into account for software development.
135904	The cost pressure of hardware components must be considered.
140550	It is unclear how each software variant can be tested on real hardware in a car.
135882	It is unclear how the testing strategy must be adapted in agile development.
135926	It is challenging to maintain the development, if requirements are becoming available late in the development process.

An exhaustive list of all automotive specific challenges can be found in Table C.5

The automotive domain is a high security and safety critical domain. It is very challenging to be compliant with standards and law (national and international) while developing a lot of different software variants. All participants mentioned that an increase of the development speed urges to validate the software with the same pace. Maintaining standards like ISO 26262 [122] and other restrictions given by law are not disputable.

A shorter development time leads to an increasing number of independent software variants, which in turn results in an additional expense of testing activity. When introducing a new feature, each affected variant must be identified and tested against the expected behavior and defined standards. An adjustable and scalable test framework is essential to ensure the test coverage within the software product line and the large amount of different software variants. However, it is challenging to scale the test framework due to the close entanglement between different departures. So far, it is unclear how the automation of tests for the large amount of variants could be realized.

Overall, 59 challenges are identified from the results of the interview study [107, 112] regarding the integration of agile software development and software product lines in the automotive domain. After publishing these challenges and presenting them at the conference [112], they were reclustered according to the feedback collected in discussion rounds. A recommendation was to differentiate these challenges even more. The differentiation leads to a fine grained view on the topic, whereof 13 new challenges were introduced leading to a total of 72 challenges overall. A complete list of all identifies challenges is presented in Appendix C.

5.2.2   Challenges Identified in Literature

In the literature review [104] (cf. Section 4.1.2), the combination of agile software development and software product lines in the automotive domain is addressed from three different perspectives. The first perspective focuses on existing agile software development in the automotive domain. It examines if software product line approaches could be combined with already implemented agile processes. None of the approaches addresses the introduction of software product line development into existing agile software development processes. The second perspective focuses on existing software product lines in the automotive domain and their combination with agile software development. This perspective reveals that software product lines within the automotive domain are widely used. However, the publications on software product lines in the automotive domain typically do not consider agile development approaches. A key finding of the literature review is that there exists no ready-made solution to combine agile software development with software product lines in the automotive domain [104]. The third perspective takes into account related research areas into account. For all three perspectives, the literature identifies challenges that need to be addressed in order to combine agile software development and software product lines. Some challenges (cf. Section 4.1.2) are also presented in additional sources and displayed in Table 5.5.

Table 5.5: Exemplary presentation of challenges identified in the literature.

ID	Category	Text
136220	organizational	It is challenging to change large organizations. *Literature Review: [50], Additional Literature: [235, 74, 149, 217, 249, 1, 9, 31]*
136283	organizational	A long-term predictability is hard to achieve with short-term agility. *Literature Review: [61]; Interview Study (cf. Section 3.2)*
136261	organizational	Intra- and inter-organizational communication practices are hard to establish and maintain. *Literature Review: [172]*
136259	software product line	It is challenging to avoid the erosion of the software architecture. *Literature Review: [86, 40, 23]*
136257	software product line	It is necessary to find the right trade-off between the management of architecture evolution and refactoring without sacrificing the principles of agility. *Literature Review: [178]*
136242	agile software development	It is challenging to deliver high-quality software within estimated costs at a fast pace. *Literature Review: [160]*
136248	agile software development	It is unclear which agile practices can be used to speed up the development. *Literature Review: [61, 59, 194], Additional Literature: [147, 68, 4]*
136232	automotive domain	It is challenging to maintain the development if requirements are changing constantly in a fast pace. *Literature Review: [17]*
136273	automotive domain	It is challenging to create documentation (process descriptions and development documentation) in a fast pace. *Literature Review:[142]; Interview Study (cf. Section 3.2), Additional Literature [120, 67, 75]*

An exhaustive list of all challenges identified in the literature can be found in Appendix C

The literature review [104] revealed that it is essential to deliver high-quality software in time and within estimated cost and effort. Time to market is an increasingly important success factor for companies. It is mandatory to know which parts of the software development process are able to become more agile and how to apply the agile practices to increase flexibility in the development [160]. Different agile methods are described to combine agile software development with a reuse strategy of software components. Well-known agile methods such as Scrum and XP are described in the literature. Furthermore, auxiliary processes are described in order to define the scope and adjust delivery time in advance. Eklund et al. [61] point out that it is unclear which agile practices can be used to speed up the development.

Furthermore, the study revealed that specific cross-cutting aspects such as architecture, scoping, or communication must be considered. Typically, agile development neglects a detailed consideration of the architecture. However, in product line development, architecture is an important aspect to consider [10, 178]. It is necessary to find the right trade-off between the management of architecture evolution and refactoring without sacrificing the principles of agility [178]. Furthermore, architecture erosion should be avoided at any time [86, 40, 23].

Intra- and inter-organizational communication practices and the awareness for software reuse is necessary within development teams, between teams, and the units they depend on, e.g. validation, production, and after sales units [172]. In addition, it is important to keep the communication overhead low [142]. The literature review [104] confirms that in the embedded domain, safety aspects are a key objective [133]. Therefore, the use of agile practices in regulated and safety-critical domains is still limited [133]. To comply with regulations and standards, process descriptions and development documentation are required.

A production of waste such as a functionality that potentially never gets shipped to a customer should be avoided [142]. Eklund et al. [61] point out the necessity to consider different development cycle-times for hardware and mechanics. It is important to synchronize these cycles and freeze the design at quality gates and milestones. Traditionally, no or minimal changes are allowed, in order to keep the development process predictable. However, a long-term predictability is hard to achieve with short-term agility [61].

Overall, 33 challenges from the literature review [104] could be identified whereof nine could also be identified in the interview study. A complete list of all challenges identified in the literature are presented in Appendix C.

5.2.3   Recommendations to Overcome the Challenges

Overall, 96 individual challenges for the combination of agile software development and software product lines within the automotive domain could be identified. To overcome these challenges, the author of this thesis identified 214 recommendations which can be used as a guideline to mitigate the risk of an unsuccessful combination. In order to obtain and propose generally valid recommendations, they are based on the literature [104], insights from workshops and discussion rounds [112] (cf. Appendix B), and include the suggestions given by participants of the interview study [107] on how to tackle the challenges.

Hence, the recommendations are based on working experience and best practice from the automotive domain [112] and further substantiated by recommendations given in the literature [104]. The combination of different perspectives leads to a large number of

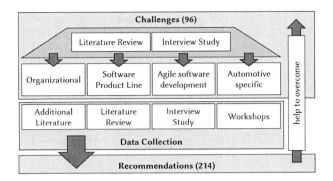

Figure 5.2: Challenge categories and recommendation sources

recommendations to combine agile software development and software product lines in the automotive domain. All 214 recommendations are linked to the corresponding challenges and related to other recommendations. These relations are presented in Appendix D by the properties "Related ↑" and "Related ↓" which help to trace each recommendation to the corresponding identified challenge. Furthermore, the source of the recommendation is provided. The "Source(s)" category denotes the original source of the recommendations and provides additional literature that supports the recommendation separated by an ";".

The following section is structured as follows: It first presents the applied method for coding and clustering the recommendations and describes the result for a high level categorization of them. Finally, the coding patterns and categories that are used to set up the ASPLA Model are introduced.

The Coding Method

For qualitative analysis, the identified recommendations are coded and clustered (cf. Figure 5.3). All recommendations were initially reviewed within a development team for embedded software in the automotive domain. Saldaña [218] defines coding as the initial step for data analysis and interpretation. In addition, Cope [41] points out that the coding is a process used for data exploration, analysis, and theory-building. She further points out that coding can be used in an exploratory, inductive way or in a more deductive manner [41]. Exploratory coding is also known from the methodology of grounded theory [117]. The selection of an appropriate coding method is essential for further analysis. Saldaña [218] suggests the application of a multistage cyclic qualitative analytical process. The applied multistage coding process is presented in Figure 5.3.

Saldaña [218] recommends an initial coding cycle, and presents different coding methods for various contexts [218]. According to the provided classification, the recommendations were coded by using descriptive and initial coding [218]. The term initial coding introduced by Saldaña [218] is synonymous to open coding as known from grounded theory (cf. [42]).

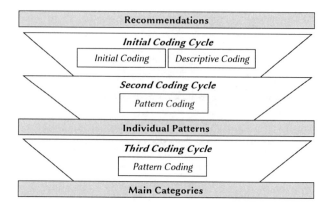

Figure 5.3: The multistage cyclic coding process

The applied coding approach for the recommendations uses the term initial coding to emphasizes the different coding cycles [218]. The goal of initial coding is to remain open to all possible directions during the coding process. As recommended by Saldaña [218], initial coding can employ other coding methods. Thereby, descriptive coding is combined with initial coding. In descriptive coding, the basic topic of a passage of qualitative data is summarized in a word or a phrase [218]. Coding phrases were assigned to each recommendation.

The second coding cycle aims at developing a thematic clustering of the codes and coding phrases from the previous coding cycle [218]. For this purpose, Saldaña [218] recommends to use pattern codes to identify common recommendations that were similarly coded.

According to Cope [41], the patterns and concepts that pertain the same topic shall be grouped into further categories. This approach leads to the third coding cycle which results in high level categories. These high level categories were generated in the same analytical process of pattern coding.

The Initial Setup of the Assessment Model

Schmid and John [222] recommend to take advantage of the existing body of knowledge. Therefore, they suggest to evaluate existing state of the art process assessment approaches valid for the desired domain and model the new approach as closely as possible to the existing one [222]. Assessments in the automotive domain cannot be conducted without considering the ASPICE model [260].

One possible approach to address the identified challenges is to modify the current ASPICE [260] standard. For this purpose the REUse processes could be extended by product lines and MANagement processes by an agile management style. However, due to the variety of recommendations and challenges it is not possible to adjust only two single ASPICE processes. The whole organization and the development processes have to change. Therefore, the ASPLA Model was developed. However, the setup of the ASPLA Model was inspired by ASPICE [260]. Furthermore, the internal structure of the model was based on the structure of ASPICE [260] to increase the acceptance of the ASPLA Model within the automotive domain.

The insights from the coding cycles are the fundamental knowledge base for setting up the ASPLA Model to support the assessment of the combination of agile software development and software product lines in the automotive domain. The initial and second coding cycle led to 64 individual coding patterns. One, exemplary pattern focuses on software product lines. The pattern phrase *"Use only one global software product line"* comprises the recommendations *"The different reuse strategies shall be merged into one approach valid worldwide [147214]"* and *"The development of features shall be standardized worldwide [147216]"*. Another pattern requests *"the software architecture [...] [to] be open to change"*. This pattern comprises the recommendations *"Monolithic Architectures shall be resolved and replaced by modular architectures [147701]"* and *"The Architecture shall be capable to manage loosely coupled software units [147703]"*.

ASPICE [260] defines two types of process performance indicators. Base Practices and Work Products are assigned to a unique process and relate to one or more process outcome. Both process performance indicators were adopted within the setup of the ASPLA Model. The 64 identified individual coding patterns were assigned to ASPLA performance indicators. However, some coding patterns did not only focus on the development process itself. Some patterns require specific attributes from the product under development. Therefore, a new category was introduced. With the focus on Product Attributes, the ASPLA Model is able to address specific requirements with regards to the product. Hence, the ASPLA Model extends the ASPICE [260] performance indicators by a product view that requests Product Attributes.

For each Base Practice and Product Attribute, the identified coding patterns were extended by a description on how to address the issue. The process focused pattern *"Use only one global software product line."* was considered as a Base Practice. The description for this Base Practice is to *"Ensure that only one software product line is used for the worldwide development of a product."*. The product focused coding pattern *"The software architecture shall be open to change"* led to a Product Attribute. The description added to the product focused coding pattern recommends to *"Ensure that the software architecture is not a monolithic architecture, by means of a modular architecture structure that is capable to manage loosely coupled software units"*. In total, 64 patterns led to 52 ASPLA Base Practices and 12 ASPLA Product Attributes.

According to ASPICE [260], each Base Practice is addressing an intended outcome. Since the ASPLA Model distinguishes between Base Practices and Product Attributes, the respective outcomes are divided as well. Therefore, Process Related Outcomes and Product Related Outcomes were introduced. The outcome of the presented Base Practice is a single software product line architecture that supports a distributed development. The Product Attribute leads to an outcome that states that the software architecture is open to changes and refactoring is possible.

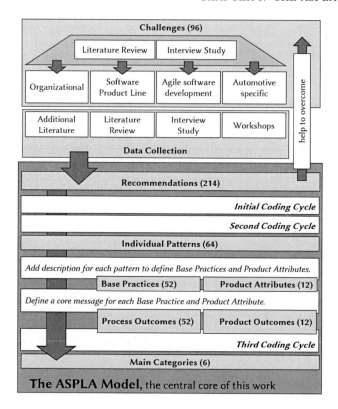

Figure 5.4: Coding the recommendations and identify main categories

To keep the model traceable, a 1-to-1 mapping of Base Practices and Product Attributes to the respective outcomes was defined. In total, this results in 52 individual Process Related Outcomes and 12 Product Related Outcomes.

According to the conducted categorization in the third coding cycle suggested by Cope [41], six high level categories were identified. These six areas are the core architecture of the ASPLA Model (cf. Section 5.3) and hence need to be considered in an assessment [111].

5.3   The ASPLA Model

Schmid and John [222] describe a process to evolve assessment approaches. They point out that assessment approaches are usually not just invented and then remain fixed forever [222]. Instead, assessment models need to be revised continuously and evolve over time. Improvements to the assessment model can be introduced by new insights and experiences from conducted assessments with the approach [222]. The proposed continuous improvement corresponds to the agile mindset. It is proposed in the inherent principles of the manifesto for agile software development [15] to reflect the current situation, decide how to become more effective, and adjust accordingly.

Therefore, one additional area was added to the ASPLA Model in order to keep the model itself flexible and adjustable to changes. With this approach, the ASPLA Model is able to evolve according to feedback and new suggestions. The improvement of the assessment model depends on the amount of information for improvement and the frequency of incorporating the feedback [222]. The introduction of iterative learning cycles ensures the possibility to update the ASPLA Model every four weeks according to provided feedback (cf. Section 6.3).

The seven identified areas are (1) Product Line Architecture, (2) Domain Requirements Engineering, (3) Agile Software Development, (4) Continuous X, (5) Continuous Model Improvement, (6) Test Strategy, and (7) Communication. The assigned number to each area randomly and does not imply any kind of prioritization. The numbers are only used to guarantee traceability.

5.3.1 The Honeycombs

In the terminology of the ASPLA Model, each identified area is called a Honeycomb (HC) (cf. Figure 5.5).

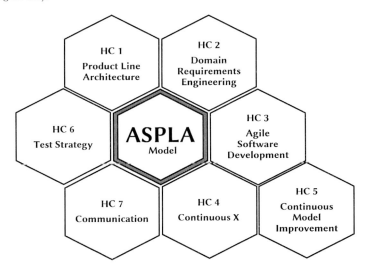

Figure 5.5: The Agile Software Product Line in Automotive (ASPLA) Model

The first sketches of the ASPLA Model and the shape of the important areas defined the term "Honeycomb". The shape of a Honeycomb was selected as it is associated with a light-weight but also stable form. Furthermore, it was not clear how many important areas will arise. With the Honeycomb shape, new arising areas can be attached to the Honeycomb structure.

The term "Honeycomb" clearly distincts the ASPLA Model from ASPICE [260]. While ASPICE focuses on processes and outcomes, ASPLA extends the process view by including a product-oriented view. For the combination of agile software development and software product lines, it is important that the product is suitable and can cope with the development. Therefore, special product properties need to be considered. Without these product properties, a combination of agile software development and software product line is not achievable. Each Honeycomb is described by the Honeycomb name and the Honeycomb purpose as follows:

Product Line Architecture (HC 1). The purpose of *Product Line Architecture* is to provide a suitable software architecture to enable the implementation of several software variants for different products with a high degree of software reuse.

Domain Requirements Engineering (HC 2). The purpose of *Domain Requirements Engineering* is to identify the reuse assets that should be developed in a software product line. This includes the identification of products and features that should be part of the product line and the definition of common and variable features.

Agile Software Development (HC 3). The purpose of *Agile Software Development* is to react faster on customer needs and legal constraints to reduce the time to market for innovative features upon a simultaneous increase of software quality.

Continuous X (HC 4). The purpose of *Continuous X* is to continuously execute tasks which lead to a more stable, compliant and better product.

Continuous Model Improvement (HC 5). The purpose of *Continuous Model Improvement* is to continuously reflect on the ASPLA Model and improve the interaction between the assessment result and the suggested improvement for the software development process.

Test-Strategy (HC 6). The purpose of *Test-Strategy* is to provide an environment to verify the correct behavior and ensure the software quality for various software variants which are developed at a fast pace.

Communication (HC 7). The purpose of *Communication* is to support the communication of all participating roles to avoid knowledge silos and react on customer needs in a flexible way.

5.3.2   The Outcomes

For each Honeycomb, a list of outcomes is associated. The outcomes denote the expected positive results of the Honeycombs. In contrast to ASPICE [260], the outcomes for the ASPLA Model are divided into Process Related Outcomes and Product Related Outcomes. Both types of outcomes represent a successful implementation of each

Honeycomb. In total, the ASPLA Model consists of 52 Process Related Outcomes and 12 Product Related Outcomes (cf. Appendix E).

Process Related Outcomes

Process Related Outcomes are expected positive results of the process performance which are related to the proper implementation of the development process.

The Process Related Outcomes define a flexible development process which is capable to handle rapid changes in requirements. This flexibility is introduced to serve different markets and model series with different software variants as well as to satisfy market specific demands. Features that are developed for one field of application can be rolled out to other markets or model series. Therefore, a software product line manages the strategic software reuse. The reuse of software leads to an enhanced reliability and quality [174]. Test automation and fast learning loops are supporting the software reuse process. The flexibility in the development process is introduced by agile practices. The agile practices foster a fast learning cycle and introduce the possibility to adjust the development. However, the selection of the agile practices to be used is not stipulated. The context for the introduction of agile practices is considered and context-specific agile practices are selected. Moreover, the flexible development process introduces new collaboration strategies that include suppliers and customers into the development process. Finally, the development processes and the ASPLA Model itself are open for new suggestions on how to improve the software development process.

The ASPLA Model denotes Process Related Outcomes as "ProcO_HC.<XX>". The name consists of the placeholder "HC", which defines the number of the related Honeycomb, and "XX", a consecutive number to identify the outcome. With this unified nomenclature, the assignment of Process Related Outcomes and Honeycombs is evident. Table 5.6 presents exemplary Process Related Outcomes and the corresponding Honeycomb. A complete list of all Process Related Outcomes can be found in Appendix E.

Table 5.6: Presentation of Process Related Outcomes.

ID	Process Related Outcome
Product Line Architecture (HC 1)	
ProcO 01.02	The software product line architecture supports a distributed development.
Domain Requirements Engineering (HC 2)	
ProcO_02.02	Rapid changes in requirements are considered and handled by the scoping process.
Agile Software Development (HC 3)	

continued on the next page.

ProcO_03.07	The use of agile practices is not stipulated, context-specific agile practices are used.

Continuous X (HC 4)

ProcO_04.01	The software development process is supported by continuous and automated tasks.

Continuous Model Improvement (HC 5)

ProcO_05.01	Suggestions to improve the software development process are proposed by the ASPLA Model.

Test-Strategy (HC 6)

ProcO_06.03	A scalable test strategy for different test hierarchies, including software variants, systems and real cars is realized.

Communication (HC 7)

ProcO_07.08	Collaboration with supplier is improved.

Product Related Outcomes

Product Related Outcomes are expected positive results of the development performance which are induced by properties of the product. The Product Related Outcomes are derived from the identified Product Attributes. In the ASPLA Model, properties for the product under development are required. This product view extends the process view as known from ASPICE [260]. The introduction of the product view is based on the coding cycles and the introduction of patterns that require specific attributes from the product under development.

Without considering the product and its properties, a successful combination of agile development and software reuse is difficult to establish. It is not possible to introduce new features into the software if its architecture is not designed to handle changes. Therefore, a dynamic adjustment of the development regarding market demands is established. The different customer needs are satisfied and a closer customer collaboration is defined. The introduced closer customer collaboration leads to a better understanding of the customer needs. As a result, the market can be serviced more purposefully. To manage the development, features are prioritized and market specific priority values for development are assigned. To retain the software quality in the multi variant development, an associated test case is assigned to each software unit. With this approach, the developed software is tested in an automated way and verification activities are conducted in regular time intervals.

The Product Related Outcomes are denoted as "ProdO_HC.XX". Table 5.7 presents exemplary Product Related Outcomes and their associated Honeycombs. Honeycomb 5 "Continuous Model Improvement" and Honeycomb 7 "Communication" do not request a demand towards the product under development. Therefore, both Honeycombs do not comprise Product Related Outcomes. A complete list of all Product Related Outcomes can be found in Appendix E.

Table 5.7: Exemplary presentation of Product Related Outcomes.

ID	Product Related Outcome
Product Line Architecture (HC 1)	
ProdO_01.02	The software architecture is open to changes, refactoring is possible.
Domain Requirements Engineering (HC 2)	
ProdO_02.03	A priority level is assigned to features.
Agile Software Development (HC 3)	
ProdO_03.01	The software satisfies customer needs and the customer is directly included into the development.
Continuous X (HC 4)	
ProdO_04.02	Software items provide the opportunity to perform verification activities with a high level of automation in regular time intervals.
Test-Strategy (HC 6)	
ProdO_06.01	For each software unit an associated test case is assigned.

5.3.3   Honeycomb Attributes

ASPICE [260] defines two types of process performance indicators. Base Practices and Work Products are mapped to an unique process and can be used by the assessor for conducting an objective assessment [260].

The ASPLA Model extends the process view and includes a product related view into the assessment. Therefore, the ASPLA Model introduces the so-called "Honeycomb attributes", which include Work Products, Base Practices, and Product Attributes. The Honeycomb attributes can be used by the assessor to define the Honeycomb maturity. During an assessment, the Honeycomb attributes are supposed to be a quickly accessible information source. They represent an exemplary implementation that the assessor can use. The internal structure of a Honeycomb is shown in Figure 5.6.

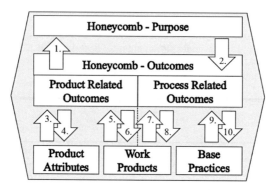

Figure 5.6: The internal structure of a Honeycomb

The relations between the purpose, the outcomes and the Honeycomb attributes are described in Table 5.8.

Table 5.8: The relationship between the purpose, the outcomes and the Honeycomb attributes.

Relation	Description
1.	*The Honeycomb-Outcomes* are the results of a successful implementation to fulfill the *Honeycomb-Purpose*.
2.	The *Honeycomb-Purpose* is characterized by the *Honeycomb-Outcomes*.
3.	*Product Attributes* indicate a successful achievement of *Product Related Outcomes*.
4.	*Product Related Outcomes* are supported by the *Product Attributes*.
5.	*Work Products* indicate a successful achievement of *Product Related Outcomes*.
6.	*Product Related Outcomes* affect the *Work Products*.
7.	*Work Products* indicate a successful achievement of *Process Related Outcomes*.
8.	*Process Related Outcomes* lead to *Work Products*.
9.	*Base Practices* indicate a successful achievement of *Process Related Outcomes*.
10.	*Process Related Outcomes* are supported by *Base Practices*.

Base Practices

Base Practices represent activity-oriented indicators. They indicate a successful achievement of the Process Related Outcomes. The ASPLA Model maps a single Base Practice to one individual Process Related Outcome. Base Practices are introduced by the definition of coding patterns in the second coding cycle (cf. Figure 5.3). Therefore, the patterns are extended by a description. The combination of pattern and description lead to 52 individual Base Practices.

The Base Practices support the assessor in assessing the current status of the development process with regards to addressing all seven Honeycombs of the ASPLA Model. As an example, the Base Practices ensure the use of a software product line. They foster the use of a single software product line for the worldwide distributed development of a product. Therefore, only one global software product line shall be used and a global software development process shall support the development of rapid changes in requirements. This is achieved by scoping meetings which ensure that rapid changes in requirements are considered in the scoping meetings.

Another example is to keep the development flexible. Therefore, agile practices shall be used whenever applicable. For this purpose, it is necessary to ensure that agile practices are suited to the context they are practiced. Furthermore, the Base Practices request the implementation of supporting tasks and a scalable test strategy. Following the Base Practices, it is ensured that supporting and repetitive tasks are included in the development process and an automated feedback is provided. In addition, a test strategy covers tests for individual software variants as well as tests in the entire systems and in real cars. The Base Practices address the process of communication and collaboration. The Base Practices foster a good and open-minded collaboration with the supplier and the supplier is participating in the process. Table 5.9 presents Base Practices for each Honeycomb. An exhaustive list of all Base Practices can be found in the description of the ASPLA Model in Appendix E.

Table 5.9: Exemplary presentation of Base Practices.

Product Line Architecture (HC 1)

BP_ProcO_01.02: Use only one global software product line. Ensure that only one software product line is used for the worldwide distributed development of a product. *[ProcO_01.02]*

===

Domain Requirements Engineering (HC 2)

BP_ProcO_02.02: Consider rapid changes in requirements in scoping meetings. Ensure that rapid changes in requirements are considered in the scoping meetings each time, even if the original feature was already assigned and prioritized for the development. *[ProcO_02.02]*

===

continued on the next page.

Agile Software Development (HC 3)

BP_ProcO_03.07: Utilize agile practices whenever applicable. Ensure agile practices are suited for the context they are practiced. *[ProcO_03.07]*

Continuous X (HC 4)

BP_ProcO_04.01: Implement supporting tasks. Ensure that supporting and repetitive tasks are included in the development process and an automated feedback is provided. *[ProcO_04.01]*

Continuous Model Improvement (HC 5)

BP_ProcO_05.01: Propose suggestion to improve the development process. Ensure that suggestions are available according to the evaluation and assessment result given by the ASPLA Model. *[ProcO_05.01]*

Test-Strategy (HC 6)

BP_ProcO_06.03: Implement a scalable test strategy. Ensure that the test strategy covers tests for individual software variants as well as tests in the entire systems and in real cars. *[ProcO_06.03]*

Communication (HC 7)

BP_ProcO_07.08: Trust the supplier. Ensure that a good and open-minded collaboration with the supplier is established and the supplier is included in the process. *[ProcO_07.08]*

Product Attributes

Product Attributes define the characteristics of the product to be developed and represent product oriented Honeycomb Attributes. In total, 12 Product Attributes are defined from the individual patterns identified in the second coding cycle and extended by a description.

For a combination of agile software development and software product lines, the implementation of a modular architecture with standardized interfaces between software units is important. A modular architecture ensures that parts of the software can be replaced or reused without affecting other parts of the software. Hence, features can be implemented independently by means of loosely coupling between software units. Based on customer feedback, a priority value for suggested features shall be assigned. This ensures that the features are customer focused and satisfy customer demands. Furthermore, the decoupling of features facilitates standalone test cases for single features. Software units can be tested for compliance by means of software items which are capable to undergo highly automated verification tasks. Table 5.10 presents Product Attributes for each Honeycomb. An exhaustive list of all Product Attributes can be found in the description of the ASPLA Model in Appendix E.

Table 5.10: Exemplary presentation of Product Attributes.

Product Line Architecture (HC 1)

PA_ProdO_01.01: The software architecture shall be modular. Ensure
that parts of the software can be replaced or reused without affecting other parts of
the software, by means of loosely coupling between software units. *[ProdO_01.01]*

Domain Requirements Engineering (HC 2)

**PA_ProcO_02.03: A priority value for software features shall be
assigned.** Ensure that the features are rated and a priority value is assigned, by
means of assigning the priority value in the requirement specification of the feature.
[ProdO_02.03]

Agile Software Development (HC 3)

PA_ProdO_03.01: The development shall focus on customer needs.
Ensure that customer feedback is integrated into the development of the product,
by means of close customer collaboration. *[ProdO_03.01]*

Continuous X (HC 4)

PA_ProdO_04.02: Continuous verification tasks shall be automated.
Ensure that the software units are tested for compliance, by means of software items
which are capable to undergo highly automated verification tasks. *[ProdO_04.02]*

Test-Strategy (HC 6)

**PA_ProdO_06.01: A test case shall be implemented for each software
unit.** Ensure that all software units, especially critical software units, do have an
associated test case, which consists of all test steps in order to be compliant with
law, by means of a traceable 1-to-1 mapping between the test cases and the software
units. *[ProdO_06.01]*

Work Products

Schmid and John [222] recommend to model new assessment approaches as closely as
possible to the existing ones, which are valid in the targeted domain. ASPICE [260]
is a well-established assessment model in the automotive domain and introduces Work
Products to judge the development processes in a result oriented way.

The ASPLA Model leverages the idea of the ASPICE Work Products [260] due to the
fact that ASPICE Work Products have to remain in full force and effect. This is required
and desired because ASPICE [260] provides a basis for mutual understanding and is an
agreed way of assessing the software development in the automotive domain. Therefore,

the ASPLA Work Products represent result oriented indicators that indicate a successful achievement of Process Related Outcomes and Product Related Outcomes. However, an extension to the ASPICE Work Products is introduced to guarantee compatibility with the combination of agile software development and software product lines.

Overall, 48 Work Products are extended and adjusted to complement missing parts from ASPICE [260] regarding agile software development and software product lines. In these ASPLA Work Products, a new section "ASPLA-complements" is introduced, which extends the content of the ASPICE Work Products. Due to the extensions, some Work Products get a wider scope and assimilate other Work Products. In total, 21 Work Products were assimilated within other ASPLA Work Products.

As an example, "08-17 Reuse Plan" is a Work Product in ASPICE [260] that includes the definition of the policy about what items should be reused, the definition of standards for the construction of reusable objects, the selection of methods for using reusable components, and the establishment of a goal for reusable components. To make the Work Product "08-17 Reuse Plan" compatible with agile software development, further properties have to be added to the ASPLA Work Product.

A faster software development in shorter development iterations leads inevitably to an increased number of software versions for all software variants. Therefore, it is necessary to maintain the management of compatible software units across all software variants at all time. The ASPLA Work Product "A_08-17 Reuse Plan"[1] requires the introduction of variant specific information to define the compatible software variants. Furthermore, the "A_08-17 Reuse Plan" assimilates the Work Product of the "12-03 Reuse Proposal". This ASPICE Work Product is further extended to "A_13-03 Reuse Proposal" to identify the intended software and variant version for a market specific release. Figure 5.7 shows a simplified representation of how Work Products are connected to Process Relates Outcomes and Product Related Outcomes. A listing of all assigned Work Products are documented in the description of the ASPLA Model in Appendix E.

Figure 5.7 shows that the Work Product "A_04-04 Software Architecture Design" is connected to Process Related Outcomes and Product Related Outcomes. In ASPICE [260], the Work Product "04-04 Software Architecture Design" describes the overall software structure such as the operative system, the inter-task/inter-process communication, and the own developed and supplied code [260]. Furthermore, it describes how variants for different models are derived [260]. The Work Product "04-04 Software Architecture Design" needs to be extended by the ASPLA-complement to fully support agile software development practices. The ASPLA-complement requires a none monolithic architecture with regard to Product Related Outcomes. Furthermore, the ASPLA-complement fosters a modular architecture structure that is capable to manage loosely coupled software units. For Process Related outcomes, auxiliary tasks to refactor the architecture are requested by the ASPLA-complement. The extension lead to the ASPLA Work Product "A_04-04 Software Architecture Design".

In ASPICE [260], the Work Product "08-50 Test Specification" consists of the test case

---

[1]The numbering of the ASPLA Work Products is based on the ASPICE numbering of Work Products. To distinguish the Work Products, the ASPLA Work Products are identified by a leading "A_".

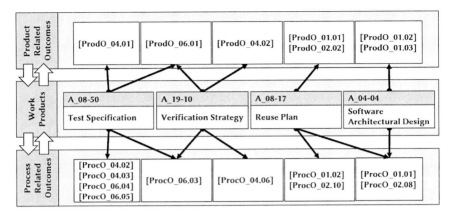

Figure 5.7: Presentation of the Work Products A_08-50, A_19-10, A_08-17, A_04-04 and their relation to the outcomes

specification and the identification of test cases for regression testing. However, to make this Work Product (Test Specification) compatible with agile software development of many software variants, further properties have to be added. The ASPLA Work Product "A_08-50 Test Specification" requires the introduction of a priority ranking of test cases. With this prioritization, the test strategy can decide in an automated test process which test cases are necessary to select and conduct. Safety critical tests shall get a higher priority and shall be preferred in test case selection.

The automated test cases selection, as proposed by the ASPLA Model, leads to adjustments in the ASPICE Work Product "19-10 Verification Strategy". ASPICE [260] defines the Work Product "Verification Strategy" as a strategy that describes verification methods, techniques, and tools [260]. The ASPLA Work Product "A_19-10 Verification Strategy" encompasses the strategy of the test coverage for all products and software variants within the software product line. To comply with legal requirements, it is necessary to pay special attention on the software variants which are produced in an iterative way with shorter development cycles. Verification methods and tools need to be capable to handle the increased amount of software variants.

Based on the fact that Work Products are mapped to several Outcomes, the Work Products are consequently influencing one or more Honeycomb. Each Honeycomb comprises individual outcomes which in turn are connected to Work Products (cf. Figure 5.6). Therefore, it is mandatory for the assessor to consider the entire ASPLA Model and not only parts of it to get a meaningful result in the assessment. The rating of each Work Product influences the calculation of the assessment result in all dependent Honeycombs. The calculation of the assessment result is described in Section 5.5.3. The influences of the Work Products on the result for each Honeycomb shall not be neglected. Table 5.11 shows the dependency structure of Honeycombs and Work Products.

Table 5.11:　Work Products and the relation to the Honeycombs.

Work Products	Product Line Architecture (HC 1)	Domain Requirements Engineering (HC 2)	Agile Software Development(HC 3)	Continuous X (HC 4)	Continuous Model Improvement (HC 5)	Test Strategy (HC 6)	Communication (HC 7)
A_01-03 Software Item			X	X			
A_01-50 Integrated Software Item				X			
A_01-51 Configuration Datasets				X			
A_02-01 Commitment/Agreement			X	X			X
A_03-03 Benchmarking Data					X		
A_03-04 Customer Satisfaction Data			X				X
A_03-06 Process Performance Data					X		
A_04-02 Domain Architecture	X	X					
A_04-03 Domain Model		X					
A_04-04 Software Architectural Design	X	X					
A_04-06 System Architectural Design	X	X					
A_07-01 Customer Satisfaction Survey			X				X
A_07-02 Field Measure			X				X
A_07-04 Process Measure					X		
A_07-05 Project Measure	X		X				
A_08-04 Configuration Management Plan						X	
A_08-12 Project Plan		X	X				
A_08-13 Quality Plan				X	X	X	
A_08-17 Reuse Plan	X	X					
A_08-28 Change Management Plan		X	X	X		X	
A_08-29 Improvement Plan					X		
A_08-50 Test Specification				X		X	
A_08-52 Test Plan				X		X	
A_09-03 Reuse Policy		X					

continued on the next page.

Work Product							
A_11-04 Product Release Package		X		X			
A_11-05 Software Unit	X		X				X	X
A_13-01 Acceptance Record			X					X
A_13-04 Communication Record	X	X	X				X	X
A_13-05 Contract Review Record								X
A_13-08 Baseline		X	X					
A_13-16 Change Request		X						
A_13-17 Customer Request			X					X
A_13-18 Quality Record					X	X		
A_13-22 Traceability Record	X					X		
A_13-50 Test Results					X	X		
A_14-01 Change History	X							
A_14-09 Work Breakdown Structure		X						
A_15-01 Analysis Report	X	X						
A_15-07 Reuse Evaluation Report		X						
A_15-13 Assessment/Audit Report					X			
A_15-16 Improvement Opportunity					X			
A_17-02 Build List				X				
A_17-03 Stakeholder Requirements		X						
A_17-05 Documentation Requirements			X					X
A_17-08 Interface Requirements Specification	X							
A_17-50 Verification Criteria					X	X		
A_18-07 Quality Criteria					X	X		
A_19-05 Reuse Strategy	X	X						
A_19-10 Verification Strategy					X	X		
A_19-11 Validation Strategy					X	X		

Furthermore, 33 ASPICE Work Products are defined to be out of scope and are not addressed within the ASPLA Model. Work Products which are out of scope for the ASPLA Model must be covered by different processes. They can be assessed, as before, by ASPICE assessments, as they are not influenced by the ASPLA Model. A complete list of all Work Products which are denoted as out of scope can be found in Appendix E.8.

For example, one of the Work Products that is excluded is "07-03 Personnel performance measure". The ASPICE Work Product [260] identifies operational performance by measuring personnel performance. The Work Product is defined to be out of scope because it is in contrast to the fostered transparency of work within a good and pleasant agile working environment. The workload is distributed in the team and may be measured at the delivered outcome. Each individual employee does one's best.

Another Work Product that is out of scope for the ASPLA Model is the "14-50 Stakeholder group list". Relevant stakeholder groups, which are ranked by their importance, are not desired to be assessed within the ASPLA Model. The reason thereof is that the ASPLA Model fosters the customer centric development without a prioritization of stakeholders. The selection of features that shall be developed is based on best business value instead of the requested demand of a high prior stakeholder group.

As a final example, the ASPICE Work Product "15-06 Project status report" is presented. The "15-06 Project status report" is considered as the current status of the project [260]. It consists of the schedule, the resources, quality goals, and project issues [260]. The ASPLA Model does not foster and require a project status report because it focuses explicitly on the direct and easy accessible communication [cf. Honeycomb 7]. The Base Practices ensure that the process and the development progress is visible and easy accessible for all involved parties (BP_ProcO_07.04). With this approach, the development process is transparent for every participant.

5.4 Addressed Aspects of Norms and Standards

Schmid and John [222] recommend to take advantage of the existing body of knowledge and to consider other valid norms and standards. The ASPLA Model is based on ASPICE [260] to ensure that the model is suitable for the automotive domain. Furthermore, ISO/IEC 26550 [128] and ISO 26262 [124] were compared to the ASPLA Model.

5.4.1 ASPICE: Process Assessment / Reference Model

The structure of the ASPLA Model is based on the structure of ASPICE [260]. ASPLA takes over the internal structure with the concept of "Outcomes", "Base Practices" and "Work Products" and extends it by a product-view (cf. Figure 5.6).

In the ASPICE Guidelines [76], specific assessment recommendations for agile environments are provided [76]. However, ASPLA and ASPICE [260] assessments have a different alignment. In ASPICE [260], the recommendations focus on down rating the assessment result in case the applied agile approach is not sufficiently implemented [76]. In contrast, ASPLA fosters the agile development and supports agile development in general. The ASPICE Guidelines [76] present recommendations that address the project life cycle, management of requirements, project planning, risk management, software architecture, software testing, quality assurance, and the use of pair programming with regard to agile development.

As denoted in the guidelines [76], "planning in [an] agile environment" requires that agile project planning is in line with the customer release planning [76]. This is addressed in the Base Practice "BP_ProcO_03.05" which requires that the agile development is synchronized with the surrounding processes and all affected parties. Table E.11 shows how the guidelines are addressed by the ASPLA Model.

5.4.2 ISO/IEC 26550: Reference Model for Product Line Engineering and Management

The ASPLA Model is compared to the "Reference model for product line engineering and management" (ISO/IEC 26550 [128]), to deal with key aspects with regard to product lines. The ISO/IEC 26550 [128] consists of two life cycles (domain engineering and application engineering) and two process groups (organizational management and technical management) for product line engineering and management [128].

ISO/IEC 26550 [128] does not prescribe the use of any particular software development methodology. However, the selected methodology should support a reuse strategy for assets [128]. Therefore, each important aspect of the life cycles and the process groups of ISO/IEC 26550 is compared with the ASPLA Model. Base Practices and Product Attributes are identified which shall address the required method or tool from ISO/IEC 26550 [128]. In total, 71 roles from ISO/IEC 26550 [128] are related to Base Practices and Product Attributes. Honeycomb 1 "Product Line Architecture" and Honeycomb 2 "Domain Requirements Engineering" are covering the majority of the required roles. As part of the domain engineering life cycle, the role "Domain requirements engineering" is covered mainly by Honeycomb 2, which has the the the same name. Domain requirements engineering includes the identification of products and features that should be part of the product line and the definition of common and variable features [128]. The management of the domain requirements helps to establish traceability between individual assets and coordinate engineering activities [128]. The ASPLA Model deals with these issues in the Base Practices of Honeycomb 2 (BP_ProcO_02.01 → BP_ProcO_02.04).

Furthermore, seven roles are not covered by the ASPLA Model and are denoted as "<out of scope>". Four roles in the technical management and three roles in the organizational management process group are not addressed by Base Practices or Product Attributes. For example, the role "Organizational-level product line planning" includes aspects such as the "organizational transition planning". This aspect deals with the initiation of the product line and defines the organizational transition planning process [128]. Transition is not addressed in the ASPLA Model. This is due to the fact that the ASPLA Model is inspired by ASPICE [260] which is a process reference and assessment model. It does not focus on the transition in detail and so does ASPLA. Both define performance indicators which could help in an organizational transition. However, a detailed plan with step-by-step instructions is not provided. This is also not expected from a reference model. A comprehensive list of the relationship between ISO/IEC 26550, Base Practices and Product Attributes can be found in the tables provided in Appendix E.10.

5.4.3 ISO 26262: Road Vehicles – Functional Safety

ISO 26262 [122] addresses the area of functional safety for road vehicles. Rothermel [215] identifies three important areas that need to be considered to satisfy the requirements given by the norm within an agile environment: (1) planning, (2) specification, and (3) the reference model.

Planning. The ISO 26262 [121] requires that functional safety activities need to be planned in advance [215].

The ASPLA Model addresses safety planning at a high level of abstraction in the Base Practice BP_ProcO_01.07.

Specification. The specification of safety requirements requires a detailed description such as the completeness or consistency of the requirements [123].

The ASPLA Model addresses the planning and specification issues at a high level of abstraction in the Base Practices (BP_ProcO_01.07, BP_ProcO_01.08, BP_ProcO_03.04, BP_ProcO_06.04).

Reference model. The ISO 26262 [122] defines a reference phase model for the software development. This phase model can be tailored to the life cycle of product development. The ASPLA Model does not predefine any specific model for software development. In all cases, the selected development approach shall be mapped to valid norms that satisfy the restrictions given by the law. This is addressed in Base Practice BP_ProcO_03.04.

5.5 Conduct an ASPLA Assessment

To conduct the ASPLA assessment, a questionnaire was designed that covers all Honeycombs and addresses Base Practices, Product Attributes and Work Products. The questionnaire was implemented as a WebApp which enables the calculation of the assessment results immediately. The WebApp is optimized for the use with mobile devices. The questionnaire poses questions for every Honeycomb. The user is guided by the WebApp to answer the questionnaire. It is not necessary to answer all questions. The user can skip the Honeycombs and check the result immediately. However, as mentioned in Section 5.3.3, the interconnections in the ASPLA Model recommend to answer all question in order to achieve a reasonable result.

5.5.1 Web Application (WebApp)

A WebApp was developed to validate the ASPLA Model and to conduct assessments with an automated evaluation and generation of the assessment result. The WebApp (www.aspla.org) is developed with the ASP.NET MVC framework. The complete ASPLA Model with all important parts such as Outcomes, Base Practices, Product Attributes, Work Products, and Assessment Questions is stored in a database. The query based development is done in two ways: First, with Entity Framework 6, and second with stored procedures for complex queries in the SQL database. The assessment results are saved and detailed evaluations are conducted.

5.5.2 Assessment Question Setup

The ASPLA Model includes 269 individual questions to assess the current status of the combination of agile software development and software product lines in the automotive domain. The author of this thesis phrased each question in a manner that each question addresses the Honeycomb Attributes. Thereby, each question addresses a single part of Process Related Outcomes, Product Related Outcomes and Work Products.

The rating scale for each ASPLA question is based on the rating scale from ISO/IEC 33020 [130]. Each question can either be "Not answered", "Not achieved", "Partially achieved", "Largely achieved" or "Fully achieved".

For each Base Practice and Product Attribute up to four questions are defined that ask for the degree of fulfillment. In total, 129 questions are defined for the fulfillment of Base Practices and Product Attributes. For example, to address BP_ProcO_03.02 *"Release product and market specific features early."*, the assessment asks for the possibility to release features into markets independent from other markets (Q_071). Furthermore, it examines if it is possible to include already released features into the software product line (Q_072). For Product Attributes, specific properties of the product under development are queried. In case of testing, the Product Attribute PA_ProdO_06.01 asks for unique test cases for each software unit. The questions that examine this issue ask for (Q_110) unique test cases, (Q_111) the test case priority of critical software units, (Q_112) the necessity to be compliant with law, and (Q_113) the assurance of traceability from software test to software unit. A comprehensive list of all questions can be found in Appendix E.9.

Table 5.12: Exemplary presentation of assessment questions for Base Practices and Product Attributes.

BP_ProcO_03.02: Release product and market specific features early.
Q_071: It is possible to release features for specific markets and products early.
Q_072: It is possible to repatriate the implemented features into the software product line.
PA_ProdO_06.01: Test case shall be implemented for each software units.
Q_110: It is ensured that each software unit has an unique test case.
Q_111: It is ensured that critical software units do have an associated test case with a high priority.
Q_112: It is ensured that all test cases consist of all test steps in order to be compliant with law.
Q_113: It is ensured that test cases are traceable to the corresponding software unit.

Work Products are addressed by 140 individual questions. The author defined the questions along the structure provided in ASPICE [260]. Questions for Work Products are adopted from ASPICE [260] without any modification. For Work Products that include an ASPLA-complement, between one and three additional questions with regard to the complement are introduced.

For the Work Product "Commitment/Agreement", the assessment questions examine (Q_141) new payment strategies and (Q_142) the use of smaller iterations. Furthermore, the assessment asks for (Q_143) an open minded collaboration and (Q_144) the collaboration with the supplier.

The "customer satisfaction survey" Work Product is extended by an ASPLA-complement. The complement elaborates the direct customer collaboration and asks for customer satisfaction (Q_155, Q_156). Furthermore, the original ASPICE [260] Work Product is addressed by one question.

Table 5.13: Exemplary presentation of assessment questions for Work Products.

Q_140: All necessary Work Product items of "Commitment/ Agreement" are available.
Q_141: It is ensured that the commitment with the customer comprises an adjusted agile commitment for incremental software delivery, such as smaller iterative commitments, payment by feature and payment by time allocation.
Q_142: It is ensured that smaller iterative commitments are possible.
Q_143: The commitment ensures an open minded collaboration.
Q_144: An agile commitment strategy with the supplier is ensured.
Q_154: All necessary Work Product items of "Customer satisfaction survey" are available.
Q_155: A mechanism to collect data on customer satisfaction is established.
Q_156: The level of customer satisfaction with products and services is determined.

5.5.3 Calculation of Assessment Results

The aggregation of the results follows the internal structure presented in Figure 5.8.

Calculation of Base Practices, Product Attributes and Work Products

For each of the 269 individual questions, the assessment user assigns a rating according the rating scale introduced in ISO/IEC 33020 [130]. Questions which are "Not answered" are not considered in the evaluation and denoted as "Not evaluated". The Web Application assigns a number to each rating level ("Not evaluated", "Not achieved", "Partially achieved", "Largely achieved", and "Fully achieved"). The assignment (cf. Formula 5.1) is based on the aggregation method described in ISO 33020 [130] and in the guidelines for ASPICE [76].

$$f\colon A \to B, x \mapsto v(x) \tag{5.1}$$

where:

A = {Not evaluated, Not achieved, Partially achieved, Largely achieved, Fully achieved}

B = {NaN, 0, 1, 2, 3}

For each Base Practice, the average value for the answers of the associated questions is calculated, according to Formula 5.2. An average value is calculated for all 52 individual Base Practices.

$$\overline{BP}_{\mathrm{i}} = \frac{1}{|Q_{\mathrm{i}}|} \sum_{q \in Q_{\mathrm{i}}} f(q) \tag{5.2}$$

where:

i	$=$	(i_1, i_2)
i_1	$=$	The identification number of the Honeycomb.
i_2	$=$	The identification number of the Base Practice.
$Q_{\mathrm{BP\_ProcO\_0}i_1.0i_2}$	$=$	The set of questions assigned to the Base Practice defined by i_1 and i_2. Unanswered questions are excluded.

Similarly, the results for the questions for Product Attributes are calculated according to Formula 5.3. For all 12 Product Attributes, an average value is calculated.

$$\overline{PA}_{\mathrm{i}} = \frac{1}{|Q_{\mathrm{i}}|} \sum_{q \in Q_{\mathrm{i}}} f(q) \tag{5.3}$$

where:

i	$=$	(i_1, i_2)
i_1	$=$	The identification number of the Honeycomb.
i_2	$=$	The identification number of the Product Attribute.
$Q_{\mathrm{BP\_ProdO\_0}i_1.0i_2}$	$=$	The set of questions assigned to the Product Attribute defined by i_1 and i_2. Unanswered questions are excluded.

Table 5.14 presents an exemplary calculation for the assessment questions defined in Table 5.13. For the classification within the ranking scale, the value is rounded up and down to the nearest integer value. The rounding rules are adopted from the assessment recommendations for ASPICE [76]. Rounding down or up is defined by the average value and if it is below or above the midpoint between consecutive integers [76]. However, for further calculations, the exact value is used.

Table 5.14: Exemplary presentation of assessment result
calculation for Base Practices and Product Attributes.

BP_ProcO_03.02: Release product and market specific features early.		
Q_071: It is possible to release features for specific markets and products early.	Largely achieved	2
Q_072: It is possible to repatriate the implemented features into the software product line.	Fully achieved	3
Average value: 2,5 → Fully achieved		

PA_ProdO_06.01: Test case shall be implemented for each software units.		
Q_110: It is ensured that each software unit has an unique test case.	Partially achieved	1
Q_111: It is ensured that critical software units do have an associated test case with a high priority.	Largely achieved	2
Q_112: It is ensured that all test cases consist of all test steps to be compliant with law.	Largely achieved	2
Q_113: It is ensured that test cases are traceable to the corresponding software unit.	Partially achieved	1
Average value: 1,5 → Largely achieved		

The results of the individual Work Products are based on the answers from the 140 questions addressing the Work Products. Unlike ASPICE [260] assessments, the ASPLA assessment uses the ranking scale to evaluate the Work Products. Therefore, the presence of the Work Product items are evaluated. An exemplary calculation for the presented Work Products is given in Table 5.15. The result is calculated according to Formula 5.4.

$$\overline{WP}_i = \frac{1}{|Q_i|} \sum_{q \in Q_i} f(q) \tag{5.4}$$

where:

i_1	=	The identification number according to ASPICE [260].
i_2	=	The identification number according to ASPICE [260].
$Q_{\text{Work Product\_A\_}i_1\text{-}i_2}$	=	The set of questions assigned to the Work Product defined by i_1 and i_2. Unanswered questions are excluded.

Table 5.15: Exemplary presentation of assessment result calculation for an ASPLA Work Product.

Q_154: All necessary Work Product items of "Customer satisfaction survey" are available.	Partially achieved	1
Q_155: A mechanism to collect data on customer satisfaction is established.	Not achieved	0
Q_156: The level of customer satisfaction with products and services is determined.	Partially achieved	1
Average value: 0,7 → Partially achieved		

Calculation of Process and Product Related Outcomes

The individual calculation for Base Practices, Product Attributes and Work Products are then combined for the Product Related Outcomes and the Process Related Outcomes. For this calculation, the exact values are used. The first step consists of calculating the average value of the assessment results of the related Work Products, according to Formula 5.5 and Formula 5.6.

$$\overline{ProcO\_WP}_{\mathrm{j}} = \frac{1}{|WP_{\mathrm{j}}|} \sum_{i \in WP_{\mathrm{j}}} \overline{WP}_{\mathrm{i}} \tag{5.5}$$

where:

j = Identifies the Process Related Outcome.

WP_j = Work Products assigned to the Process Related Outcome.

$$\overline{ProdO\_WP}_{\mathrm{j}} = \frac{1}{|WP_{\mathrm{j}}|} \sum_{i \in WP_{\mathrm{j}}} \overline{WP}_{\mathrm{i}} \tag{5.6}$$

where:

j = Identifies the Product Related Outcome.

WP_j = Work Products assigned to the Product Related Outcome.

The second step of the calculation requires no additional calculation, due to the 1-to-1 mapping of Base Practices onto Process Related Outcomes and the mapping of Product Attributes to Product Related Outcomes. The overall result for each Base Practice and Product Attribute combined with the Work Product result is calculated according to Formula 5.7 and Formula 5.8. Exemplary, the calculation is shown in Table 5.16 for ProdO_06.01.

$$\overline{ProcO_j} = \frac{\overline{ProcO\_WP_j} + \overline{BP_j}}{2} \tag{5.7}$$

where:

j   =   Identifies the Process Related Outcome.

$$\overline{ProdO_j} = \frac{\overline{ProdO\_WP_j} + \overline{PA_j}}{2} \tag{5.8}$$

where:

j   =   Identifies the Product Related Outcome.

Table 5.16: Exemplary presentation of assessment result
for ProdO_06.01.

ProdO_06.01 For each software unit an associated test case is assigned.		
PA_ProdO_06.01: A test case shall be implemented for each software unit.		1,5
A_08-13 *Quality Plan*	1	
A_08-50 *Test Specification*	1,3	
A_08-52 *Test Plan*	1,6	
A_11-05 *Software Unit*	1,5	
A_17-50 *Verification Criteria*	3	
A_19-10 *Verification Strategy*	3	
A_19-11 *Validation Strategy*	2	
Work Products Average Value		**1,9**
Result for ProdO_06.01: 1,7 → Largely achieved		

Calculation of Honeycomb Result

The last calculation step is the calculation of the overall assessment result regarding the Honeycombs. For this purpose, the average of all corresponding Process Related Outcomes and Product Related Outcomes is calculated. The overall result is displayed by means of a radar chart (cf. Section 6.4) and calculated by Formula 5.9.

$$\overline{Honeycomb_j} = \frac{\sum_{i \in ProcO_j} \overline{ProcO_i} + \sum_{i \in ProdO_j} \overline{ProdO_i}}{(|ProcO_j| + |ProdO_j|)} \tag{5.9}$$

where:

j   =   The identification number of the Honeycomb

5.5.4 Improvement Potential and Recommendation List

At the end of the assessment process, the ASPLA Model displays the results for each assessment user. An overview of the assessment results is presented in a radar chart (cf. Section 6.4.5). Furthermore, a detailed overview of each outcome is given. The results are separated by Base Practices, Product Attributes and Work Products as shown in Figure 5.8 and calculated according to Formula 5.7 and Formula 5.8.

ProcO_01.01
Improve
Define a software product line architecture. A software product line architecture is defined that enables the development of various software variants for different products.
Base Practice
Fully
Work Products
Partially

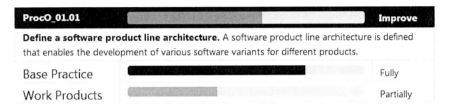

Figure 5.8: Detailed evaluation for ProcO_01.01 as presented by the ASPLA Model assessment results. (Screenshot from www.aspla.org)

Furthermore, the ASPLA Model identifies improvement potential and assigns recommendations for each outcome. The assessment user can work with these recommendations in two different ways. First, the assessment user can examine the results for the respective outcome separately. For this purpose, the user can display the recommendations for the specific outcome he wants to improve and select the recommendations to address. Figure 5.9 displays the list of recommendations for the corresponding outcome.

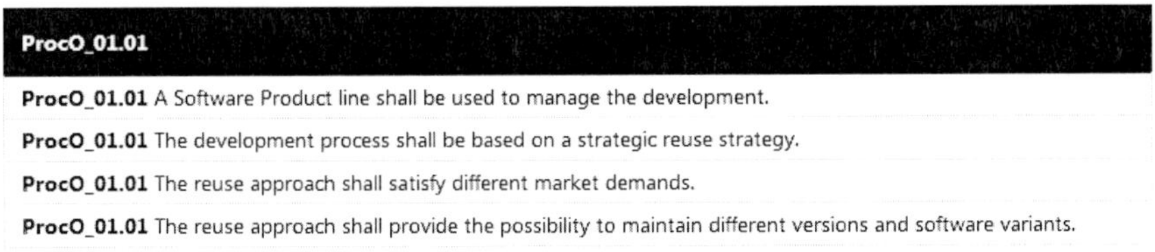

ProcO_01.01
ProcO_01.01 A Software Product line shall be used to manage the development.
ProcO_01.01 The development process shall be based on a strategic reuse strategy.
ProcO_01.01 The reuse approach shall satisfy different market demands.
ProcO_01.01 The reuse approach shall provide the possibility to maintain different versions and software variants.

Figure 5.9: Recommendations to improve the assessment result for ProcO_01.01 as identified by the ASPLA Model.

The second possibility is to let the ASPLA Model decide which recommendations should be addressed first. Thereby, the assessment user can configure the amount of recommendations that should be proposed.

5.6 Chapter Summary

This chapter introduces the type of the artifact, following the guidelines for conducting Design-Science Research proposed by Hevner et al. [100]. In Design-Science Research the artifact must be a viable and technology-based solution to an existing and relevant problem [100]. The relevant challenges in combining agile software development with software product lines were identified in real-life and in the literature (cf. Chapter 4). These challenges were categorized in four categories that need to be addressed.

Recommendations to overcome the challenges were extracted from the results of the interview study (cf. Section 3.2), the literature review and several workshops (cf. Appendix B). Coding the recommendations ended up in six main areas that need to be addressed for combining agile software development and software product lines. In order to manage the recommendations, they were integrated in a structured approach. Therefore, the artifact described within this thesis is the so-called ASPLA Model. The ASPLA Model is an assessment and improvement model to combine agile software development and software product lines in the automotive domain. Furthermore, the model gives recommendations to foster the combination.

The ASPLA Model consists of six main areas, called Honeycombs that are assessed. One additional Honeycomb "Continuous Model improvement" is not used in the assessment, but needed for the evolution of the model. The Honeycombs consist of 52 Process Related Outcomes and 12 Product Related Outcomes. Each Process Related Outcome is addressed by a Base Practice and each Product Related Outcome by a Product Attribute. ASPLA Work Products, Base Practices and Product Attributes are summarized under the Honeycomb Attributes. ASPLA is based on the structure of ASPICE[260], in line with the recommendation given by Schmid and John [222]. Therefore, the ASPLA Model was compared to the standards ASPICE [260], ISO/IEC 265502 [128] and ISO 26262 [122]. Furthermore, ASPICE [260] Work Products were adjusted to support the combination of agile software development and software product lines.

269 individual questions were defined to assess the current status. The author of this thesis phrased each question in a manner that each question addresses the Honeycomb Attributes. The assessment can be conducted online in a Web Application. The Web Application calculates the assessment results using the aggregation method described in ISO 33020 [130] and in the guidelines for ASPICE [76]. Depending on the results, a list of recommendations is created.

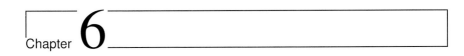

Chapter 6

Validation of the ASPLA Model

The ISO 9000:2015 [7] defines validation as the confirmation that requirements for a specific intended use or application have been fulfilled. The definition of validation is also specified in CMMI [243]. CMMI defines the purpose of validation to "demonstrate that a product or product component fulfills its intended use when placed in its intended environment" [243, p.393]. This chapter presents the validation of the ASPLA Model. Section 6.1 describes the hypotheses and the validation strategy. Section 6.3 presents the iterative learning cycles to collect feedback by experts in the areas of assessments, automotive, software product lines and agile software development. The learning cycles collect feedback to cover the most important areas to consider. This ensures that the ASPLA Model is general valid and accepted by the users. Section 6.4.2 compares the results of an assessment conducted by experts with the results generated by the use of the ASPLA Model assessment.

6.1 Hypotheses

The following section summarizes the research hypotheses stated in Section 1.6, defines the criteria for validating them, and presents a corresponding validation strategy. All three hypotheses are examined by comparing the ASPLA Model with assessment results of experienced experts. The selection of the experts and case study participants is described in Section 6.4.3.

Hypothesis 1: The results from applying the assessment model is in agreement with the recommendations of the experts that assess the current development process. The ASPLA Model is meaningful and in agreement with the recommendations of experts that assess the presented development process (cf. Section 6.4). The ASPLA Model provides a list of recommendations in order to foster the combination of agile software development and software product lines. These recommendations are in agreement with the recommendations given by the experts. In total, the number of recommendations given by the model is deviating by less than 30% compared to the recommendations given by the experts.

Hypothesis 2: **The results from applying the assessment model are not missing important recommendations given by the experts that assess the current development process.** The ASPLA Model covers the recommendations of the experts that assess the presented development process (cf. Section 6.4). The number and content of the recommendations given by the experts is in agreement to the recommendations provided by the assessment model. In total, the number of missing recommendations given by the model is less than 10% compared to the recommendations given by the experts.

Hypothesis 3: With the developed assessment model, the time for conducting an assessment could be reduced by a factor of 2 compared to the assessments conducted by experts. The ASPLA Model reduces the time for conducting an assessment by a factor of 2 compared to the assessments conducted by the experts.

6.2 Two-Step Validation Strategy

The research presented within this thesis follows the Design-Science Research guidelines proposed by Hevner and Chatterjee [99] (cf. Section 1.3). Hevner et al. [100] point out that evaluation is one relevant component of the research process. They mention that evaluation includes the integration of the developed artifact within the technical infrastructure of the business environment [99]. Furthermore, it needs to be ensured that the assessment model is relevant for the environment for which it is developed. The utility, quality, and efficacy of the assessment model can be shown via well-executed evaluation methods [100]. In order to evaluate the ASPLA Model as described in this thesis, the chosen validation strategy was divided into two consecutive phases, an iterative learning phase and a case study. The validation strategy is shown in Figure 6.1.

The first phase (*iterative learning*) aimed at getting a more comprehensive understanding of the applicability of the ASPLA Model. As described in the guidelines by Hevner et al. [100], design is inherently an iterative and incremental activity. Accordingly, they define the evaluation phase which provides essential feedback to the construction phase [100]. The first phase included iterative learning cycles. These learning cycles were used to verify that all key aspects are covered within the model and model improvements can be integrated. Therefore, the industry and the academic community was asked to give feedback on the initial model. The iterative learning cycles ensure that every four weeks, the model is updated according to the provided feedback. Based on the clustered and evaluated feedback, a new model increment is then generated. Through the usage of the iterative learning cycles, the model itself is flexible and can be adjusted to the software development.

The second validation phase (*case study*) followed Guideline 3 "Design Evaluation" proposed by Hevner et al. [100]. They point out that well-executed evaluation methods help to demonstrate the utility, quality, and efficacy of the design artifact [100]. The design artifact that was evaluated in the case study was the ASPLA Model in Version V1.02.

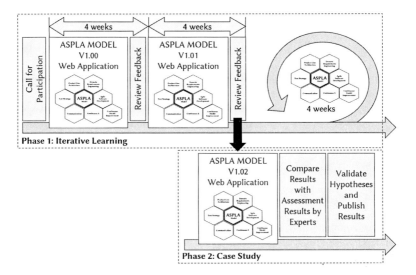

Figure 6.1: The two-step validation approach: The iterative learning cycles and the case study.

A case study was selected because it is an observational design evaluation method. The evaluation requires the execution of the assessment model within the technical infrastructure of the business environment [100]. In the case study, the results of the ASPLA Model were compared against the assessment results of experts (cf. Section 6.4.3).

The results were used to verify the hypotheses. Improvements and adjustments to the model which arise during the case study were considered in V1.03 of the ASPLA Model.

6.3 Phase 1: Iterative Learning

The implementation of iterative learning cycles was adopted from agile software development and from the selected research approach of Design-Science Research. In Design-Science Research, so-called build-and-evaluate loops are conducted repeatedly [100]. These loops provide feedback information and results in order to better understand the problem. With the gained knowledge, the quality of the created artifact can be improved [100]. Following the purposed approach, iterative feedback cycles were used to incrementally update the ASPLA Model.

6.3.1   Context

The ASPLA Model was implemented as a Web Application (WebApp) (cf. Section 5.5.1). The WebApp is divided into two parts. The first part provides detailed information about the model, while the second one enables online assessments and identifies improvement potential. The first part gives explanations about the defined Honeycombs, the Base Practices, the Product Attributes, the Work Products and their linkages. Furthermore, the WebApp provides all publications on partial results which are published in the context of the creation of the ASPLA Model. This information is freely accessible. A feedback form is provided to give the website visitors the possibility to provide anonymous feedback about the model. In order to categorize the received feedback, six questions to the feedback providers are posed. Two questions deal with the role of the feedback provider and the industry domain. Further two questions deal with the skill levels regarding agile development and software product lines. The last two questions ask for the feedback providers' personal opinion on the model.

6.3.2   Feedback Collection Process

The "call for participation" to provide feedback on the ASPLA Model was distributed on social media via Twitter, XING, LinkedIn and ResearchGate. Furthermore, personalized emails were send to 50 researchers in the area of software product lines and agile software development. Each contacted researcher was identified and selected according to the area of his/her research and active participation at conferences that deal with agile software development and software product lines. Conferences that were considered are the International Conference on Product-Focused Software Process Improvement (PROFES) and the International Systems and Software Product Line Conference (SPLC). The first iterative learning cycle started in July 2018. Feedback was collected using the feedback form on the WebApp.

Received Feedback in Learning Cycles

The first two learning cycles led to six feedbacks from the anonymous feedback form. Nevertheless, one data set was excluded because it contained only dummy data. In total, five complete feedback forms were received. The anonymous reviewers were divided into three reviews from the automotive domain and two reviews from academia. An overview about the anonymous reviewers and their capabilities with regard to agile software development and software product lines is shown in Table 6.1.

Table 6.1:   Overview about the reviewers providing anonymous feedback on the Web Application.

Reviewer 01	Automotive Domain - Software Developer
Software Product Line	Competent
Agile Software Development	Proficient

continued on the next page.

Reviewer 02	Automotive Domain - Consultant
Software Product Line	Advanced Beginner
Agile Software Development	Expert

Reviewer 03	Automotive Domain - Assessor
Software Product Line	Competent
Agile Software Development	Competent

Reviewer 04	Academia
Software Product Line	Competent
Agile Software Development	Competent

Reviewer 05	Academia
Software Product Line	Competent
Agile Software Development	Competent

Personal Feedback

Although the number of the anonymous feedback received was low, ten additional reviewers provide direct feedback by email or telephone. As Reviewer 06 stated, it was "easier to email directly, rather than through the feedback form on the website ... mostly due to the length" (Reviewer 06). The email responses provide feedback on a detailed level. Feedback was given for Base Practices and on ASPLA-complements for individual Work Products. Furthermore, some reviewers requested a telephone or Skype™ call to discuss the ASPLA Model in more detail. In these calls, questions regarding the assessment and the set-up of the ASPLA Model were answered and further feedback on the ASPLA Model was provided by the reviewers. The results and feedback was recorded by the author of this thesis.

This section gives an overview of the reviewers which gave direct feedback by email or telephone call. The categorization for the company size is defined as "very large company" (more than 2500 employees), "large company" (251 - 2499 employees), "medium company" (51 - 250 employees), "small company" (11-50 employees), and micro company (1 - 10 employees). Each reviewer was classified by knowledge, skills and experiences in software product lines and agile software development. The skill levels with regard to agile software development and software product lines are classified as "Novice", "Advanced Beginner", "Competent", "Proficient", or "Expert". Not all reviewers provided information about their company size or their experience in the areas of software product lines and agile software development. If no information was provided, it is marked as "unknown" in Table 6.2.

Table 6.2: Overview of the reviewers who provided direct feedback.

Reviewer 06	Industry - Quality Representative
Company Size	Very large

continued on the next page.

Software Product Line	Competent
Agile Software Development	Competent
Correspondence	Email, telephone, personal contact
Reviewer 07	**Industry - Agile Coach**
Company Size	Micro
Software Product Line	Competent
Agile Software Development	Expert
Correspondence	Email
Reviewer 08	**Industry - Agile Coach**
Company Size	Micro
Software Product Line	Competent
Agile Software Development	Expert
Correspondence	Email, Skype™, personal contact
Reviewer 09	**Industry - Assessor and Agile Coach**
Company Size	Micro
Software Product Line	Proficient
Agile Software Development	Proficient
Correspondence	Email, Skype™
Reviewer 10	**Industry - Change Agent, Agile Consultant and Researcher**
Company Size	Unknown
Software Product Line	Competent
Agile Software Development	Proficient
Correspondence	Email
Reviewer 11	**Industry - Unknown**
Company Size	Unknown
Software Product Line	Unknown
Agile Software Development	Advanced Beginner
Correspondence	Email
Reviewer 12	**Academia**
Company Size	Unknown
Software Product Line	Proficient
Agile Software Development	Proficient
Correspondence	Email

6.3.3 ASPLA Model Feedback Results and Adjustments

The adjustments to the ASPLA Model were based on the received feedback provided by the anonymous feedback form via the Web Application as well as on the review comments resulting from direct correspondence (email, telephone, Skype™, personal contact) with the reviewers listed in Table 6.2. All adjustments were reviewed by the author of this thesis and discussed with two experienced ASPICE assessors. After approval has been granted, the ASPLA Model was adjusted. All adjustments resulting from one iterative learning cycle were then released to the ASPLA Model and available in the next iterative learning cycle (cf. Figure 6.1).

Anonymous Feedback

Reviewer 01 suggested to introduce an additional Honeycomb for the developers and employees. As he[1] pointed out, the main agile idea is based on the statement "Manage the people not the processes" (Reviewer 01). Furthermore, he proposed to offer special agile training and support the agile development by an agile consultant. The review comments by Reviewer 01 are similar to the review comments provided by Reviewer 09.

Reviewer 02 assumed that the model is useful for both agile self-assessment and assessment by an independent assessor. The intention behind the implementation of the ASPLA Model is to enable developers to assess their current development processes. According to the assessment result, recommendations are given to foster a development process that supports agile software product lines. However, the ASPLA Model can be a helpful tool for an experienced assessor as well.

Reviewer 03 from the automotive domain stated that it is often not possible to work in a collaborative way because of incompatible tool chains that prevent an easy to handle data exchange between departments. Furthermore, the reviewer mentioned that the development departments are introducing "quick and dirty" in-house software solutions that are precisely tailored to their needs. However, this hinders a collaboration with other departments. This issue is addressed within the recommendations for Base Practice BP_ProcO_01.03, which requires the management of the software product line by means of suitable tools. The recommendation proposes to avoid "quick and dirty" and not maintainable software solution for managing the software product line (Recommendation ID 147669). Furthermore, this leads to the recommendation proposed by the reviewer that the tool chain is suitable for the context in which it is used. To address this issue, another recommendation for Base Practice BP_ProcO_01.03 was added to the ASPLA Model. "The tool chain shall be as simple as possible, and as extensive as necessary" (Recommendation ID 147673).

Reviewer 04 indicated that the connection of the ASPLA Model with ISO 26262 [127] is not presented in detail. The reviewer mentioned that it is unclear how safety requirements are addressed. Furthermore, risk classification according to the Automotive Safety Integrity Level (ASIL) is not addressed. This introduced an additional recommendation for risk analysis to identify potential hazard. The Base Practice BP_ProcO_01.07: "Analyze and consider safety regulations" was extended by the recommendation that "an ASIL shall be assigned for all features" (Recommendation ID 147691). Furthermore, Reviewer 04 liked the idea to initiate the improvement process using an assessment model to determine the current status. He pointed out that the automotive domain is familiar with assessments and it could be adopted easily.

---

[1]For reasons of readability and to ensure anonymity, only the masculine form is used to address reviewers comments.

Reviewer 05 was not convinced by the adoption of the term "Honeycomb". He suggested to select a better naming schema consistent with ASPICE (MAN, SYS, SWE, SUP, and similar). The term "Honeycomb" clearly distinguishes the ASPLA Model from ASPICE [260]. While ASPICE focuses on processes and outcomes, ASPLA extends the process view and comprises a product-oriented view. Therefore, the naming was not changed within the ASPLA Model.

In addition to the presented feedback, the anonymous feedback form provided a priority ranking for Honeycombs. Each reviewer assigned a priority value to the Honeycombs. However, this feedback is not yet used in the selection of recommendations. As mentioned in Section 10.2 the priority ranking could be used in future work in order to identify recommendations according to the Honeycomb priority value.

Direct Feedback

Reviewer 06 mentioned several incorrect assignments from Base Practices and Honeycombs, which are out of place. The faulty assignments could be resolved in the database of the WebApp. Furthermore, typos within the ASPLA Model were mentioned by Reviewer 06 and resolved in the first learning cycle of the ASPLA Model. In addition, Reviewer 06 referred to the Product Attributes PA_ProdO_02.03 and PA_ProdO_02.04 and assumed that the term "criticality", as used in the ASPLA Model, is the same as the term "severity". The wording was adjusted to avoid misunderstandings. He raised the question if there is a known case in the automotive development area where the priority value is in opposition to the severity. In the discussion with Reviewer 06, he pointed out that it is easy to see the difference between criticality and priority. For instance, a bug which causes data loss but is rarely encountered would have a high severity, but could have a low priority. In no case shall a severe issue be handled at a low priority. The ASPLA Model emphasizes also to prioritize safety critical tests with high priority. The two different priority values in the ASPLA Model were introduced to have opportunities to handle the business point of view and the technical and risk point of view on requirements separately.

Reviewer 06 pointed out that some agile terms, such as "Definition of Done (DoD)" or "Retrospectives" are interpreted in various ways across the agile community. In his agile experience, a retrospective is primarily for the team itself to improve its internal development processes. This contradicts with the Process Related Outcome ProcO_03.08. The outcome states that knowledge is transferred to other variants in the software product line by retrospectives. Reviewer 06 mentioned that "retrospectives are not so much for external consumption". However, he pointed out that suggestions to "improve interaction with other teams, process changes, etc. are valid points that should be externalized". The ASPLA Model aims at establishing an open minded collaboration of development teams and to break down the knowledge silos within the development. Therefore, lessons learned as they arise in retrospectives shall be distributed to other teams to avoid the repetition of mistakes.

Reviewer 06 suggested to consider agile metrics such as "velocity improvement or consistency, rate of reopened issues,[...] issues found after release, or [...] committed versus completed" to measure "things like improving speed, quality and process improvement" (Reviewer 06). The ASPLA Model does not prescribe metrics. However, the organization is encouraged in Honeycomb 5 to measure company-specific values to trace the improvement.

In addition, Reviewer 07 addressed metrics and mentioned that the efficiency is mainly evaluated in Honeycomb 5. He pointed out that "agile is actually more about effectiveness". In the context of the ASPLA Model, effectiveness is considered to be a precondition to evaluate the efficiency in Honeycomb 5.

Furthermore, Reviewer 07 mentioned that it is good that the ASPLA Model does not stipulate specific agile practices or methods and welcomed the recommendation of using context specific practices. However, the reviewer detected that Honeycomb Continuous X "covers a lot of things mentioned in DevOps" (Reviewer 07). Therefore, he suggested to mention the term "DevOps" explicitly. However, the term "DevOps" is not mentioned in the description and definition of the Honeycomb in order to not confuse the assessment users. The term "DevOps", such as the term "agile" in general is often interpreted in different ways. The ASPLA Model aims at Best Practices and Outcomes and does not care about naming.

Reviewer 08 inquired for the intention behind the ASPLA Model. He considered the ASPLA Model as an "ordinary SPICE Model flavored with some agile aspects" (Reviewer 08). He pointed out that Honeycomb 3 (Agile Software Development) "is not agile at all" (Reviewer 08). Furthermore, he argued that the reuse of software will not make the development more agile. He doubted that the agile development requests for a strategic reuse and vice versa. Nevertheless, he pointed out that the ASPLA Model could be helpful in case of process optimization, however, not in introducing pure agility. He recommended to "compare the ASPLA Model to the Cynefin Model by Dave Snow" (Reviewer 08). The ASPLA Model is based on ASPICE according to the recommendation for setting up assessment models by Schmid and John [222]. The ASPICE [260] structure with Base Practices and Work Products is adopted within the ASPLA Model. Therefore, in the first glance, it might look like an ordinary SPICE assessment. However, the ASPLA Model introduces a product-oriented view and extends the Work Products by ASPLA-complements. The need to combine a structured reuse of software in combination with agile software development is identified in the case study and motivated by the gap in literature.

In this thesis, the ASPLA Model was not compared with the Cynefin Model as proposed by Reviewer 08. Comparing all existing agile assessment models would be beyond the scope of this thesis. However, the identified maturity models in Section 4.2 influenced the implementation of the ASPLA Model. Challenges and recommendations were identified and addressed in the implementation of the ASPLA Model. Each challenge and recommendation provides the source and links to the corresponding identified literature and source of recommendation (cf. Section D).

Reviewer 09 pointed out that the power of agile shall not be limited by an assessment framework such as represented by the ASPLA Model. He mentioned that there exists no target state in agile development, as agile is always evolving and searching for better solutions. Thought has been given to develop an add-on to the ASPLA Model to evolve the Model using Honeycomb 5. A detailed description of the idea is given in Section 10.2.

Furthermore, Reviewer 09 complained about the lack of consideration with regard to employees, corporate culture and changing mindset. He suggested to accompany the assessments by an agile consultant to consider the needs of the employees in more detail. He characterized agile organizations as organizations which successfully have implemented network structures instead of hierarchical structures. In addition, he mentioned that organizations need to set up lean processes. These processes provide the employee an environment for self-determined work.

The ASPLA Model does not explicitly provides a Honeycomb for empowering people or establishing a new company culture. However, the agile aspects mentioned by Reviewer 09 are addressed in the ASPLA Model. The agile mindset pervades the ASPLA Model in various Base Practices and recommendations. The mentioned self-determined work is recognized in the Base Practices BP_ProcO_02.04 *"Permit low hierarchy levels to scope features"*, BP_ProcO_03.07 *"Utilize agile practices whenever applicable"*, BP_ProcO_07.06 *"Overcome hierarchies"* and BP_ProcO_07.08 *"Trust the supplier"*.

For the aspect of empowering people and agile coaching mentioned by Reviewer 01 and Reviewer 09, three new recommendations were deployed to the ASPLA Model. The Base Practice BP_ProcO_03.07 fosters the selection of applicable agile practices and methods. However, the employees need the knowledge to decide which practice could be used in the given context. Therefore, the employees shall be trained in agile practices and methods (Recommendation ID 149157). Furthermore, employees shall be empowered to take decisions, solve problems, and develop innovative solutions (Recommendation ID 149159) and agile coaches shall advise people to rethink and change the way they go about development (Recommendation ID 149161).

The feedback received by Reviewer 10 aims at a better understanding of the ASPLA Model itself. This includes several identified typos in the initial ASPLA Model. Furthermore, he pointed out that the selected names in the ASPLA Model are hard to understand in the first glance. The naming was not changed as it is an uniform nomenclature that helps to provide a consistent traceability within the ASPLA Model. However, as a result of the first learning cycle, the description of individual constituents of the ASPLA Model were extended and described in more detail. This was also addressed in the feedback provided by Reviewer 11.

Furthermore, it was not evident to Reviewer 10 why special attention to the product line architecture process is given. This is resulting from the setup of the ASPLA Model (cf. Section 5.2) and the focus on software reuse in current development practices in the automotive domain [208]. The advantages arising from the use of software product lines, such as an increased software quality by reuse and customization and individualization of customers' requirements, should not be neglected. Therefore, the ASPLA Model aims at maintaining the advantages introduced by the software product line and addresses some areas (e.g. Product Line Architecture, Domain Requirements Engineering) at a different abstraction level.

Reviewer 10 was curious about the ostensible neglect of other processes such as system requirements and risk management. He recognized that these processes are not addressed by an individual Honeycomb within the ASPLA Model. The setup of the ASPLA Model is based on the emerging patterns found in literature and in a case study (cf. Section 5.2). The mentioned processes by Reviewer 10 are important to address. However, from the starting point of the emerging patterns, they are not addressed by a separate Honeycomb. The structure of the ASPLA Model is based on ASPICE [260] and the mentioned processes are covered by the ASPICE [260] framework and in the ASPLA Work Products (e.g. A_07-05, A_15-01). In addition, Reviewer 10 pointed out that Honeycomb 5 is irrelevant for developers in a self-assessment. This is true as Honeycomb 5 offers the possibility to keep the ASPLA Model itself flexible and adjustable to changes.

Reviewer 11 pointed out that the model is too complex to understand. However, he admitted that his lack of experience with regard to assessment models made it hard to follow the process and to give qualitative feedback on the maturity of the model.

Reviewer 12 suggested to include insights from further publications to make the ASPLA Model "more reliable, valid and exhaustive" (Reviewer 12).

6.4 Phase 2: Case Study

Hevner et al. [100] propose to validate artifacts in IT regarding relevant quality attributes such as functionality, completeness, consistency, accuracy, reliability, and usability. The second evaluation phase of the ASPLA Model was designed as a comparative case study [216, 268]. Yin [268] proposes different approaches such as comparative or chronological procedures for reporting case studies. The conducted comparative case study was addressing the same case to compare alternative descriptions, explanations and points of view [268]. Therefore, data from four different assessors were collected and compared to the assessment results acquired by the ASPLA Model.

6.4.1 Case Study Design

The objective of the case study was to investigate the hypotheses presented in Section 6.1. The data collection in this case study was based on assessments of four experts (cf. Section 6.4.3). Therefore, a development process for the implementation of embedded software used in automotive Electronic Control Units (ECUs), presented in Section 6.4.2, was assessed. The assessments took place in September 2018 at the development side in Germany. In the assessments, the process owner described the current development process to the experts and the experts were asked to give recommendations on how to combine agile software development practices and software product lines within the presented development process. Each assessment started with a presentation of the process owner about the current development and challenges the development faces when introducing agile practices. In addition, the assessor asked questions regarding the development.

The author of this thesis observed the assessment sessions conducted by the process owner and the assessors. According to Dresch et al. [55], the observer was not an active participant and the observations were conducted in a real environment [55]. Furthermore, the observer recorded the session in writing.

In addition, two datasets were generated by developers from the presented development department in a self-assessment assisted by the ASPLA Model. This datasets include the assessment results and recommendation lists for improvement. The ASPLA Model assessment results were compared with the assessment results provided by the experts and their recommendations.

6.4.2   Research Site

The data for the research presented in this thesis was gathered in the development departments for embedded software at an OEM. This section describes the research context, including the background of the software development process, which is selected for the assessment of the current state with regard to agile software development and software product lines. The presented development process is considered as a representative of embedded software development for Electronic Control Units (ECUs) in the automotive domain. The development process for the ECU software is based on the V-Model as recommended by ISO 26262 [121]. The preferred use of the V-Model is confirmed by Schloßer et al. [221]. They identify "mainly sequential V-Models to develop e.g. engine control software with millions of lines of code controlling highly complex physical systems while satisfying tremendous demands on quality and safety requirements" [221, p. 490].

For the evaluation of the ASPLA Model, assessments were conducted in the context of software development process for ECUs. The ECUs control the engine during combustion, injection and address thermodynamics behavior as well as exhaust treatment. The development is distributed worldwide and located in several affiliates. Furthermore, the development process is managed by means of a software product line for common and market-specific features. New desired features are confirmed on a global level and assigned to the common software base line or to a market-specific solution. Therefore, the requirements for each feature are analyzed and an impact analysis is conducted. After that, the requirements are approved, prioritized and scheduled for the next software version. The feature is implemented and integrated in the scheduled version. Subsequent process steps verify the software implementation by Hardware in the Loop (HIL) tests and vehicle tests in the real car.

6.4.3   Case Study Participants

The case study participants were selected from employees of the Daimler AG. The participants were divided into three groups with different roles. The first group assessed the presented development process as external assessors, the second group was conducting a self-assessment by means of the ASPLA Model, and the third group served as a contact for the assessors in case of questions regarding the process.

Group 1: Assessors. The selection of case study participants, which conduct the assessment without the ASPLA Model was based on two criteria: First, they had to have sufficient knowledge, skills and experiences regarding software product lines and agile software development. The skill levels are classified as "Novice", "Advanced Beginner", "Competent", "Proficient", or "Expert". For considering a participant as an expert which is capable to conduct the assessments, the level of knowledge for both skill levels was at least "Competent". Second, the case study participants had to have a work experience of more than eight years in the field of automotive software engineering. Furthermore, they had to be familiar with assessments in the automotive domain.

Four experts were selected for assessing the presented development process. Table 6.3 gives an overview of the experts.

Table 6.3: Overview of experts who conducted assessments and provided recommendations.

Expert 1	Scrum Master with extensive knowledge in software product lines
Software Product Line	Expert
Agile Software Development	Expert
Expert 2	Agile Facilitator
Software Product Line	Competent
Agile Software Development	Expert
Expert 3	Agile Facilitator
Software Product Line	Expert
Agile Software Development	Proficient
Expert 4	Scrum Master
Software Product Line	Proficient
Agile Software Development	Expert

Group 2: Developers. The selection of case study participants that conducted a self-assessment guided by the ASPLA Model, was based the following criteria: It was required that the participants had the necessary skills and knowledge regarding the development process.

Two participants both working in the presented development process (cf. Section 6.4.2) were selected to conduct a self-assessment guided by the ASPLA Model. Both are actively developing embedded software for ECU functionality and have a working experience of more than ten years in embedded software development in the automotive domain. Table 6.4 gives an overview of their skill levels.

Table 6.4: Overview of the participants who conducted an assessment by means of the ASPLA Model.

Developer 1	Current Position: Software Developer
Software Product Line	Expert
Agile Software Development	Proficient

continued on the next page.

Developer 2	Current Position: Software Developer
Software Product Line	Expert
Agile Software Development	Proficient

Group 3: Process Owner. The selected process owner is in charge of the development process described in Section 6.4.2 for more than ten years. In this case study, he provided the requested information for the assessment.

6.4.4 Assessment Executions

All experts conducted an assessment for the presented development process. The procedure for the assessments was done in the same way for all four assessors. Each assessment session took between one and two hours. In the beginning, the process owner presented the current development process and pointed out the peculiarities in the given context. Following this, the process owner and the expert discussed how an agile transformation can be initiated and which recommendations the assessor could provide to improve the combination of agile software development and software product lines in the presented context. The discussion was recorded for detailed analysis. Expert 2 and Expert 3 decided to conduct the assessment session together in order to complement each other with their knowledge and experience. Expert 4 requested information and documentation about the process, including process description and the participating roles prior to the assessment.

In addition to the external assessments, the developers (cf. Table 6.4) conducted self-assessments using the WebApp.

6.4.5 Results

This section presents the results obtained by the assessments and relates them to the hypotheses presented in Section 6.1. Taking into account the recommendation by Runeson and Höst [216] this section is structured by the assessment results and includes evaluation and the validity.

Assessment Result: Experts

Two central questions were defined and presented to each expert prior to the assessment. The first question dealt with an agile transformation process for the described development process and how it could be initiated. The second questions asked for a prioritized list of recommendations.

Expert 1. Expert 1 pointed out that for the introduction of agile into the presented development process, great importance must be given to quality assurance. He emphasized the importance of software quality to obtain stability in the development. He further mentioned that the quality assurance starts with well-written requirements and includes assignments that focus on unit tests, coverage metrics, and Continuous Integration (CI). In fact, CI serves as a quality assurance in early development stages. In addition, he pointed out that it is necessary to automate software tests. However, for this a well-skilled development team is needed and test expertise must be present in the team. Furthermore, he mentioned that it is important for the agile transformation of complex development processes to build up agile know-how and involve agile coaches in the transformation process.

Expert 1 defined the term "agile" as being more flexible in case of unforeseeable changes. He further emphasized that agile does not necessarily mean a faster development. However, he admitted that being flexible and work in an agile way is difficult in classic development processes. Therefore, he recommended that parts of the V-process should be rebuilt into a Scrum process. Scrum could serve as the basis to define new roles and to separate the agile development from the slow surrounding processes. To synchronize the agile development with the other departments, synchronization points must be introduced. These synchronization points as well as the time for refactoring the software are important to prevent the erosion of the software product line. In case of the assessed development process, Expert 1 recommended to set up six Scrum teams. Furthermore, he pointed out that Product Owners (POs) need to be appointed who serve as a proxy for global agreement on feature implementation. However, he added that the responsibility of how a feature is implemented and the architectural decision lies within the development team. The recommendations given by Expert 1 are summarized in Table 6.5.

Table 6.5: Recommendation list based on the assessment conducted by Expert 1.

Improvement potential 1	He recommends to automate software test and introduce CI. Furthermore, he suggests to extend the test procedures to handle virtual integration.
Improvement potential 2	He recommends to introduce an existing agile framework, such as Scrum, and follow the instructions of the framework strictly. He emphasizes not to change anything in the process of the selected framework. Changes will introduce discussion and therefore lower performance of the team.
Improvement potential 3	He recommends to organize regular training and certification of the employees.
Improvement potential 4	He points out that the agile approaches are only intended for the context of software development. He recommends to define clear boundaries to the surrounding processes. Hardware development processes and other processes shall be synchronized but the clear separation between the different processes shall be remain.

Expert 2 and Expert 3. Expert 2 considered great potential in the demand and requirements management. He mentioned that from his experience, requirements and how they are documented always offer a potential to foster the introduction of an agile way of working. Therefore, he emphasized that it is important to write requirements from the customer's point of view, so-called user stories. Expert 3 elaborated that with a different perspective on requirements it is possible to neglect a specification in some cases. Both experts did not specify the mentioned cases exactly but requested for a more detailed discussion on the context where a specification can be replaced by a user story to comply with legal requirements.

Both experts pointed out that the customer contact must be intensified in order to better understand the customer. However, this also requires shorter development loops. Therefore, requirements are specified in a continuous process in close collaboration between customers and developers. Expert 2 mentioned that this helps to identify problems early in the development and enables the developers to understand customer wishes correctly. It furthermore offers the advantage that software tests are not only at the end of the development cycle but in a continuous process.

Expert 2 mentioned that it is important for agile software development to introduce a strategy team which defines the strategic direction. He emphasized that features must be selected according to their priority. The priority value helps to manage the development process and set the scope for the next development iteration. Expert 3 highlighted that it is not allowed to change the features to be implemented in one sprint. The strict rejection of amendments during a sprint is necessary because otherwise, the productivity of the team suffers. Moreover, for the consistent development within a development sprint, it is important to identify dependencies in features and software units (Expert 2).

Therefore, Expert 2 recommended the implementation of Scrum as a framework for agile software development. He emphasized that Scrum is not mandatory, however Scrum has proven itself in the agile software development. However, he admitted that the introduction of Scrum in the development is only the first step to start an agile transformation in the presented development process. He recommended to transform the whole organization to obtain the benefits of an agile way of working. For him, key elements are collaboration and communication within the organization and an open feedback culture (Expert 3).

Expert 3 identified the need to change the mindset of employees in the presented development process. He pointed out that "agile means, how do I treat my employees respectfully" (Expert 3). He promoted to bring employees together in one room to support an open communication between them and to establish openness in the team. Expert 2 pointed out that this requires to teach the employees in the agile mindset. Furthermore, he suggested to establish a close partnership with agile coaches. These coaches will help in the people management and in the development of soft skills among employees. "Confidence, transparency and the willingness to admit mistakes are part of a changed mindset" (Expert 2).

Expert 2 recommended that the cooperation with suppliers must be changed. Therefore, it must be regulated, when the supplier is allowed to provide software functionality. This is an important fact to consider, if the software development process is organized in small development iterations. Expert 2 reconfirmed the importance to identify dependencies in the functionality that is provided by the supplier and software that is implemented in-house.

In order to define a test process that is used in the combination of agile software development and software product lines, both experts recommended a Design Thinking Workshop. The Design Thinking Workshop could come up with solutions such as virtual integration, testing against models or the use of test vehicles to address the challenges in the development and testing process. They pointed out that the best solutions are often found by the team itself and the Design Thinking Workshop could help to better understand the current issues. The recommendations given by Expert 2 and 3 are summarized in Table 6.6.

Table 6.6: Recommendation list based on the assessment conducted by Expert 2 and 3.

Improvement potential 1	The experts recommend to establish a close customer contact and collect feedback from the customer directly. With a close customer collaboration, user stories instead of requirements can be written and specifications can be avoided in some cases.
Improvement potential 2	The experts recommend to establish short iterative development cycles, best addressed by the implementation of Scrum.
Improvement potential 3	The experts recommend to change the mindset of the employees. This can be achieved by the involvement of agile trainers who help to change the mindset and further teach employees' soft skills.
Improvement potential 4	The experts recommend to solve existing problems in the agile transformation and in the agile test strategy for various software variants by means of Design Thinking Workshops within the teams.

Expert 4. Expert 4 pointed out that the current development processes should not be taken for granted. To adopt an agile way of working, the whole organization must change their internal management methods and processes. He identified the current development process as a necessity for maintaining the distributed development. The process ensures that common features are identified. However, he pointed out that the process is slowed down by decisions on feature development which have to be obtained from different roles at different hierarchy levels. To improve the coordination and to make it more efficient, he suggested that only one person decides on feature implementation. However, he recognized that the limitation to one "decision maker" is not suitable for the distributed development in the automotive domain. The responsible person must have an overview of all model series and markets and needs extensive knowledge in the implementation and architecture of the software to be able to decide correctly. Therefore, he noted that several specialists are needed for different areas and communication between them plays a crucial role.

Furthermore, he proposed to retain the established processes to coordinate the development and introduce context-specific agile practices. Therefore, he suggested a clear separation of the software development process to other processes, e.g. the decoupling of hardware and software. He pointed out that this separation requires a clearly defined interface between the processes. In addition, he proposed to make the requirements and approval process more flexible. He recommended to "Avoid Waste". Instead of specifying and approving requirements which will never be implemented, the decision to implement them should be as early as possible. This can help to specify the requirements which are needed. For him "agile" means a clear "definition of ready" to define a uniform standard for requirements. In order to have the same understanding on requirements, the team members should be trained. This is also necessary to be able to prioritize correctly. He recommended to consider the business value and avoid to prioritize the features redundantly. Beside the importance of prioritization, coordination, and requirements elicitation, the ratio of software development to the entire process needs to be improved.

For the combination of agile software development and software product lines the test process needs to be adapted as well. Expert 4 suggested that the test process should be automated by means of setting up a CI environment. Furthermore, he recommended to reduce the release cycles and integrate the software into a real vehicle. He mentioned that this requires several vehicles for testing. However, this will increase the product responsibility of the developers and will build up necessary test know-how on the developer side. The recommendations given by Expert 4 are summarized in Table 6.7.

Table 6.7: Recommendation list based on the assessment conducted by Expert 4.

Improvement potential 1	He recommends to centralize the decision on feature implementation and the coordination of the distributed development, while retaining the benefits of the existing development process and introduce context-specific agile elements to it.
Improvement potential 2	He recommends to make the requirements and approval process more flexible. He points out to "Avoid Waste" and only specify the requirements which are needed.
Improvement potential 3	He recommends to automate software test and introduce CI. Furthermore, he suggests to extend the test procedures and integrate the software into real vehicles as often as possible.
Improvement potential 4	He recommends to foster the collaboration between the teams, by building up technical expertise and strengthening the product responsibility of each developer. An open communication between all participants is crucial.

Assessment Result: Developers

The assessment by means of the ASPLA Model Web Application was conducted by the selected developers (cf. Table 6.4). Both software developers work in the presented development context (cf. Section 6.4.2) and assessed the same process. The results of both assessment sessions match closely. It took them both less than half an hour to conduct the assessment. Developer 1 conducted the assessment in 26 minutes, Developer 2 in 28 minutes. The result of the assessment conducted by Developer 1 is shown in Figure 6.2, the result of Developer 2 in Figure 6.3.

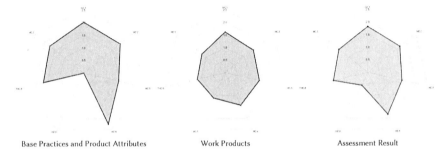

   Base Practices and Product Attributes   Work Products   Assessment Result

Figure 6.2: Overview of the assessment result as calculated by the ASPLA Model for Developer 1

Honeycomb 5 is not directly assessed by the ASPLA Model. Therefore, no questions for Base Practices and Product Attributes are asked for this Honeycomb. This leads to a result of "0" for Base Practices and Product Attributes in this Honeycomb. However, Work Products are connected to this Honeycomb (cf. Appendix E.5). Answers for these Work Products are connected to the result for this Honeycomb. Therefore, the Honeycomb 5 is shown in the final assessment result.

At the end of the assessment process, the ASPLA Model displays the results in a radar chart, identifies improvement potential and assigns recommendations to each outcome. One possibility (cf. Section 5.5.4) is to let the ASPLA Model decide which recommendations should be addressed first. Therefore, a configurable amount of recommendations can be proposed by the ASPLA Model. Based on the results of the pilot tests, the selection of recommendations for the case study was limited to three Honeycombs. Therefore, the ASPLA Model selected the three Honeycombs with the lowest assessment result. Within those, the three outcomes with the lowest assessment results were selected. According to the pilot testers, this limitation leads to a manageable amount of recommendations. Based on the identified Honeycombs and outcomes, the improvement potential was defined and a list of recommendations was created.

Both assessment results show the same tendency and led to an overall assessment result of "Partially fulfilled". This leaves a leeway for future improvement. However, Developer 2 assessed the development in a more reserved way than Developer 1. Due to this more re-

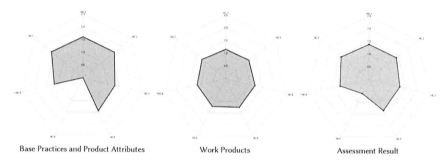

Base Practices and Product Attributes   Work Products   Assessment Result

Figure 6.3: Overview of the assessment result as calculated by the ASPLA Model for Developer 2

served assessment, the ASPLA Model identified slightly different Honeycombs to improve. For Developer 1, the ASPLA Model recommends to improve Honeycomb 3 (Agile Software Development), Honeycomb 6 (Test Strategy) and Honeycomb 7 (Communication) with a high priority. For Developer 2, the ASPLA Model identifies Honeycomb 3 (Agile Software Development), Honeycomb 4 (Continuous X) and Honeycomb 6 (Test Strategy). The fact that Honeycomb 4 is included in the improvement plan for Developer 2 but not in the plan for Developer 1 appears to be consistent with the fact that Developer 1 is responsible for the Continuous Integration (CI) strategy and supervised the CI environment. Hence, he has better insight into the continuous tasks and the assessment result is better for this Honeycomb.

In total, the ASPLA Model identified 35 recommendations for Developer 1 and 34 recommendations for Developer 2. The complete list of recommendations for Developer 1 can be found in Table A.1 and correspondingly in Table A.2 for Developer 2. The two recommendation lists overlap each other in 19 recommendations that address four different Base Practices. Combining these two assessments, the improvement plan can be summarized in four important improvement potentials that need to be addressed first.

Table 6.8: Combined recommendation list based on both assessments to identify the improvement potential for the assessed department.

Improvement potential 1	It is recommended to organize the development in short iterative cycles. These cycles shall be adjustable, according to the developers team needs. With adjusted development cycles, the iterative development process is capable to react on changes in the market situation. New requirements can be taken into account and addressed in a shorter time.

continued on the next page

Improvement potential 2	It is recommended to adjust the collaboration with suppliers to fit with an agile development process. Therefore, it is necessary that the purchase department provides working contract arrangements for the collaboration with suppliers that comprise an agile payment strategy. This payment strategy is flexible to address the needs of the development team and provides the supplier the ability to work in an agile way.
Improvement potential 3	It is recommended not to stipulate agile methods and practices to the development process. The employees shall be empowered to decide for themselves on how to solve problems and develop innovative solutions. Therefore, it is necessary that the employees are trained in agile basics to know the available practices and methods. Agile coaches can support the selection of suitable practices.
Improvement potential 4	It is recommended to establish a consistent and bidirectional traceability between software units, test cases and the corresponding results. The established consistency is a prerequisite for automated testing of various software variants and to fulfill legal requirements.

Summary of Results

According to Seaman [226], there exists two general techniques to analyze qualitative data with respect to hypotheses. First, hypotheses could be generated in the analysis of the qualitative data. Second, hypotheses could be confirmed by the data [226]. The following section focuses on the second approach by confirming the hypotheses presented in Section 6.1. Seaman points out that "a hypothesis cannot be proven, it can only be supported or refuted" [226, p. 13]. Therefore, Seaman [226] recommends to "build up a 'weight of evidence' in support of a particular proposition, not to prove it" [226, p. 13]. The qualitative data gained in the assessments conducted by the experts and the developers provide explanatory information and help in confirming the hypotheses. In addition, Seaman [226] emphasizes the necessity to ensure the validity of the method for data collection. This objection of validity is addressed in Section 6.4.6.

Wohlin et al. [266] propose to use tabulation as a useful analysis technique. Thereby, the data is arranged in tables to get an overview of the data [266]. They point out that the selection of how to organize the data must be decided for every case study [266]. For analyzing the recommendations provided by the experts and the ASPLA Model, each recommendation is represented by a row in Table 6.9. Also, the recommendations given by the ASPLA Model are summarized. For example, the term *"Adjust payment strategy for suppliers"* in Table 6.9 covers the recommendations *"The payment strategy should be able to be changed, according to the developers team needs."*, *"The payment strategy shall provide the suppliers the ability to work in an agile way."*, and *"The payment strategy shall be adjustable."* (cf. Appendix A). With this approach, the 35 recommendations for

Developer 1 are reduced to 16 and the 34 recommendations for Developer 2 are reduced to 14. The columns define the corresponding source of the recommendation.

Table 6.9: Comparison of recommendations given by the experts and provided by the ASPLA Model.

Recommendation	Expert 1	Expert 2	Expert 3	Expert 4	Experts combined	Developer 1	Developer 2	Developers combined
Adjust payment strategy for suppliers						X	X	X
Improved collaboration with suppliers		X			X	X	X	X
Adjustable development iterations		X	X	X	X	X	X	X
No stipulated agile framework						X	X	X
Employee training	X				X	X	X	X
Responsibility on lower hierarchy levels	X			X	X	X	X	X
Introduce agile coaches	X				X	X	X	X
Shorten release cycles	X				X	X	X	X
Focus on market and customer demands		X	X		X	X	X	X
Establish tracing in the development process						X	X	X
Prioritize testing activities	X			X	X	X	X	X
Satisfy requirements for legal restrictions	X				X	X	X	X
Automate testing and selection of test cases	X	X	X	X	X	X	X	X
Establish feedback channels		X	X	X	X	X		X
Include customer feedback		X	X		X	X		X
Make the process visible to all participants						X		X
Introduce CI and Virtual Integration	X			X	X		X	X
Introduce Scrum by the book	X	X	X	X	X			
Replace requirements with User Stories		X	X		X			
Foster employees' mindset change		X	X	X	X	<out of scope>		
Conduct Design Thinking Workshops		X	X		X	<out of scope>		

Combining the results of the experts (cf. 5th column in Table 6.9) lead to 17 recommendations in total. However, two recommendations which focus on the change of the employees' mindset, are defined to be <out of scope>. As defined in Section 5.2.1, the mindset change will be the result of a slow and stepwise integration of agile methods into the rigid and inflexible surrounding processes [107]. The focus of this thesis and the presented research artifact is to address the "context" forces (cf. Section 3.4.2) that support the combination of agile software development and software product lines. This reduces the number of recommendations for the combined experts to 15 recommendations. The recommendations for the developers are also combined and lead to a total number of 17 recommendations when clustered, as shown in Table 6.9.

The assessments conducted by the developers by means of the ASPLA Model lead to similar results. In contrast, the results of the experts are different in some cases. This indicates that it could be helpful to use a structured approach to assess the combination of agile software development and software product lines.

Hypothesis 1. *The results from applying the assessment model are in agreement with the recommendations of the experts that assess the current development process.*

This hypothesis is to support the meaningfulness of the ASPLA Model. Therefore, the ASPLA Model recommendations are compared with recommendations given by the experts that assessed the presented development process (cf. Section 6.4). The ASPLA Model evaluates the assessment result and provides recommendations to establish an agile software product line. Therefore, the ASPLA Model was configured to return only recommendations for the three Honeycombs with the lowest assessment result (cf. Section 5.5.4). These recommendations are in agreement with the recommendations given by the experts. In total, the number of recommendations given by the model is deviating by less than 30% compared to the recommendations given by the experts.

As shown in Table 6.9, this leads to a total number of 17 recommendations for the ASPLA Model, 15 recommendations for the experts and a deviation of 13%. The ASPLA Model covers more recommendations than given by the experts. This result supports the Hypothesis 1 that results from applying the ASPLA Model are generally in line with the recommendations of the experts.

Hypothesis 2. *The results from applying the assessment model are not missing important recommendations given by experts that assess the current development process.*

The ASPLA Model is complete and covers the recommendations of experts that assess the presented development process (cf. Section 6.4). The number and the content of the recommendations given by the experts are in line with the recommendations provided by the ASPLA Model. In total, the number of missing recommendations given by the ASPLA Model is less than 10% compared to the recommendations given by the experts.

Two recommendations given by the experts are not addressed in the ASPLA Model. The first one is the recommendation to "Introduce Scrum by the book". This recommendation contradicts with the recommendation in the ASPLA Model that proposes to "not stipulate an agile framework". From the direct feedback in the iterative learning cycle given by Reviewer 07, this is one key benefit of the ASPLA Model. Klünder et al. [147] point out that it is necessary to select agile practices for the specific context in which they should be used. Furthermore, they point out that a wrong selection of agile practices could lead to a rejection of agile development in general [147]. Therefore, the recommendation to "Introduce Scrum by the book" is not purposed by the ASPLA Model.

The second recommendation to "Replace requirements with User Stories" is also not addressed by the ASPLA Model. The ASPLA Model intends to be an easy to use assessment model in particular for self-assessments. Employees with different skills in agile development practices shall be able to conduct an assessment. The development in the automotive domain must comply with legal restrictions and documentation obligations. Therefore, the ASPLA Model is not proposing to write user stories. This is also connected to the previous recommendation not to stipulate a specific agile practice. User stories could be introduced with the help of agile coaches but only if the context allows to move to user stories with regard to legal requirements.

Two recommendations compared to a total number of 19 recommendations lead to a deviation of 10,5%. Even if the proposed 10% of missing recommendations given by the ASPLA Model compared to the recommendations given by the expert are not fulfilled, the result suggests that Hypothesis 2 is supported by the result. If the second recommendation is considered as a consequence of the first recommendation not to stipulate a specific agile practice, it could considered as <out of scope>. By not considering the recommendation "Replace requirements with User Stories", the deviation reduces on 5%. Therefore, the results indicate that Hypothesis 2 is supported and the ASPLA Model is not missing important recommendations given by experts.

Hypothesis 3. *With the developed assessment model, the time for conducting an assessment could be reduced by a factor of 2 compared to the assessments conducted by experts.*

The Web Application measures the time for each assessment session. The assessment session conducted by Developer 1 lasted 26 minutes. In addition, Developer 2 finished the assessment within 28 minutes. This in turn leads to an average time duration of 27 minutes to conduct the assessment by means of the ASPLA Model. The resulting assessment time was comparable to the time for assessments conducted in five pilot tests (30 minutes).

The experts assessed the presented development process in an average time of 71 minutes. The assessment of Expert 1 took 90 minutes. Expert 2 and Expert 3 evaluated the process within 60 minutes, and the assessment of Expert 4 took 75 minutes to finish.

This time duration is quite fast if it is compared to ASPICE assessments in general. The Process Owner (cf. Section 6.4.3) points out that he was quite surprised that the assessments took only 71 minutes in average. Furthermore, he appreciates that the assessment was set up as a discussion with the experts, to elaborate the question how agile software development could be introduced in the presented development process managed by a software product line. Compared to the assessment time for ASPICE [260] (about 1 week), this is clearly an improvement.

The numbers indicate that with an average time of 27 minutes, the ASPLA Model assessment is 2,6 times faster than the assessments conducted by the experts. Based on this result, Hypothesis 3 is supported by the data. The data indicates that the time for assessing a development process can be reduced by following the structured approach provided by the ASPLA Model.

6.4.6 Threats to Validity

Wohlin et al. [266] point out that it is important to consider the validity of a study. The mention that the credibility of the results shall not be influenced by the researcher [266]. Furthermore, they recommend to distinguish between construct validity, internal validity, external validity, and reliability as the four aspects of validity [266].

Construct Validity

The construct validity defines to what extend the study outcomes really represent the original intention of the research [266].

A threat to the construct validity is the fact that only the author of this thesis observed and recorded the assessment sessions conducted by the experts and process owner. Therefore, the result can be biased by the subjectivity of the author of this thesis. To verify that the correct recommendations and improvement potentials are recorded, the process owner reviewed the recorded meeting minutes.

Internal Validity

The internal validity addresses causal relations [266]. This could occur if more than one factors affect another factor, but not all factors are identified by the researcher [266]. If one is not aware of all influencing factors, this is a threat to internal validity [266].

The scope of the case study was very narrow, containing only one selected development process that is assessed in the case study. This may neglect other software development processes. In order to address this threat, more ASPLA assessments should be conducted also in different development processes. The case study was conducted within one OEM. Therefore, it was not possible to control company specific effects related to the development process. The selection of case study participants was limited by the assessed development process and the selection criteria for selecting the developers (cf. Section 6.4.3). The selection of experts was limited by the knowledge in the automotive software development and agile skills. The strict selection criteria for experts tried to address the issue that a non-representative set of case study participants was selected. However, the small number of experts conducting the assessment can be a threat. For the given context, and based on the knowledge of the experts, it is accepted as a valid sample size. The internal validity can be threaten by the fact that the process to be assessed was always represented by the same person.

External Validity

According to Wohlin et al. [266], this aspect of validity addresses the generalization of results. Furthermore, it is defined to what extent the findings are of interest outside of the investigated case [266].

The case study was conducted in an embedded software development process in the automotive domain. The assessed process contained a global distributed software product line and aims at introducing agile software development practices into the development.

It cannot be generalized from the case study results that the ASPLA Model will provide similar recommendations in other contexts. Furthermore, this case study only covers a small part of the ASPLA Model. However, the ASPLA Model is based on ASPICE [260] and can be used to assess all processes addressed with an ASPICE assessment.

Reliability

The aspect of reliability is used in qualitative data analysis [266]. According to Wohlin et al. [266], the counterpart in quantitative data analysis is known as the conclusion validity. Reliability addresses to what extent the data and the analysis are affected by the specific researchers [266].

It could be the case that the presence of the researcher may affect the behavior of the experts during the assessment. The researcher was taking notes without interfering the discussion between the experts and the process owner. After the assessments, the process owner reviewed the meeting minutes to avoid wrong recording of the assessment session. Furthermore, this helps with the issue that the researcher loose its objectivity by being too closely involved in the setting being observed and influenced by the implementation of the ASPLA Model. Data triangulation for the results of the experts and developers could help to overcome researcher bias.

6.5 Chapter Summary

This chapter presents the validation of the ASPLA Model. According to Hevner et al. [99], the ASPLA Model was integrated within the technical infrastructure of the business environment. This helped to ensure that the ASPLA Model is relevant for the environment for which it was developed. For the first evaluation phase, the ASPLA Model was implemented as a Web Application (WebApp) (cf. Section 5.5.1). The received feedback led to two increments of the ASPLA Model. Furthermore, it turned out that the ASPLA Model is considered to be useful for the combination of agile software development and software product lines. Missing recommendations were addressed and the model was incremented accordingly. Version 1.02 of the ASPLA Model was selected for the second step of validation.

The case study compares the recommendations supposed by the assessment tool with the recommendations given by experts. Therefore, data from four different experts were collected and compared with the two assessment conducted by developers. The qualitative data analysis helped to build up a "weight of evidence" to support the hypotheses (cf. Section 6.1). The evaluation of the ASPLA Model indicated that the assessment can help to foster the combination of agile software development with software product lines in the automotive domain. In comparison with experts' assessments and recommendations, the model produced similar or even better results.

Chapter 7

Results

Hevner et al. [100] propose to communicate the results effectively to the audience. Therefore, this chapter summarizes the findings of the research addressed by the general research question: *How to establish an agile software product line in the automotive domain?* The findings are presented by each research questions RQ1.1 - RQ1.5.

7.1 Appropriate Methods to Establish an Agile Software Product Line

RQ1.1: What are appropriate methods to establish an agile software product line?
Section 3.1 describes the current development practice in the automotive domain, comprising software reuse strategies and structured by standardized processes. These processes are considered as too inflexible to keep pace with fast changing market demands [23, 63]. Hence, the development processes need to be redesigned in a way that it is possible to learn and adapt continuously at a fast pace [111] (cf. Section 3.1.1).

The interview study (cf. Section 3.2) revealed that agile development methods are not used in many organizational units or only very rudimentary in the automotive domain. Furthermore, the study revealed that agile software development and the reuse of software is not addressed at the same time. This combination is only addressed individually in different development contexts in the automotive domain. Therefore, the first research question identified three possible strategies to establish an agile software product line. The first strategy is to enrich a working software product line development with agile methods and practices. Second, agile development processes can be extended by a software reuse strategy. Finally, both approaches can be introduced at the same time. Depending on the initial situation and the context, the appropriate methods and the suitable strategy to establish an agile software product line varies.

Furthermore, Münch et al. [183] identify two general ways to introduce changes into existing processes in organizations. The two possible approaches identified by them are the big-bang and the phased approach [183]. In the big-bang approach, the complete organization is changed at the same time. Therefore, the old processes and ways of working

123

are abandoned. From that point in time, only the new processes are used. However, a big-bang introduction of agile software product lines in the automotive domain is hard to address [183, 140]. With the phased approach, the changed processes are introduced in a phased way [183]. Münch et al. [183] emphasis that it does not matter which strategy is used. However, it is necessary to know the current process and the desired new way of working [111].

In the automotive domain, process assessments are currently used to evaluate and improve the processes of the organizational units against a predefined process assessment model. Standards in the automotive domain are Automotive SPICE® (ASPICE) [260] and Capability Maturity Model Integration (CMMI) [243]. However, neither CMMI [243] nor ASPICE [260] focus explicitly on the combination of agile development practices and software product lines and foster an introduction of agile software product lines. Hence, there exists a need for an assessment model that deals with agile software product lines in the automotive domain.

7.2   Transformation Tasks towards Agile Software Product Lines

RQ1.2: Which tasks are relevant for improvement and transformation towards agile software product lines?

Sharp and Hall [229] identify that the introduction of agile practices often starts in an uncoordinated way. The combination of agile software methods and software product lines in the automotive domain often fails due to the lack of a structured improvement approach. Identifying the relevant tasks for a structured transformation towards an agile software product line is always context-specific [146]. Klünder et al. [146] identify models for different contexts such as small or large companies. The identified model focus on different aspects such as human factors or development methods [146]. However, they did not find any transformation model preserving or supporting software product line engineering [146]. They identify that an assessment of the current situation is a first and relevant task towards agile software product lines.

The research artifact of this thesis is the ASPLA Model which is an assessment model to foster the adoption of agile software product lines in the automotive domain. Therefore, the model covers six important areas that need to be considered for the combination [111]. According to the results of the assessment, a prioritized list of recommendation is generated (cf. Section 5.5.4). There exists no silver bullet for the combination of agile software development and software product lines. The selection of relevant tasks for improvement and transformation towards agile software product lines is context-specific [111].

7.3 Challenges of Agile Assessment Models

RQ1.3: What are problems with using assessment models for introducing agile software product lines?
This research question is addressed in the literature review in Section 4.2. The literature review identified a general problem when using assessment models for the introduction of agile development approaches. Gren et al. [85] question the applicability of maturity models as a way to assess agility. Fontana et al. [70] point out that agile practitioners do not necessarily demand an agile maturity model. This aversion to assessment models to introduce agility was also mentioned by Reviewer 08 in the learning cycles of the ASPLA Model (cf. Section 6.3.3).

Furthermore, the literature review revealed that current assessment models are only covering parts of the development cycle or just focusing on specific agile methods.

For example, the Agile, Hybrid Assessment Method for the Automotive Industry (AHAA) by McCaffery et al. [176]. This assessment considers safety-critical development and aims to be a low-overhead assessment method, based on CMMI [243] and ASPICE [260], for small-to-medium sized organizations [176]. Furthermore, the AHAA aims at assessing organizations that wish to be automotive software suppliers but does not consider a strategic software reuse strategy as it is common in the automotive domain [176]. In addition, Özcan-Top and Demirörs [198] identify nine assessment models and 37 assessment tools that address agility. However, none of the identified models cover the specific peculiarities of the automotive domain. Other assessment models, such as the Reuse Capability Maturity Model (RCMM) by Jasmine and Vasantha [134] focus only on a structured reuse. The RCMM aims to ensure a well-planned and controlled reuse oriented software development [134]. However, Jasmine and Vasantha did not evaluate the suggested model so far [134]. It is too early to be certain that this model also fits for automotive software development.

The literature review identified that there exists no assessment tool for the combination of software product lines and agile development. Therefore, the ASPLA Model was developed. The model can be used to determine the current status of the combination of agile development and software product lines in the automotive domain [111].

7.4 Automotive Specific Aspects in Agile Software Product Line Assessments

RQ1.4: What are the automotive specific aspects that need to be addressed in an assessment of agile software product lines?
Katumba and Knaus [140] mention that the introduction of agile methods into the automotive software development is hindered by special peculiarities of the automotive domain. The automotive context is restricted by rigid quality and safety requirements [245]. Furthermore, complex relationships between hardware and software development must be considered. The development process involves a lot of suppliers which are closely linked and integrated in the development. It is essential to consider all aspects introduced by

the need for functional safety, security, robustness, legal compliance, and modularity [59]. The introduced agile adoption forces model presents hindering factors that need to be addressed to combine agile software development and software product lines in the automotive domain (cf. Section 3.4).

Existing assessment models like ASPICE [260] do not predefine any agile practice or method [76]. The guidelines for conducting an Automotive SPICE assessment in the development of software-based systems recommend that the selected agile approach shall be compliant with required rules and standards [76]. Therefore, assessment recommendations for agile environments are provided [76]. However, the recommendations do not support agile development or foster the introduction of agile elements into the development. Rather, it is recommended to down rate the assessment result if the applied agile approach is not sufficiently implemented. By extending the assessment recommendations of ASPICE [76], this thesis identifies the demands on an assessment model for the combination of agile development and software product lines with respect to the specific peculiarities of the automotive domain. One aspects that needs to be considered is, for example, an improved test strategy to handle the large amount of software variants in a distributed development process. According to Hunt [164], "if you cannot get software automatically and reliably out of your pipeline for continuous delivery, [...] then all the other stuff like talking to users and so on does not matter" [164].

7.5   The Modification of Existing Assessment Models

RQ1.5: How do existing assessment models need to be modified to introduce and improve agile software product lines?

The literature review in Section 4.2 revealed that existing assessment models do not aim at introducing agile and software reuse strategies at the same time. Furthermore, none of the identified assessment models address the specific peculiarities of the automotive domain. According to Fontana et al. [70], existing assessment models shall not be modified to introduce and improve agile development. They mention that maturity models to assess agility cannot be based on traditional maturity models [70].

This contradicts with the recommendation given by Schmid and John [222]. They point out that a new assessment model benefits from being based on an existing assessment framework [222]. The introduced ASPLA Model is based on the ASPICE [260] structure. The ASPLA Model is tailored to the specifics of the automotive domain, fosters agile transformation due to providing a detailed overview on the current situation and supports the transformation due to specific recommendations given to the assessment user. An iterative learning cycle (cf. Section 6.3) keeps the model adjustable to emerging innovations and leads to continuous improvement of the model. By means of a case study (cf. Section 6.4), the results of the model were compared with the result of experts assessing the same development process. The results indicate that the ASPLA Model is a useful tool for conducting assessments in the automotive domain with regard to agile software product lines.

Chapter 8

Related Work

The definition of maturity in software development is covered by models such as ASPICE [260], CMMI [243] or ISO/IEC 15504 [127]. These models provide assistance on how to manage and optimize development processes and provide detailed processes with Work Products and Best Practices. However, these models do not address agile maturity in detail (cf. Section 4.2).

Fontana et al. [70] identify possible approaches that increase the maturity of agile software development. They identify two possible approaches to determine agile software development maturity [69]. First, the combination of existing maturity models with agile aspects, and second the disengagement of existing maturity models and the implementation of sole agile maturity models [70].

Therefore, Fontana et al. [69] propose a definition of agile software development maturity as a set of best practices and team characteristics. They point out that communication within a team is important. Furthermore, they define that the team "cares about customers and software quality, allows requirements to change, shares knowledge, manages source code and tests using tools, methods and metrics supported by infrastructure appropriate for agility, self-organizes at a sustainable pace, standardizes and continuously improves agile practices, and generates perceived outcomes for customers and management" [69, p. 152].

As they point out, their objective is not to propose an agile maturity model [69]. They mention that the implementation of agility is context-dependent and needs to be considered separately for each context. Furthermore, they claim that agile maturity models cannot be based on traditional maturity models and identify that agile practitioners do not necessarily demand an agile maturity model [70].

In the context of automotive software development, assessment models are a well-used approach to determine the capability and maturity of organizational processes to develop software. Assessments are accepted by management to manage and foster improvement. The introduced ASPLA Model helps to fill the identified gap of current automotive assessment models that combine agile software development with software product lines. The introduction of a maturity model contradicts with the findings from Fontana et al. [70]. However, in the structured development of automotive software, it is beneficial

127

to start with what already works and what is widely accepted and adopted within the automotive domain [222]. The ASPLA Model helps introducing agile software product lines and identifies specific aspects that need to be addressed with respect to the specific peculiarities of the automotive domain.

Stallinger and Neumann [236] point out that the established software process life cycle models such as ISO/IEC 12207 [131] do not consider strategic software reuse and lack product management practices at system level [236]. They propose to extend system life cycle processes as presented in ISO/IEC 12207 [131] with strategic reuse and product-orientation [236]. Therefore, they propose the development of a process reference model and suggest to use it as an add-on for software development process assessments [236]. The presented reference model is compliant with ISO/IEC 15504 [127] and provides product management and reuse practices on a high level [236].

The presented approach follows the guidelines proposed by Schmid and John [222]. Stallinger and Neumann [236] use an established software process life cycle model and extend some parts of it for strategic reuse and product-orientation [236]. For the initial set up of the ASPLA Model it was proposed to extend the REUse processes to better cover product lines and the MANagement processes to cover an agile management style. In contrast to Stallinger and Neumann [236], the ASPLA Model addresses the combination of agile software development and software product lines in the automotive domain. The reference model by Stallinger and Neumann [236] does not focus on the automotive domain in particular and does not consider agile development practices. However, both, the ASPLA Model and the model by Stallinger and Neumann [236] focus on product-orientation.

Diebold et al. [53] describe how agile practices do support ASPICE [260] requirements (Base Practices and Work Products). They combine the outcome of literature reviews with expert opinions to map 155 agile practices onto 185 ASPICE [260] requirements [53]. This resulted in 772 mappings [53]. They point out that most ASPICE Base Practices are supported by agile practices (96%) [53]. In addition, they observe less support for work products (87%) [53]. Instead, Diebold et al. [53] suggest to introduce some agile practices (backlog, product owner or templates and standards). Those practices are promising a large coverage of ASPICE [260].

The less support for ASPICE [260] Work Products, as identified by Diebold et al. [53], fosters the introduction of ASPLA-complements for ASPLA Work Products. To make Work Products more compatible with agile software development, the ASPICE [260] Work Products are extended by ASPLA-complements. Within the ASPLA Model, a product-oriented view is introduced and agile practices are not stipulated.

Turetken et al. [253] present the SAFe maturity model that prioritizes the improvement actions for adopting agile in combination with SAFe practices. The SAFe maturity model is based on the agile maturity model by Sidky [234]. Agile practices from the agile maturity model by Sidky [234] are adopted within the SAFe framework. Turetken et al. [253] point out that the SAFe maturity model guides and structures the adoption of SAFe by providing a practical mechanism to assess agility [253]. The agility levels are "based on the extent of successfully performed practices" [253, p. 16]. However, the SAFe maturity model is not yet validated.

Further related work could be identified in the literature review presented in Section F.2.

Sidky [234] introduces a structured approach to adopt agile practices by identifying areas within the organization that require improvement before the adoption effort starts [234]. He presents an agile adoption framework that defines an agile measurement index with five agile levels (Collaborative, Evolutionary, Effective, Adaptive and Encompassing) for measuring agility. Each level implements agile practices that include the introduction of communication and collaboration practices, continuous software delivery, improved software quality, the capability of address changes, and an environment to sustain agility [234]. Furthermore, Sidky [234] introduces a process to assist agile adoption by guiding assessments.

The ASPLA Model addresses several important areas such as communication which are also identified in the agile adoption framework by Sidky [234]. However, the ASPLA Model does not propose to adapt agile practices in different levels. Communication and collaboration, as well as the improved software quality and the capability to address changes, are all addressed by the ASPLA Base Practices, Product Attributes and Work Products.

Hayashi et al. [94] introduce an iterative development process that combines agile development methods and management methods for multiple product lines of automotive software systems. In contrast to the proposed approach by Hayashi et al. [94], the ASPLA Model addresses the whole organization and not only the management of the software product line. Furthermore, Hayashi et al. [94] do not offer an assessment model to identify the current status of the software development with regard to agile software product lines.

Özcan-Top and Demirörs [198] identify nine assessment models and seven assessment tools that partially automate the assessment process for agility. However, none of the identified models cover the specific peculiarities of the automotive domain. In contrast to the ASPLA Model, a systematic reuse of software within the automotive domain is not addressed [198].

The AHAA model by McCaffery et al. [176] considers safety-critical development and is a low-overhead assessment method, based on CMMI [243] and ASPICE [260], for small to medium sized organizations [176]. In contrast to the ASPLA Model, the AHAA model does not explicitly focus on software reuse and aims at small and medium enterprises that want to become automotive suppliers [176].

Hantke [92] presents a development process that includes both requirements for SCRUM [225] and SPICE [127]. He presents first results, such as clearer and more transparent requirements, an improved team communication, and a better understanding of project goals within the team. Furthermore, he mentions that the coverage of the SPICE practices by the SCRUM [225] activities is relative large. He presents a method for implementing the combination in a pilot project. In contrast to the ASPLA Model, Hantke [92] does not focus on software product lines. The potential benefits of the strategic software reuse are not considered in the comparison of SPICE [127] and SCRUM [225].

In summary, there exists currently no approach to combine agile software development and software product lines in the automotive domain. This section and the literature review in Section 4.2 reveals that current assessment models are only covering some parts of the development cycle or just focusing on specific agile methods. One difference to the identified assessment models is that the ASPLA Model does not stipulate an agile framework. Instead, the ASPLA Model focuses on software reuse and agile development and addresses agile software product lines in the automotive domain.

Chapter 9

Discussion

The ASPLA Model, as implemented and presented by the author in this thesis, is an assessment model to foster the adoption of agile software product lines in the automotive domain. Related assessment models are identified in the literature review (cf. Section 4.2) and in Chapter 8. The ASPLA Model addresses the identified gap in literature and expands the collection of different assessment models to address the combination of agile software development and software product lines in the automotive domain.

9.1 Critical Appraisal

The ASPLA Model is an assessment and improvement model to foster the adoption of agile software product lines in the automotive domain. An assessment model was selected as the research artifact for the design-science research. However, it must be mentioned that assessment models are not the only approach for software process improvement. Shewhart [231] introduced a circular model that consists of three steps (Specification, Production, Inspection) and constitutes a dynamic scientific process of acquiring knowledge. This model forms the basis for several improvement models such as the Deming-Cycle (plan–do–check–act) [49] or the improvement guide introduced by Langley et al. [153].

The combination of agile software development and software product lines is probably better addressed by this improvement approaches instead of the selected assessment model. One reason for the selection of an assessment model is the fact that assessments are a standardized and accepted way to change organizational processes [64] in the automotive domain. According to the recommendation given by Schmid and John [222], the development of the ASPLA Model was based on an existing state of the art process assessment approach that is valid for the automotive domain.

The ASPLA Model is based on ASPICE [260] and can be used to assess all processes addressed with an ASPICE assessment. The fact that the ASPLA Model is based on the structure of ASPICE limits its applicability to the automotive domain. It extends ASPICE by focusing on the developed product, agile aspects and software product lines.

Furthermore, the origin of the ASPLA Model is based on challenges and recommendations identified in practice. The results of the interview study were compared and extended with findings from the literature. The conclusions drawn from these studies were systematically derived and directly related to the identified challenges. A case study (cf. Section 6.4) showed that the ASPLA Model supports the hypotheses. In the case study, four experts assessed the development processes and the results were compared to the results of the ASPLA Model assessments conducted by two skilled developers. The assessed process contained a globally distributed software product line and aims at introducing agile software development practices into the development. Hence, it cannot be ensured that the ASPLA Model identifies the most suitable recommendations for a highly agile development without any software reuse strategy. Although this case was considered during the development of the ASPLA Model, further empirical studies are needed to validate whether problems in the combination of agile software development and software product lines can be identified correctly in practice.

It cannot be generalized from the case study results that the ASPLA Model will provide similar recommendations to other contexts. The assessment and improvement model described in this thesis may be applicable to similar domains other than automotive software engineering. However, this is not its intended purpose. Other domains generally have different peculiarities, so the model might not be applicable or must be tailored to the context specific characteristics.

Furthermore, the assessment user needs experience in the assessed development process. With limited knowledge of the development process, it cannot be ensured that the assessment result is correct and the ASPLA Model provides the correct recommendations. The given recommendations are a good starting point to reconsider the development processes and improve them accordingly. However, the ASPLA Model does not provide a transformation model on how to introduce or adapt the recommendations to a specific context. Upcoming trends and new legal restrictions are not addressed in the model because they were simply not known when developing it. Therefore, it cannot be ensured that the model identifies the correct tasks for upcoming challenges such as safety and security. To address this flaw, Honeycomb 5 offers the possibility to learn from best practices and evolve the ASPLA Model. Further feedback on the model and recommendations can be introduced every four weeks in the learning cycles (cf. Section 6.3) in order to further develop the model.

A last remark concerns the acceptance of the ASPLA Model. As recognized in the feedback on the model and identified in literature [85, 70], agile enthusiasts do not like the idea of introducing agility by means of an assessment model. However, the ASPLA Model received positive feedback from the industry and is also accepted by the agile community. For example, it is registered in the list of "Tools and Checklists for agile self-assessments [1]". Agile coaches recognize the benefits of assessment models, as they can give assistance for the introduction of agile practices. Introducing agile practices by the book are often doomed to fail due to the previously mentioned peculiarities of software development in the automotive domain.

---

[1] https://www.benlinders.com/tools/agile-self-assessments/

9.2 Adherence to Design-Science Research Guidelines

Hevner et al. [100] regard design-science in information systems research as a problem solving process. According to them, the fundamental principle of Design-Science Research is to find a solution for a relevant business problem [100]. The process to find a solution, the so-called artifact, to an identified problem is based on knowledge and continuous learning [100]. Hevner et al. [100] propose to follow the seven guidelines for conducting Design-Science Research. If these guidelines are fulfilled, the research process can be called Design-Science Research. This section introduces the guidelines, as proposed by Hevner et al. [100]. Each guideline is addresses individually.

Guideline 1: Design as an Artifact. "Design-science research must produce a viable artifact in the form of a construct, a model, a method, or an instantiation" [100, p. 83]. The viable artifact described in this thesis is the so-called ASPLA Model. The ASPLA Model is an assessment model to foster the adoption of agile software product lines in the automotive domain.

Guideline 2: Problem Relevance. "The objective of Design-Science Research is to develop technology-based solutions to important and relevant business problems" [100, p. 83]. The interview study (cf. Section 3.2) and the literature reviews (cf. Chapter 4) identify relevant challenges with regard to the combination of agile software development and software product lines in the automotive domain. The findings revealed that there exists a relevant problem which could be addressed by a tailored assessment model that deals with the current status of agile software product lines in the automotive domain. This need was further confirmed by the feedback collection process in the iterative learning cycles (cf. Section 6.3).

Guideline 3: Design Evaluation. "The utility, quality, and efficacy of a design artifact must be rigorously demonstrated via well-executed evaluation methods" [100, p. 83]. The utility and efficacy of the ASPLA Model is evaluated in the case study presented in Section 6.4. The results indicate that the presented hypotheses (cf. Section 6.1) are supported by the ASPLA Model. The quality of the model every four weeks is ensured by the continuous learning cycles and the possibility to update the model according to the received feedback.

Guideline 4: Research Contributions. "Effective Design-Science Research must provide clear and verifiable contributions in the areas of the design artifact, design foundations, and/or design methodologies" [100, p. 83]. Hevner et al. [100] point out that "design-science research holds the potential for three types of research contributions based on the novelty, generality, and significance of the designed artifact" [100, p. 87]. They point out that at least one of these contributions must be part of Design-Science Research. The novelty is based on the fact that the ASPLA Model and the associated publications about the model are closing an important gap in the literature (cf. Section 4). The applicability is limited to the automotive domain. The ASPLA Model is based on

ASPICE [261] and bundles agile aspects and software product line approaches into the assessment in an innovative way. It further identifies potential improvement areas and gives recommendations on how to introduce agile software product lines in the assessed context. The significance of the research is evidenced by the number of published contributions to the knowledge base (cf. Appendix G) and the interest and feedback of the research community.

Guideline 5: Research Rigor. "Design-science research relies upon the application of rigorous methods in both the construction and evaluation of the design artifact" [100, p. 83]. The research relies on the results obtained through the interview study (cf. Section 3.2), two literature reviews (cf. Section 4.1 and Section 4.2) and five workshops (cf. Appendix B). The data collection followed rigorous methods and is described in the corresponding sections. For setting up the ASPLA Model, the qualitative analysis was based on the coding methods described by Saldaña [218] (cf. Figure 5.3). Furthermore, an observational case structure was conducted, to evaluate the ASPLA Model. The selection of the evaluation method was based on the classification by Hevner et al. [100]. They recommend to study the artifact in depth in one business environment. A complete description of the case study and the research process can be found in Section 6.4.

Guideline 6: Design as a Search Process. "The search for an effective artifact requires utilizing available means to reach desired ends while satisfying laws in the problem environment" [100, p. 83]. Hevner et al. [100] point out that the search for the best suitable solution for an identified problem is often inherently iterative. They recommend two ways to search for the optimal solution. First, it is common in Design-Science Research to simplify a problem by decomposing into smaller problems and only consider these small parts. These smaller parts can be addressed separately in order to verify that the solution is suitable to address the problem [100].

The decomposition as part of the search process has been applied to the ASPLA Model. The ASPLA Model and partial solutions were continuously presented to the academic community and practitioners from industry (cf. Appendix G). The feedback obtained supported the verification that the solution is suitable to address the identified problem to combine agile software development and software product lines in the automotive domain. The verification strategy with iterative learning cycles also helped to verify that the solution still fits to the customers' demands and within close proximity of an optimal solution [100].

The second way to search for the optimal solution is to compare the solution "with those constructed by expert human designer[s] for the same problem situation" [100, p. 90]. This was addressed by the case study presented in Section 6.4. The case study compared the results from the ASPLA Model with the assessment results of experts.

Guideline 7: Communication of Research. "Design-science research must be presented effectively both to technology-oriented as well as management-oriented audiences" [100, p. 83]. This guideline is addressed by the publications and presentations at international conferences (cf. Appendix G) and the workshops conducted with participants in the industry (cf. Appendix B). In summary, the presented research process to set up the ASPLA Model fulfills the guidelines proposed by Hevner et al. [100]. Therefore, the ASPLA Model is a viable artifact that addresses the identified gap in research and the demand in industry.

9.3 Fulfillment of Assessment Criteria

Maier et al. [169] present guidelines for developing maturity grids that are categorized by the four phases (1) planning, (2) development, (3) evaluation, and (4) maintenance. The ASPLA Model is compared to these four phases by Maier et al. [169].

9.3.1 Phase 1: Planning

The planning phase specifies the intended audience, "the purpose of the assessment, the scope, and success criteria" [169, p. 149].

Specify Audience. Maier et al. [169] recommend to specify the expected users before the development of a new assessment model starts. They further recommend to differentiate between different audiences [169]. The development of the ASPLA Model faces real-life challenges from the developers' point of view. Furthermore, it contains best practices that are identified in the literature. Therefore, the primary intention for the ASPLA Model is to provide self-assessments within the development team. The audience, as defined by Maier et al. [169], are developers that conduct self-assessments in order to identify improvement potential in the development process.

However, the iterative learning cycles (cf. Section 6.3) and the case study (cf. Section 6.4) lead to the awareness that the ASPLA Model can guide assessors through the assessment. Therefore, the audience of the ASPLA Model is extended to guide assessors in an assessment that fosters the adoption of agile software product lines in the automotive domain. Furthermore, Maier et al. [169] define another user group, the so-called *improvement entity*. This user group will work with the recommendations, based on the assessment results, to improve the process.

Define Aim. The definition of the aim categorizes the improvement approach either into an analytical or a benchmarking improvement initiative [169]. According to Maier et al. [169], benchmarking initiatives identify best practices that have proved to add value in a particular context [169]. Maier et al. [169] take CMMI [243] as an example for a benchmarking approach. Due to the fact that the ASPLA Model is based on the structure of ASPICE [260], the ASPLA Model can be categorized into the benchmarking improvement initiatives.

Clarify Scope. The research scope of this thesis which can be described along the three areas *Automotive Domain, Agile Software Development* and *Software Product Lines* (cf. Figure 1.1) limits the scope of ASPLA Model. Therefore the scope of the ASPLA Model is to assess software development processes in order to foster the adoption of agile software product lines in the automotive domain. The ASPLA Model may be applicable to domains other than automotive software engineering. However, this is not its intended purpose. Other domains generally have different peculiarities, so the assessment model might not be applicable or must be tailored to the context specific characteristics.

Define Success Criteria. Maier et al. [169] point out that it is challenging to determine the success of an assessments model. They recommend to define success criteria in the form of high-level requirements, such as usability and usefulness of the Model. For the ASPLA Model, hypotheses have been defined as success criteria (cf. Section 1.6).

9.3.2   Phase 2: Development

The second phase defines the assessment architecture. Furthermore, the rating scale and the process areas are selected [169].

Select Process Areas (Content). Meier et al. [169] recommend to define relevant process areas for an effective assessment. To make the ASPLA Model accessible to teams and departments who might fear significant overhead when assessing their agile development, the ASPLA Model is based on the ASPICE [260] framework. The selection of important process areas is adopted from ASPICE [260] and defined by the VDA-Scope (cf. Section 2.1.4). Rather than being another standard or process to adhere to, the ASPLA Model provides insights on how processes could be improved to align with agile principles and software product lines.

Select Maturity Levels (Rating Scale). In the presented guidelines by Meier et al. [169], the next step in the development of an assessment is the definition of the maturity levels. The rating scale in the ASPLA Model is based on the process capability levels and process attributes of ASPICE [260]. The capability levels are in accordance with the six capability levels taken from ISO/IEC 33020 [130] (cf. Section 2.1.3).

Formulate Cell Text (Intersection of Process Areas and Maturity Levels). This step identifies the characteristics for the process capability [169]. Therefore each level of maturity needs to be described. In the ASPLA Model, only the capability Level 1 from ISO/IEC 33020 [130] is addressed. This restriction is introduced by the structure of ASPICE [260] used for the ASPLA Model. Level 1 defines that the process Outcomes, the Base Practices and the Work Products are achieved [260]. For higher levels, generic practices from ISO/IEC 33020 [130] are applied. The ASPLA Model follows the structure as introduced by ASPICE [260].

Define Administration Mechanism. The administrative mechanism supports the infrastructure to conduct the assessment [169]. Meier et al. [169] identify that "approaches aiming at benchmarking seem to prefer electronic distribution systems for questionnaires to reach a wide variety and large number of participants" [169, p. 151]. Furthermore, they propose that the overall assessment assumes processes which are all of the same importance [169]. To make the ASPLA Model accessible for a large number of assessment users, it is developed within a Web Application (cf. Section 5.5.1). The calculation of the assessment result is based on the average calculation as proposed by Maier et al. [169].

9.3.3 Phase 3: Evaluation

Maier et al. [169] suggest to refine the assessment model in an iterative evaluation until the assessment reaches a saturation point which is being reached if no more significant changes are suggested by participants [169].

Validation. Maier et al. [169] propose to populate the assessment model and test its relevance. In the ASPLA Model, the iterative learning cycles validate the relevance of the assessment. For this purpose, the Web Application offers the possibility to submit feedback (cf. Section 6.3). Furthermore, pilot tests are conducted to check the relevance of the assessment and to determine if the recommendations given by the ASPLA Model could help the assessment user.

Verification. The verification is referring to the success criteria and requirements defined in Phase 1: *Define Success Criteria*. The high-level requirements defined in the first phase address the usability and the usefulness of the model [169]. The usability is verified by the implementation of the Web Application that guides the user through the ASPLA Model. Furthermore, the usability of the ASPLA Model benefits from the known structure of ASPICE [260]. The results of the case study (cf. Section 6.4) confirm the usefulness of the ASPLA Model. The recommendation list which is the key output from the assessment proposes an effective plan to improve the situation under assessment.

9.3.4 Phase 4: Maintenance

The maintenance phase is adjusting the assessment model continuously. This phase includes the storage of data in an accurate way and requires that the assessment tool is updated according to technical innovations [169]. Furthermore, maintenance comprises the documentation and communication of the assessment design process to the academic community [169]. In this thesis, the design process is published. Furthermore, the iterative learning cycle will keep the model up to date and offers the possibility that the model improves with new technical innovations in the automotive domain.

Chapter **10**

Conclusion and Future Work

10.1 Conclusion

This thesis presented the ASPLA Model, an assessment and improvement model to foster the adoption of agile software product lines in the automotive domain.

The research is focused on the complex and distributed software development in the automotive domain [267]. In order to manage the complexity in the software and keep the software development for vehicles cost efficient, the development is based on a software reuse strategy across different model series [86]. Nowadays, the development is heavily structured by standardized processes which are seen as too inflexible in order to keep pace with the fast changing market demands [23, 63]. Agile practices are promising approaches to improve software development, thereby reducing the time to market and increasing the speed of learning [109].

Based on the results of an interview study (cf. Section 3.2), benefits for combining agile software development with software product lines in the automotive domain were defined. The interview study revealed the *agile adoption forces model* which includes forces that either support or hinder an agile adoption within the automotive domain [107]. Furthermore, the interview study revealed that agile software product lines are currently not used in many organizational units in the automotive domain. A strategic software reuse strategy enriched with a high amount of agile methods is the desired way to develop software in the future. However, it is not yet clear how to combine agile software development and software product lines in the automotive domain.

The two literature reviews were conducted in a way to find a solution on how to combine agile software development and software product lines in the automotive domain. The first literature review (cf. Section 4.1) revealed that currently there exists no automotive specific combination approach. However, some related domains provide many insights on how a combination could look like in the automotive domain. These insights are the starting points to modify automotive software development processes in a way that they can benefit from both agility and systematic reuse through product lines. A second literature review revealed that there exists currently no assessment model to assess the current status of agile software product lines in the automotive domain. Presented assessment models do only cover some parts of the development cycle or just focus on specific agile methods.

Therefore, the ASPLA Model was developed as artifact within this thesis. The ASPLA Model is an assessment model to identify the current status of agile software product lines in the automotive domain. Furthermore, the model gives recommendations to foster the combination. The development is based on relevant challenges that were identified in real-life and in the literature. These challenges were categorized in four categories that need to be addressed. Recommendations to address the challenges were extracted from the results of the interview study (cf. Section 3.2), the literature reviews (cf. Chapter 4) and several workshops (cf. Appendix B). When coding these recommendations, six main areas (so-called Honeycombs) were identified that need to be addressed for combining agile software development and software product lines. In order to manage the recommendations effectively, they were integrated in a structured approach.

The Honeycombs comprise 52 Process Related Outcomes and 12 Product Related Outcomes. Each Process Related Outcome is addressed by a Base Practice and each Product Related Outcome by a Product Attribute. As recommended by Schmid and John [222], ASPLA is based on the structure of ASPICE [260]. Therefore, the ASPLA Model was compared to the standards ASPICE [260], ISO/IEC 265502 [128] and ISO 26262 [122]. Furthermore, ASPICE [260] Work Products were adjusted to support the combination of agile software development and software product lines. ASPLA Work Products, Base Practices and Product Attributes are summarized under the Honeycomb Attributes. For this assessment, 269 individual questions were defined. These specific questions were phrased by the author of this thesis to address the Honeycomb Attributes. The assessment can be conducted online in a Web Application. The Web Application calculates the assessment results based on the aggregation method described in ISO 33020 [130] and in the guidelines for ASPICE [76]. Depending on the results, a list of recommendations is created.

According to Hevner et al. [99], the ASPLA Model was integrated within the technical infrastructure of the business environment. This helped to assure that the ASPLA Model is relevant for the environment for which it is developed. In order to evaluate the ASPLA Model, the validation strategy was divided into two consecutive phases, an iterative learning phase and a case study. In the first validation phase, feedback was collected in the Web Application. In addition direct feedback was received by mail and telephone. The ASPLA Model was adjusted to the received feedback and released for the next learning cycle. The second validation phase conducted a study in a selected development process to evaluate the applicability of the ASPLA Model. For this purpose, data from four different experts was collected and compared with two assessments conducted by developers who used the ASPLA Model. The qualitative data analysis helps to build up a "weight of evidence" to support the hypothesis (cf. Section 6.1).

It became apparent that the results of the ASPLA Model are consistent with the assessment results of the experts. The recommendations received by the experts and the ASPLA Model support the hypotheses that the results from applying the assessment model are in line with the recommendations of experts. Furthermore, the results from applying the assessment model reveal that the ASPLA Model is not missing important recommendations given by experts and the time for conducting an assessment could be reduced by a factor of 2 when compared to the assessments conducted by the experts.

10.2 Future Work

As the ASPLA Model attract attention in the research community and the industry, further development and evaluation of the ASPLA Model will take place. Based on the feedback received in the learning cycles, the industry desires an easy to use assessment model that can be conducted by developers in a short time. With a suggestion schema that is based on the assessment results, the developers can learn how to introduce agile elements into their daily work and what they should address in their development processes.

Therefore, the ASPLA Model will develop further in the context of the four weeks learning cycles (cf. Section 6.3) in order to address the current demands of the assessment user as well as the markets' and the legal restrictions. In general, there is potential for future work in the following areas:

- The recommendations of anonymous users shall be displayed and evaluated in a discussion forum to determine their relevance. Therefore, the feedback form shall also ask for the type of software the user is implementing. With this, a distinction could be realized and the model could evolve into different types of software without getting too generic.

- The recommendation list shall be adjustable. Thereby, the user shall be able to reorganize the recommendation in the recommendation list. With this approach, it is possible to learn from best practices of the users and transfer this knowledge back into the ASPLA Model. Therefore, a value needs to be assigned to a recommendation to specify its relevance. This could also be specific for the type of software.

- Consider other peculiarities such as safety and security for the automotive domain and introduce them to the ASPLA Model in a more detailed way.

- Make the ASPLA Model freely accessible and collect further feedback comments.

Bibliography

[1] I. Aaen. Essence: Facilitating agile innovation. In P. Abrahamsson, R. Baskerville, K. Conboy, B. Fitzgerald, L. Morgan, and X. Wang, editors, *Agile Processes in Software Engineering and Extreme Programming*, volume 9 of *Lecture Notes in Business Information Processing*, pages 1–10. Springer, 2008.

[2] F. A. Z. Abidin, D. N. Jawawi, and I. Ghani. Agile transition model based on human factors. *International Journal of Innovative Computing*, (Vol. 7):23–32, 2017.

[3] P. Abrahamsson. *Agile software development methods: Review and analysis*, volume 478 of *VTT publications*. VTT, Espoo, 2002.

[4] C. O. Albuquerque, P. O. Antonino, and E. Y. Nakagawa. An investigation into agile methods in embedded systems development. In D. Hutchison, T. Kanade, J. Kittler, J. M. Kleinberg, F. Mattern, J. C. Mitchell, M. Naor, O. Nierstrasz, C. Pandu Rangan, B. Steffen, M. Sudan, D. Terzopoulos, D. Tygar, M. Y. Vardi, G. Weikum, B. Murgante, O. Gervasi, S. Misra, N. Nedjah, A. M. A. C. Rocha, D. Taniar, and B. O. Apduhan, editors, *Computational Science and Its Applications – ICCSA 2012*, volume 7335 of *Lecture Notes in Computer Science*, pages 576–591. Springer Berlin Heidelberg, 2012.

[5] V. Antinyan, M. Staron, W. Meding, P. Osterstrom, E. Wikstrom, J. Wranker, A. Henriksson, and J. Hansson. Identifying risky areas of software code in agile/lean software development: An industrial experience report. In S. Demeyer, editor, *Software Evolution Week - IEEE Conference on Software Maintenance, Reengineering and Reverse Engineering (CSMR-WCRE), 2014*, pages 154–163. IEEE, 2014.

[6] A. F. Arbain, I. Ghani, and S. R. Jeong. A systematic literature review on secure software development using feature driven development (fdd) agile model. *Journal of Korean Society for Internet Information*, 15(1):13–27, 2014.

[7] ASQ/ANSI/ISO 9000. Quality management systems - fundamentals and vocabulary, 2015.

[8] M. J. Atherton and S. T. Collins. 9.2.1 developing product lines in engine control systems: Systems engineering challenges. *INCOSE International Symposium*, 23(1):184–198, 2013.

[9] J. Auvinen, R. Back, J. Heidenberg, P. Hirkman, and L. Milovanov. Software process improvement with agile practices in a large telecom company. In J. Münch and M. Vierimaa, editors, *Product-focused software process improvement*, volume 4034 of *Lecture Notes in Computer Science*, pages 79–93. Springer, 2006.

[10] M. A. Babar, T. Ihme, and M. Pikkarainen. An industrial case of exploiting product line architecturesin agile software development. In Carnegie Mellon University, editor, *Proceedings of the 13th International Software Product Line Conference*, pages 171–179. 2009.

[11] M. Balbino, E. S. de Almeida, and Silvio Romero de Lemos Meira. An agile scoping process for software product lines & knowledge engineering. In SEKE 2011, editor, *Proceedings of the 23rd International Conference on Software Engineering & Knowledge Engineering*, pages 717–722. 2011.

[12] K. Beck. Extreme programming: A humanistic discipline of software development. In E. Astesiano, editor, *Fundamental Approaches to Software Engineering*, volume 1382 of *Lecture Notes in Computer Science*, pages 1–6. Springer, 1998.

[13] K. Beck. *Extreme programming explained: Embrace change*. Addison-Wesley, Reading Mass. u.a., 3. print edition, 2000.

[14] K. Beck. *Test driven development: By example*. The Addison-Wesley signature series. Addison-Wesley, Boston, Mass., 2003.

[15] K. Beck, M. Beedle, A. van Bennekum, A. Cockburn, W. Cunningham, M. Fowler, J. Grenning, J. Highsmith, A. Hunt, R. Jeffries, J. Kern, B. Marick, R. C. Martin, S. Mellor, K. Schwaber, J. Sutherland, and D. Thomas. Manifesto for agile software development http://agilemanifesto.org/iso/en/: (retrieved 15.10.2018), 2001.

[16] F. Besemer, T. Karasch, P. Metz, and J. Pfeffer. Clarifying myths with process maturity models vs. agile: White paper, 06.08.2014.

[17] S. Black, P. P. Boca, J. P. Bowen, J. Gorman, and M. Hinchey. Formal versus agile: Survival of the fittest. *Computer*, 42(9):37–45, 2009.

[18] B. Blau and T. Hildenbrand. Product line engineering in large-scale lean and agile software product development environments - towards a hybrid approach to decentral control and managed reuse. In *Sixth International Conference on Availability, Reliability and Security (ARES), 2011*, pages 404–408. IEEE, 2011.

[19] B. Boehm and R. Turner. Balancing agility and discipline: evaluating and integrating agile and plan-driven methods. In IEEE Computer Society Washington,

editor, *Proceedings of the 26th International Conference on Software Engineering*, pages 718–719. IEEE Computer Society, 2004.

[20] B. Boehm and R. Turner. Management challenges to implementing agile processes in traditional development organizations. *IEEE Software*, 22(5):30–39, 2005.

[21] B. W. Boehm. Managing software productivity and reuse. *IEEE Computer*, 32(9):111–113, 1999.

[22] G. Booch. *Object oriented design: With applications*. The Benjamin, Cummings series in Ada and software engineering. Benjamin/Cummings, Redwood City, Calif., [nachdr.] edition, 1993.

[23] J. Bosch and P. M. Bosch-Sijtsema. Introducing agile customer-centered development in a legacy software product line. *Software: Practice and Experience*, 41(8):871–882, 2011.

[24] J. Bosch, G. Florijn, D. Greefhorst, J. Kuusela, J. H. Obbink, and K. Pohl. Variability issues in software product lines. In F. Linden, editor, *Software Product-Family Engineering*, volume 2290 of *Lecture Notes in Computer Science*, pages 13–21. Springer-Verlag Berlin Heidelberg, 2002.

[25] M. Broy. Challenges in automotive software engineering. In *Proceedings of the 28th International Conference on Software Engineering*, ICSE '06, pages 33–42. ACM, 2006.

[26] M. Broy, I. H. Krüger, A. Pretschner, and C. Salzmann. Engineering automotive software. *Proceedings of the IEEE*, 95(2):356–373, 2007.

[27] Bruce Douglass. Chapter 21 - agile development for embedded systems. In Robert Oshana and Mark Kraeling, editors, *Software Engineering for Embedded Systems*, pages 731–766. Newnes, 2013.

[28] A. Bryman. *Social research methods*. Univ. Press, Oxford, 2. ed. edition, 2004.

[29] G. Buckle, P. C. Clements, J. D. McGregor, D. Muthig, and K. Schmid. Calculating roi for software product lines. *IEEE Software*, 21(3):23–31, 2004.

[30] J. N. Buxton and B. Randell. *Software engineering techniques: Report on a conference sponsored by the NATO Science Committee*. [NATO Science Committee and available from Scientific Affairs Division, NATO], [Brussels], 1970.

[31] A. S. Campanelli, D. Bassi, and F. S. Parreiras. Agile transformation success factors: A practitioner's survey. In E. Dubois and K. Pohl, editors, *Advanced Information Systems Engineering*, pages 364–379. Springer International Publishing, 2017.

[32] A. S. Campanelli, F. S. Neto, and F. S. Parreiras. Assessing agile transformation success factors. *CoRR*, abs/1711.04188, 2017.

[33] S. Chong, C.-B. Wong, H. Jia, H. Pan, P. Moore, R. Kalawsky, and J. O'Brien. Model driven system engineering for vehicle system utilizing model driven architecture approach and hardware-in-the-loop simulation. In *2011 IEEE International Conference on Mechatronics and Automation*, pages 1451–1456, 2011.

[34] M. B. Chrissis, M. Konrad, and S. Shrum. *CMMI for development: Guidelines for process integration and product improvement*. The SEI series in software engineering. Addison-Wesley, Upper Saddle River, NJ, 3rd ed. edition, 2011.

[35] F. Cilliers and H. Greyvenstein. The impact of silo mentality on team identity: An organisational case study. *SA Journal of Industrial Psychology*, 38(2), 2012.

[36] P. Coad, E. Lefebvre, and J. DeLuca. *Java modeling in color with UML®: Enterprise components and process*. Prentice Hall, Upper Saddle River NJ u.a., 1999.

[37] A. Cockburn. *Crystal clear: A human-powered methodology for small teams*. The agile software development series. Addison-Wesley, Boston Mass. u.a., 2005.

[38] K. Conboy and B. Fitzgerald. Toward a conceptual framework of agile methods. In N. Mehandjiev, P. Brereton, K. Bennett, D. Budgen, and P. Layzell, editors, *Proceedings of the 2004 ACM workshop on Interdisciplinary software engineering research - WISER '04*, page 37. ACM Press, 2004.

[39] M. Contag, G. Li, A. Pawlowski, F. Domke, K. Levchenko, T. Holz, and S. Savage. How they did it: An analysis of emission defeat devices in modern automobiles. In *2017 IEEE Symposium on Security and Privacy (SP)*, pages 231–250. IEEE, 2017.

[40] B. Cool, C. Knieke, A. Rausch, M. Schindler, A. Strasser, M. Vogel, O. Brox, and S. Jauns-Seyfried. From product architectures to a managed automotive software product line architecture. In S. Ossowski, editor, *Proceedings of the 31st Annual ACM Symposium on Applied Computing - SAC '16*, pages 1350–1353. ACM Press, 2016.

[41] M. Cope. Coding qualitative data. pages 223–233, 2010.

[42] J. Corbin and A. Strauss. Grounded theory research: procedures, canons and evaluative criteria, 1990.

[43] I. F. Da Silva. An agile approach for software product lines scoping. In Unknown, editor, *the 16th International Software Product Line Conference*, page 225, 2012.

[44] I. F. Da Silva, P. A. Da Mota Silveira Neto, P. O'Leary, E. S. de Almeida, and S. R. De Lemos Meira. Agile software product lines: A systematic mapping study. *Software: Practice and Experience*, 41(8):899–920, 2011.

[45] I. F. Da Silva, P. A. Da Mota Silveira Neto, P. O'Leary, E. S. De Almeida, and S. R. De Lemos Meira. Using a multi-method approach to understand agile software product lines. *Information and Software Technology*, 57(1):527–542, 2015.

[46] I. F. Da Silva, P. A. Da Mota Silveira Neto, P. O'Leary, E. S. De Almeida, and S. R. Meira. Software product line scoping and requirements engineering in a small and medium-sized enterprise: An industrial case study. *Journal of Systems and Software*, 88(1):189–206, 2014.

[47] C. de O. Melo, D. S. Cruzes, F. Kon, and R. Conradi. Interpretative case studies on agile team productivity and management. *Information and Software Technology*, 55(2):412–427, 2013.

[48] S. Deelstra, M. Sinnema, and J. Bosch. A product derivation framework for software product families. In F. van der Linden, editor, *Software product-family engineering*, volume 3014 of *Lecture Notes in Computer Science*, pages 473–484. Springer, 2004.

[49] W. E. Deming. *Out of the Crisis*. MIT Press Ser. MIT Press, Cambridge, 2000.

[50] J. Díaz, J. Pérez, P. P. Alarcón, and J. Garbajosa. Agile product line engineering- a systematic literature review. *Software: Practice and Experience*, 41(8):921–941, 2011.

[51] J. Díaz, J. Pérez, and J. Garbajosa. Agile product-line architecting in practice: A case study in smart grids. *Information and Software Technology*, 56(7):727–748, 2014.

[52] J. Diaz, J. Pérez, A. Yagüe, and J. Garbajosa. *Tailoring the Scrum Development Process to Address Agile Product Line Engineering*. E.U. de Informática (UPM), 2011.

[53] P. Diebold, T. Zehler, and D. Richter. How do agile practices support automotive spice compliance? In R. Bendraou, D. Raffo, H. LiGuo, and F. M. Maggi, editors, *Proceedings of the 2017 International Conference on Software and System Process - ICSSP 2017*, pages 80–84. ACM Press, 2017.

[54] T. Dingsøyr, S. Nerur, V. Balijepally, and N. B. Moe. A decade of agile methodologies: Towards explaining agile software development. *Journal of Systems and Software*, 85(6):1213–1221, 2012.

[55] A. Dresch, D. P. Lacerda, and J. A. V. Antunes Jr. *Design Science Research*. Springer International Publishing, Cham, 2015.

[56] B. S. Drummond and J. F. Unson. Yahoo! distributed agile: Notes from the world over. In G. Melnik, editor, *Conference Agile, 2008*, pages 315–321. IEEE Computer Soc, 2008.

[57] DSDM Consortium. What is dsdm? (retrieved 15.10.2018), 2017.

[58] S. Easterbrook, J. Singer, M.-A. Storey, and D. Damian. Selecting empirical methods for software engineering research. In F. Shull, J. Singer, and D. I. K. Sjøberg, editors, *Guide to Advanced Empirical Software Engineering*, pages 285–311. Springer-Verlag London Limited, 2008.

[59] U. Eklund and J. Bosch. Applying agile development in mass-produced embedded systems. In W. van der Aalst, J. Mylopoulos, M. Rosemann, M. J. Shaw, C. Szyperski, and C. Wohlin, editors, *Agile Processes in Software Engineering and Extreme Programming*, volume 111, pages 31–46. Springer Berlin Heidelberg, 2012.

[60] U. Eklund and H. Gustavsson. Architecting automotive product lines: Industrial practice. *Science of Computer Programming*, 78(12):2347–2359, 2013.

[61] U. Eklund, H. Holmström Olsson, and N. J. Strøm. Industrial challenges of scaling agile in mass-produced embedded systems. In T. Dingsøyr, N. B. Moe, R. Tonelli, S. Counsell, C. Gencel, and K. Petersen, editors, *Agile Methods. Large-Scale Development, Refactoring, Testing, and Estimation*, volume 199, pages 30–42. Springer International Publishing, 2014.

[62] U. Eliasson, R. Heldal, E. Knauss, and P. Pelliccione. The need of complementing plan-driven requirements engineering with emerging communication: Experiences from volvo car group. In D. Zowghi, editor, *2015 IEEE 23rd International Requirements Engineering Conference (RE)*, pages 372–381. IEEE, 2015.

[63] U. Eliasson, R. Heldal, J. Lantz, and C. Berger. Agile model-driven engineering in mechatronic systems - an industrial case study. In J. Dingel, W. Schulte, I. Ramos, S. Abrahão, and E. Insfran, editors, *Model-Driven Engineering Languages and Systems*, volume 8767 of *Lecture Notes in Computer Science*, pages 433–449. Springer International Publishing, 2014.

[64] K. E. Emam and D. R. Goldenson. An empirical review of software process assessments. In *Emphasizing Distributed Systems*, volume 53 of *Advances in Computers*, pages 319–423. Elsevier, 2000.

[65] F. Farahani and R. Ramsin. Methodologies for agile product line engineering: A survey and evaluation. In *Conference: The 13th International Conference on Intelligent Software Methodologies, Tools, and Techniques*, volume 2014.

[66] Federal Office for Administrative Affairs. Das v-modell ® xt, 2005.

[67] B. Fitzgerald, K.-J. Stol, R. O'Sullivan, and D. O'Brien. Scaling agile methods to regulated environments: An industry case study. In D. Notkin, editor, *35th International Conference on Software Engineering (ICSE), 2013*, pages 863–872. IEEE, 2013.

[68] M. Fletcher, W. Bereza, M. Karlesky, and G. Williams. Evolving into embedded develop. In J. Eckstein, editor, *Agile 2007*, pages 150–155. IEEE Computer Soc, 2007.

[69] R. M. Fontana, I. M. Fontana, P. A. da Rosa Garbuio, S. Reinehr, and A. Malucelli. Processes versus people: How should agile software development maturity be defined? *Journal of Systems and Software*, 97:140–155, 2014.

[70] R. M. Fontana, S. Reinehr, and A. Malucelli. Maturing in agile: What is it about? In G. Cantone and M. Marchesi, editors, *Agile Processes in Software Engineering and Extreme Programming*, pages 94–109. Springer International Publishing, 2014.

[71] M. Fowler. *Refactoring: Improving the design of existing code*. Addison-Wesley object technology series. Addison-Wesley, Reading Mass. u.a., 1999.

[72] Fred A. Cummins. Chapter 10 - the agile organization structure. In Fred A. Cummins, editor, *Building the Agile Enterprise (Second Edition)*, The MK/OMG Press, pages 301–332. Morgan Kaufmann, 2017.

[73] M. Galster and P. Avgeriou. Supporting variability through agility to achieve adaptable architectures. In *Agile Software Architecture*, pages 139–159. Elsevier, 2014.

[74] T. J. Gandomani, H. Zulzalil, A. A. Abd Ghani, and A. B. M. Sultan. *Towards comprehensive and disciplined change management strategy in agile transformation process*. Maxwell Science Publication, 2013.

[75] K. Gary, A. Enquobahrie, L. Ibanez, P. Cheng, Z. Yaniv, K. Cleary, S. Kokoori, B. Muffih, and J. Heidenreich. Agile methods for open source safety-critical software. *Software: practice & experience*, 41(9):945–962, 2011.

[76] German Association of the Automotive Industry. *Joint Quality Management in the Supply Chain Automotive SPICE® Guidelines: Process assessment using Automotive SPICE in the development of software-based systems*. Verband der Automobilindustrie e. V. (VDA), Qualitätsmanagement-Center (QMC), Berlin, 1st. edition edition, September 2017.

[77] Y. Ghanam, D. Andreychuk, and F. Maurer. Reactive variability management in agile software development. In *2010 AGILE Conference*, pages 27–34.

[78] Y. Ghanam and F. Maurer. An iterative model for agile product line engineering. In B. Geppert, editor, *12th International Software Product Line Conference, 2008*. IEEE, 2008.

[79] Y. Ghanam and F. Maurer. Extreme product line engineering – refactoring for variability: A test-driven approach. In W. van der Aalst, J. Mylopoulos, N. M. Sadeh, M. J. Shaw, C. Szyperski, A. Sillitti, A. Martin, X. Wang, and E. Whitworth, editors, *Agile Processes in Software Engineering and Extreme Programming*, volume 48 of *Lecture Notes in Business Information Processing*, pages 43–57. Springer Berlin Heidelberg, 2010.

[80] Y. Ghanam, F. Maurer, P. Abrahamsson, and K. Cooper. A report on the xp workshop on agile product line engineering. *ACM SIGSOFT Software Engineering Notes*, 34(5):25, 2009.

[81] Y. Ghanam, S. Park, and F. Maurer. A test-driven approach to establishing & managing agile product lines limerick, ireland, september 8-12, 2008, proceedings. second volume (workshops). In S. Thiel and K. Pohl, editors, *Software Product Lines, 12th International Conference, SPLC 2008, Limerick, Ireland, September 8-12, 2008, Proceedings. Second Volume (Workshops)*, pages 151–156. Lero Int. Science Centre, University of Limerick, Ireland, 2008.

[82] B. Gottschalk and R. Kalmbach. *Mastering Automotive Challenges*. Kogan Page Series. Kogan Page, 2007.

[83] S. P. Gregg, R. Scharadin, E. LeGore, and P. C. Clements. Lessons from aegis. In S. Gnesi and A. Fantechi, editors, *Proceedings of the 18th International Software Product Line Conference on - SPLC '14*, pages 264–273. ACM Press, 2014.

[84] L. Gren, R. Torkar, and R. Feldt. Work motivational challenges regarding the interface between agile teams and a non-agile surrounding organization: A case study. In *26th Euromicro Conference on Real-Time Systems (ECRTS), 2014*, pages 11–15. IEEE, 2014.

[85] L. Gren, R. Torkar, and R. Feldt. The prospects of a quantitative measurement of agility: A validation study on an agile maturity model. *Journal of Systems and Software*, 107:38–49, 2015.

[86] A. Grewe, C. Knieke, M. Körner, A. Rausch, M. Schindler, A. Strasser, and M. Vogel. Automotive software product line architecture evolution: Extracting, designing and managing architectural concepts. *International Journal on Advances in Intelligent Systems*, (vol 10 no 3 & 4):203–222, 2017.

[87] I. Habli, T. Kelly, and I. Hopkins. Challenges of establishing a software product line for an aerospace engine monitoring system. In *11th International Software Product Line Conference, 2007*, pages 193–202. IEEE Computer Society, 2007.

[88] A. Haghighatkhah, A. Banijamali, O.-P. Pakanen, M. Oivo, and P. Kuvaja. Automotive software engineering: A systematic mapping study. *Journal of Systems and Software*, 128:25–55, 2017.

[89] G. K. Hanssen. *From agile software product line engineering towards software ecosystems: Avhandling (ph.d.) - Norges teknisk-naturvitenskapelige universitet, Trondheim, 2010*, volume 2010:219 of *Doctoral theses at NTNU*. Norwegian University of Science and Technology Faculty of Information Technology Mathematics and Electrical Engineering Department of Computer and Information Science, Trondheim, 2010.

[90] G. K. Hanssen. Agile software product line engineering: Enabling factors. *Software: Practice and Experience*, 41(8):883–897, 2011.

[91] G. K. Hanssen and T. E. Fægri. Process fusion: An industrial case study on agile software product line engineering. *Journal of Systems and Software*, 81(6):843–854, 2008.

[92] D. Hantke. An approach for combining spice and scrum in software development projects. In T. Rout, R. V. O'Connor, and A. Dorling, editors, *Software Process Improvement and Capability Determination*, volume 526 of *Communications in Computer and Information Science*, pages 233–238. Springer International Publishing, 2015.

[93] K. Hayashi, M. Aoyama, and K. Kobata. A concurrent feedback development method and its application to automotive software development. In *2015 Asia-Pacific Software Engineering Conference (APSEC)*, pages 362–369.

[94] K. Hayashi, M. Aoyama, and K. Kobata. Agile tames product line variability. In M. Cohen, A. Ruiz-Cortés, D. Benavides, M. Acher, L. Fuentes, D. Schall, J. Bosch, R. Capilla, E. Bagheri, Y. Xiong, and J. Troya, editors, *Proceedings of the 21st International Systems and Software Product Line Conference - Volume A on - SPLC '17*, pages 180–189. ACM Press, 2017.

[95] L. T. Heeager and P. A. Nielsen. A conceptual model of agile software development in a safety-critical context: A systematic literature review. *Information and Software Technology*, 2018.

[96] J. Heidenberg, M. Matinlassi, M. Pikkarainen, P. Hirkman, and J. Partanen. Systematic piloting of agile methods in the large: Two cases in embedded systems development. In M. Ali Babar, M. Vierimaa, and M. Oivo, editors, *Product-Focused Software Process Improvement*, pages 47–61. Springer Berlin Heidelberg, 2010.

[97] W. Heider, M. Vierhauser, D. Lettner, and P. Grunbacher. A case study on the evolution of a component-based product line. In *2012 Joint Working IEEE/IFIP Conference on Software Architecture (WICSA) & European Conference on Software Architecture (ECSA)*, pages 1–10.

[98] R. Heimgärtner, A. Solanki, and H. Windl. Cultural user experience in the car—toward a standardized systematic intercultural agile automotive ui/ux design process. In G. Meixner and C. Müller, editors, *Automotive User Interfaces: Creating Interactive Experiences in the Car*, pages 143–184. Springer International Publishing, 2017.

[99] A. Hevner and S. Chatterjee. Design science research frameworks. In A. Hevner and S. Chatterjee, editors, *Design Research in Information Systems*, volume 22, pages 23–31. Springer US, 2010.

[100] A. R. Hevner, S. T. March, J. Park, and S. Ram. Design science in information systems research. *MIS Q*, 28(1):75–105, 2004.

[101] J. A. Highsmith. *Adaptive software development: A collaborative approach to managing complex systems*. Dorset House, New York NY, 2000.

[102] J. A. Highsmith. *Agile software development ecosystems*. The agile software development series. Addison-Wesley, Boston Mass. u.a., 1. print edition, 2002.

[103] P. Hohl. Agile software development and structured software reuse: Daimler confidential data, 2016.

[104] P. Hohl, J. Ghofrani, J. Münch, M. Stupperich, and K. Schneider. Searching for common ground: Existing literature on automotive agile software product lines. In R. Bendraou, D. Raffo, H. LiGuo, and F. M. Maggi, editors, *Proceedings of the 2017 International Conference on Software and System Process - ICSSP 2017*, pages 70–79. ACM Press, 2017.

[105] P. Hohl, J. Ghofrani, J. Münch, M. Stupperich, and K. Schneider. Searching for common ground: Existing literature on automotive agile software product lines. In M. Tichy, editor, *GI Edition Proceedings Band 279 Software Engineering und Software Management 2018*, pages 55–57. Köllen, 2018.

[106] P. Hohl, J. Klünder, A. van Bennekum, R. Lockard, J. Gifford, J. Münch, M. Stupperich, and K. Schneider. Back to the future: Origins and directions of the "agile manifesto": - views of the originators -. *Journal of Software Engineering Research and Development*, accepted, to be published in 2019.

[107] P. Hohl, J. Münch, K. Schneider, and M. Stupperich. Forces that prevent agile adoption in the automotive domain. In P. Abrahamsson, A. Jedlitschka, A. Nguyen Duc, M. Felderer, S. Amasaki, and T. Mikkonen, editors, *Product-Focused Software Process Improvement: 17th International Conference, PROFES 2016, Trondheim, Norway, November 22-24, 2016, Proceedings*, volume 10027, pages 468–476. Springer International Publishing, 2016.

[108] P. Hohl, J. Münch, K. Schneider, and M. Stupperich. Real-life challenges on agile software product lines in automotive. In M. Felderer, D. Méndez Fernández, B. Turhan, M. Kalinowski, F. Sarro, and D. Winkler, editors, *Product-Focused Software Process Improvement: 18th International Conference, PROFES 2017, Innsbruck, Austria, November 29–December 1, 2017, Proceedings*, pages 28–36. Springer International Publishing, 2017.

[109] P. Hohl, J. Münch, and M. Stupperich. Forces that support agile adoption in the automotive domain. In *Software Engineering*, 2017.

[110] P. Hohl, M. Stupperich, J. Münch, and K. Schneider. Die variantenvielfalt agil managen: Agile software-produktlinien im automobilsegment. In *Tagungsband -*

Embedded Software Engineering Kongress 2016 : 28. November bis 2. Dezember 2016, Sindelfingen, pages 427–433, 2016.

[111] P. Hohl, M. Stupperich, J. Munch, and K. Schneider. An assessment model to foster the adoption of agile software product lines in the automotive domain. In G. Baltes and M. König, editors, *IEEE International Conference on Engineering, Technology and Innovation (ICE/ITMC)*, pages 1–9. IEEE, 2018.

[112] P. Hohl, M. Stupperich, J. Munch, and K. Schneider. Combining agile development and software product lines in automotive: Challenges and recommendations. In G. Baltes and M. König, editors, *IEEE International Conference on Engineering, Technology and Innovation (ICE/ITMC)*, pages 1–10. IEEE, 2018.

[113] P. Hohl, S. Theobald, M. Becker, M. Stupperich, and J. Münch. Mapping agility to automotive software product line concerns. In *Proc. of PROFES'18*. 2018.

[114] H. Holdschick. Challenges in the evolution of model-based software product lines in the automotive domain. In I. Schaefer and T. Thüm, editors, *the 4th International Workshop*, pages 70–73, 2012.

[115] H. Holmström Olsson, J. Bosch, and H. Alahyari. Customer-specific teams for agile evolution of large-scale embedded systems. In *2013 39th EUROMICRO Conference on Software Engineering and Advanced Applications (SEAA)*, pages 82–89.

[116] H. Holmström Olsson, J. Bosch, and H. Alahyari. Towards r&d as innovation experiment systems: A framework for moving beyond agile software development. In E. P. Klement, editor, *Proceedings of the IASTED multiconferences*. Acta Press, 2013.

[117] J. Holton. The coding process and its challenges. 9:21–40, 2010.

[118] O. Hummel and C. Atkinson. Supporting agile reuse through extreme harvesting. In G. Concas, editor, *Agile processes in software engineering and extreme programming*, volume 4536 of *Lecture Notes in Computer Science*, pages 28–37. Springer, 2007.

[119] A. Hunt and D. Thomas. *The pragmatic programmer: From journeyman to master*. Addison-Wesley, Boston Mass u.a., 2000.

[120] D. Hutchison, T. Kanade, J. Kittler, J. M. Kleinberg, F. Mattern, J. C. Mitchell, M. Naor, O. Nierstrasz, C. Pandu Rangan, B. Steffen, M. Sudan, D. Terzopoulos, D. Tygar, M. Y. Vardi, G. Weikum, J. Heidrich, M. Oivo, A. Jedlitschka, and M. T. Baldassarre, editors. *Product-Focused Software Process Improvement*, volume 7983. Springer Berlin Heidelberg, Berlin, Heidelberg, 2013.

[121] ISO 26262-4:2011. *Road vehicles — Functional safety — Part 4: Product development at the system level*. International Organization for Standardization, 1 edition, 2011.

[122] ISO 26262-6:2011. *Road vehicles — Functional safety — Part 6: Product development at the software level.* International Organization for Standardization, 1st edition.

[123] ISO 26262-8:2011. *Road vehicles — Functional safety — Part 8: Supporting processes.* International Organization for Standardization, 1st edition.

[124] ISO 26262-9:2011. *Road vehicles – Functional safety – Part 9: Automotive Safety Integrity Level (ASIL)-oriented and safety-oriented analyses,* volume 43.040.10 Electrical and electronic equipment. International Organization for Standardization, 1 edition, 2011.

[125] ISO/IEC 12207:2008. *Systems and software engineering – Software life cycle processes,* volume 35.080 Software. International Organization for Standardization, 2 edition, 2008.

[126] ISO/IEC 15504-5:2006. *Information technology – Process Assessment – Part 5: An exemplar Process Assessment Model,* volume 35.080. International Organization for Standardization, 1 edition, 2006.

[127] ISO/IEC 15504-5:2012. *Information technology – Process assessment – Part 5: An exemplar software life cycle process assessment model,* volume 35.080. International Organization for Standardization, 2 edition, 2012.

[128] ISO/IEC 26550:2015. *Software and systems engineering — Reference model for product line engineering and management.* International Organization for Standardization, 2 edition, 2015.

[129] ISO/IEC 33004:2015. *Information technology – Process assessment – Requirements for process reference, process assessment and maturity models,* volume 35.080 Software. International Organization for Standardization, 1 edition, 2015.

[130] ISO/IEC 33020:2015. *Information technology – Process assessment – Process measurement framework for assessment of process capability,* volume 35.080 Software. International Organization for Standardization, 1 edition.

[131] ISO/IEC/IEEE 12207:2017. *Systems and software engineering – Software life cycle processes,* volume 35.080 Software. International Organization for Standardization, 1 edition, 2017.

[132] ISO/IEC/IEEE 15288:2015. *Systems and software engineering – System life cycle processes,* volume 35.080 Software. International Organization for Standardization, 1 edition, 2015.

[133] C. R. Jakobsen and K. A. Johnson. Mature agile with a twist of cmmi. In G. Melnik, editor, *Conference Agile, 2008,* pages 212–217. IEEE Computer Soc, 2008.

[134] K. S. Jasmine and R. Vasantha. A new capability maturity model for reuse based software development process. *International Journal of Engineering and Technology*, 2(1):112, 2010.

[135] T. Javdani Gandomani and M. Ziaei Nafchi. An empirically-developed framework for agile transition and adoption: A grounded theory approach. *Journal of Systems and Software*, 107:204–219, 2015.

[136] H. Jonsson, S. Larsson, and S. Punnekkat. Agile practices in regulated railway software development. In *2012 IEEE International Symposium on Software Reliability Engineering Workshops (ISSREW)*, pages 355–360.

[137] M. Kaisti, V. Rantala, T. Mujunen, S. Hyrynsalmi, K. Könnölä, T. Mäkilä, and T. Lehtonen. Agile methods for embedded systems development - a literature review and a mapping study. *EURASIP Journal on Embedded Systems*, 2013(1):15, 2013.

[138] T. Kakola. Standards initiatives for software product line engineering and management within the international organization for standardization. In *2010 43rd Hawaii International Conference on System Sciences*, pages 1–10. IEEE, 2010.

[139] A. Kasoju, K. Petersen, and M. V. Mäntylä. Analyzing an automotive testing process with evidence-based software engineering. *Information and Software Technology*, 55(7):1237–1259, 2013.

[140] B. Katumba and E. Knauss. Agile development in automotive software development: Challenges and opportunities. In A. Jedlitschka, P. Kuvaja, M. Kuhrmann, T. Männistö, J. Münch, and M. Raatikainen, editors, *Product-Focused Software Process Improvement*, volume 8892, pages 33–47. Springer International Publishing, 2014.

[141] Y. Khramov. The cost of code quality. In J. Chao, editor, *Agile Conference, 2006*, pages 119–125. IEEE Computer Society, 2006.

[142] M. Kircher and P. Hofman. Combining systematic reuse with agile development. In E. Santana de Almeida, editor, *Proceedings of the 16th International Software Product Line Conference - Volume 1*, page 215. ACM, 2012.

[143] B. Kitchenham. Guidelines for performing systematic literature reviews in software engineering, 9 July, 2007.

[144] J. Klünder, P. Hohl, M. Fazal-Baqaie, S. Krusche, S. Küpper, O. Linssen, and C. R. Prause. Helena study: Reasons for combining agile and traditional software development approaches in german companies. In M. Felderer, D. Méndez Fernández, B. Turhan, M. Kalinowski, F. Sarro, and D. Winkler, editors, *Product-Focused Software Process Improvement*, pages 428–434. Springer International Publishing, 2017.

[145] J. Klünder, P. Hohl, S. Krusche, P. Lous, M. Fazal-Baqaie, S. Küpper, and C. R. Prause. Towards a better understanding of the motivation of german organizations to apply certain development methods. In *Proceedings of 3rd HELENA Workshop*, 2018.

[146] J. Klünder, P. Hohl, and K. Schneider. Becoming agile while preserving software product lines: An agile transformation model for large companies. In M. Kuhrmann, R. V. O'Connor, and D. Houston, editors, *Proceedings of the 2018 International Conference on Software and System Process - ICSSP '18*, pages 1–10. ACM Press, 2018.

[147] J. Klünder, A. Schmitt, P. Hohl, and K. Schneider. Fake news: Simply agile. In *Gesellschaft für Informatik, Projektmanagement und Vorgehensmodelle, Darmstadt*, 2017.

[148] E. Knauss, M. Staron, W. Meding, O. Soder, A. Nilsson, and M. Castell. Supporting continuous integration by code-churn based test selection. In *2015 IEEE/ACM 4th SEMAT Workshop on a General Theory of Software Engineering (GTSE)*, pages 19–25. IEEE, 2015.

[149] J. P. Kotter and L. A. Schlesinger. Choosing strategies for change. In D. Asch and C. Bowman, editors, *Readings in Strategic Management*, pages 294–306. Macmillan Education UK, 1989.

[150] KUGLER MAAG CIE GmbH. Agile in automotive – state of practice 2015, April 2015.

[151] R. Kurmann. Agile spl–scm agile software product line configuration and release management.

[152] P. Kuvaja. Bootstrap 3.0—a spice1 conformant software process assessment methodology. *Software Quality Journal*, 8(1):7–19, 1999.

[153] G. J. Langley, R. D. Moen, K. M. Nolan, T. W. Nolan, and C. L. Norman. *The improvement guide: A practical approach to enhancing organizational performance*. Jossey-Bass, San Francisco, Calif., 2. ed. edition, 2009.

[154] Lee Copeland. Extreme programming: How-to, 2001.

[155] D. Leffingwell, R. Knaster, I. Oren, and D. Jemilo. *SAFe reference guide: Scaled Agile Framework for lean enterprises*. Pearson, [United States], 2018.

[156] A. Leitner and C. Kreiner. Software product lines – an agile success factor? In R. V. O'Connor, J. Pries-Heje, and R. Messnarz, editors, *Systems, Software and Service Process Improvement*, volume 172 of *Communications in Computer and Information Science*, pages 203–214. Springer-Verlag GmbH Berlin Heidelberg, 2011.

[157] A. Leitner, R. Mader, C. Kreiner, C. Steger, and R. Weiß. A development methodology for variant-rich automotive software architectures. *e & i Elektrotechnik und Informationstechnik*, 128(6):222–227, 2011.

[158] F. Linden. Family evaluation framework overview & introduction, 29 August, 2005.

[159] B. Linders. *Agile Self-assessment Game: The Map for your Agile Journey.* 2018.

[160] M. Lindvall, D. Muthig, A. Dagnino, C. Wallin, M. Stupperich, D. Kiefer, J. May, and T. Kahkonen. Agile software development in large organizations. *Computer*, 37(12):26–34, 2004.

[161] R. Lockard. *Agile Uprising - Agile Manifesto Review: Alistair Cockburn.* http://agileuprising.libsyn.com/manifesto-co-author-interview-alistair-cockburn (Retrieved 31.01.2017), 2016.

[162] R. Lockard and J. Gifford. *Agile Uprising - Agile Manifesto Review: Mike Beedle.* http://agileuprising.libsyn.com/manifesto-co-author-interview-mike-beedle, (Retrieved 31.01.2017), 2016.

[163] R. Lockard and J. Gifford. *Agile Uprising - Agile Manifesto Review: Robert C. Martin.* http://agileuprising.libsyn.com/manifesto-co-author-interview-bob-martin, (Retrieved 31.01.2017), 2016.

[164] R. Lockard and J. Gifford. *Agile Uprising Agile Manifesto Review: Andy Hunt,.* http://agileuprising.libsyn.com/podcast/manifesto-co-author-interview-andy-hunt (Retrieved 31.01.2017), 2016.

[165] R. Lockard and J. Gifford. *Agile Uprising Agile Manifesto Review: Brian Marick.* http://agileuprising.libsyn.com/podcast/manifesto-co-author-interview-brian-marick, (Received 26.01.2017), 2016.

[166] R. Lockard and J. Gifford. *Agile Uprising - Agile Manifesto Review: James Grenning.* https://coalition.agileuprising.com/t/podcast-released-interview-with-james-grenning/613?u=ryan, (Retrieved 26.01.2017), 2017.

[167] R. Lockard and J. Gifford. *Agile Uprising Agile Manifesto Review: JimHighsmith.* http://agileuprising.libsyn.com/manifesto-co-author-interview-jim-highsmith, (Retrieved 02.02.2017), 2017.

[168] R. Lockard and J. Gifford. *Agile Uprising Agile Manifesto Review: Stephen Mellor.* http://podcast.agileuprising.com/manifesto-co-author-interview-stephen-mellor/, (Retrieved 26.10.2017), 2017.

[169] A. M. Maier, J. Moultrie, and P. J. Clarkson. Assessing organizational capabilities: Reviewing and guiding the development of maturity grids. *IEEE Transactions on Engineering Management*, 59(1):138–159, 2012.

[170] P. Manhart and K. Schneider. Breaking the ice for agile development of embedded software: an industry experience report. In *Proceedings. 26th International Conference on Software Engineering*, pages 378–386, 23-28 May 2004.

[171] J. Martinez, J. Diaz, J. Pérez, and J. Garbajosa. Software product line engineering approach for enhancing agile methodologies. In W. van der Aalst, J. Mylopoulos, N. M. Sadeh, M. J. Shaw, C. Szyperski, P. Abrahamsson, M. Marchesi, and F. Maurer, editors, *Agile Processes in Software Engineering and Extreme Programming*, volume 31 of *Lecture Notes in Business Information Processing*, pages 247–248. Springer Berlin Heidelberg, 2009.

[172] A. Martini, L. Pareto, and J. Bosch. Enablers and inhibitors for speed with reuse. In E. Santana de Almeida, editor, *Proceedings of the 16th International Software Product Line Conference - Volume 1*, page 116. ACM, 2012.

[173] A. Martini, L. Pareto, and J. Bosch. Communication factors for speed and reuse in large-scale agile software development. In S. Jarzabek, editor, *Proceedings of the 17th International Software Product Line Conference*, page 42. ACM, NY : ACM, 2013.

[174] A. Mateen, S. Kausar, and A. R. Sattar. A software reuse approach and its effect on software quality, an empirical study for the software industry. *CoRR*, abs/1702.00125, 2017.

[175] A. Maurya. The science of how customers buy anything: The motivational forces that drive customers to buy.

[176] F. McCaffery, M. Pikkarainen, and I. Richardson. Ahaa –agile, hybrid assessment method for automotive, safety critical smes. In W. Schäfer, editor, *Companion of the 30th international conference on Software engineering*, page 551. ACM, 2008.

[177] J. D. McGregor. Agile software product lines - a working session. In *2008 12th International Software Product Line Conference (SPLC)*, page 364.

[178] J. D. McGregor. Mix and match. *The Journal of Object Technology*, 7(6):7, 2008.

[179] S. J. Mellor and M. J. Balcer. *Executable UML: A foundation for model-driven architecture*. Addison-Wesley, Boston and San Francisco and New York, 2002.

[180] A. Metzger and K. Pohl. Software product line engineering and variability management: achievements and challenges. In M. Dwyer and J. Herbsleb, editors, *Future of Software Engineering (FOSE 2014)*, pages 70–84. Association for Computing Machinery, Inc, 2014.

[181] K. Mohan, B. Ramesh, and V. Sugumaran. Integrating software product line engineering and agile development. *IEEE Software*, 27(3):48–55, 2010.

[182] M. Mueller-Eberstein. Agility // assessing your situation: Competing and winning in a tech-savvy marketplace. In M. Mueller-Eberstein, editor, *Agility: Competing and Winning in a Tech–Savvy Marketplace*, pages 147–170. John Wiley & Sons, Inc, 2012.

[183] J. Münch, O. Armbrust, M. Kowalczyk, and M. Soto. *Software Process Definition and Management*. Springer Berlin Heidelberg, Berlin, Heidelberg, 2012.

[184] J. Münch, K. Schmid, and H. D. Rombach. *Perspectives on the future of software engineering: Essays in honor of Dieter Rombach*. Springer, Heidelberg, 2013.

[185] K. Münzel, W. Boon, K. Frenken, and T. Vaskelainen. Carsharing business models in germany: Characteristics, success and future prospects. *Information Systems and e-Business Management*, 22:493, 2017.

[186] P. Naur and B. Randell, editors. *Software engineering: Report on a conference ... Garmisch, Germany, 7th to 11th October 1968*. NATO Scientific Affairs Div, Brussels, 1969.

[187] G. S. Neves and P. Vilain. Reactive variability realization with test driven development and refactoring engineering, hyatt regency, vancouver, bc, canada, july 1-3, 2013. In M. Reformat, editor, *The 26th International Conference on Software Engineering and Knowledge Engineering, Hyatt Regency, Vancouver, BC, Canada, July 1-3, 2013*, pages 100–105. Knowledge Systems Institute Graduate School, 2014.

[188] M. A. Noor, R. Rabiser, and P. Grünbacher. Agile product line planning: A collaborative approach and a case study. *Journal of Systems and Software*, 81(6):868–882, 2008.

[189] M. Northover, A. Boake, and D. G. Kourie. Karl popper's critical rationalism in agile software development. In H. Schärfe, editor, *Conceptual structures: inspiration and application*, volume 4068 of *Lecture notes in computer science Lecture notes in artificial intelligence*, pages 360–373. Springer, 2006.

[190] L. M. Northrop and P. C. Clements. A framework for software product line practice, 2012.

[191] H. F. R. Nuhn, J.-P. Martini, and A. Kostron. Hybride strukturen in der automobilindustrie - studie zu agilen praktiken in forschungs- und entwicklungsprozessen. In M. Engstler, M. Fazal-Baqaie, E. Hanser, O. Linssen, M. Mikusz, and A. Volland, editors, *Projektmanagement und Vorgehensmodelle 2016, Lecture Notes in Informatics (LNI)*,, pages 29–36. Gesellschaft für Informatik e.V, 2016.

[192] P. O'Leary, M. Ali Babar, S. Thiel, and I. Richardson. Product derivation process and agile approaches:exploring the integration potential. *2nd IFIP CEE Conference on Software Engineering Techniques (CEE-SET 2007)*, 2007.

[193] P. O'Leary, F. McCaffery, I. Richardson, and S. Thiel. Towards agile product derivation in software product line engineering, 2009.

[194] P. O'Leary, F. McCaffery, S. Thiel, and I. Richardson. An agile process model for product derivation in software product line engineering. *Journal of Software: Evolution and Process*, 24(5):561–571, 2012.

[195] O. Oliinyk, K. Petersen, M. Schoelzke, M. Becker, and S. Schneickert. Structuring automotive product lines and feature models: An exploratory study at opel. *Requirements Engineering*, 22(1):105–135, 2017.

[196] P. Oliveira, A. L. Ferreira, D. Dias, T. Pereira, P. Monteiro, and R. J. Machado. An analysis of the commonality and differences between aspice and iso26262 in the context of software development. In J. Stolfa, S. Stolfa, R. V. O'Connor, and R. Messnarz, editors, *Systems, Software and Services Process Improvement: 24th European Conference, EuroSPI 2017, Ostrava, Czech Republic, September 6– 8, 2017, Proceedings*, pages 216–227. Springer International Publishing, 2017.

[197] Ö. Özcan-Top and O. Demirörs. Assessment of agile maturity models: A multiple case study. In T. Woronowicz, T. Rout, R. V. O'Connor, and A. Dorling, editors, *Software Process Improvement and Capability Determination*, pages 130–141. Springer Berlin Heidelberg, 2013.

[198] Ö. Özcan-Top and O. Demirors. Application of a software agility assessment model – agilitymod in the field. *Computer Standards & Interfaces*, 2018.

[199] R. F. Paige, X. Wang, Z. R. Stephenson, and P. J. Brooke. Towards an agile process for building software product lines. In D. Hutchison, T. Kanade, J. Kittler, J. M. Kleinberg, F. Mattern, J. C. Mitchell, M. Naor, O. Nierstrasz, C. Pandu Rangan, B. Steffen, M. Sudan, D. Terzopoulos, D. Tygar, M. Y. Vardi, G. Weikum, P. Abrahamsson, M. Marchesi, and G. Succi, editors, *Extreme Programming and Agile Processes in Software Engineering*, volume 4044 of *Lecture Notes in Computer Science*, pages 198–199. Springer Berlin Heidelberg, 2006.

[200] J. Pedersen Notander, M. Höst, and P. Runeson. Challenges in flexible safety-critical software development – an industrial qualitative survey. In D. Hutchison, T. Kanade, J. Kittler, J. M. Kleinberg, F. Mattern, J. C. Mitchell, M. Naor, O. Nierstrasz, C. Pandu Rangan, B. Steffen, M. Sudan, D. Terzopoulos, D. Tygar, M. Y. Vardi, G. Weikum, J. Heidrich, M. Oivo, A. Jedlitschka, and M. T. Baldassarre, editors, *Product-Focused Software Process Improvement*, volume 7983, pages 283–297. Springer Berlin Heidelberg, 2013.

[201] K. Peffers, T. Tuunanen, M. A. Rothenberger, and S. Chatterjee. A design science research methodology for information systems research. *Journal of Management Information Systems*, 24(3):45–77, 2007.

[202] P. Pelliccione, E. Knauss, R. Heldal, M. Agren, P. Mallozzi, A. Alminger, and D. Borgentun. A proposal for an automotive architecture framework for volvo cars. In *2016 Workshop on Automotive Systems/Software Architectures (WASA)*, pages 18–21.

[203] P. Pelliccione, E. Knauss, R. Heldal, S. Magnus Ågren, P. Mallozzi, A. Alminger, and D. Borgentun. Automotive architecture framework: The experience of volvo cars. *Journal of Systems Architecture*, 77:83–100, 2017.

[204] Per Runeson and Emelie Engström. Chapter 7 - regression testing in software product line engineering. In Ali Hurson and Atif Memon, editors, *Advances in Computers*, volume 86 of *Advances in Computers*, pages 223–263. Elsevier, 2012.

[205] K. Petersen, R. Feldt, S. Mujtaba, and M. Mattsson. Systematic mapping studies in software engineering. In British Computer Society, editor, *Proceedings of the 12th International Conference on Evaluation and Assessment in Software Engineering*, EASE'08, pages 68–77. 2008.

[206] J. K. Philipp Hohl. Agile manifesto: Review and future directions: Workshop, 18.10.2017.

[207] P. Pohjalainen. Bottom-up modeling for a software product line: An experience report on agile modeling of governmental mobile networks. In E. Almeida, editor, *2011 15th International Software Product Line Conference (SPLC 2011)*, pages 323–332. IEEE, 2011.

[208] K. Pohl, G. Böckle, and F. Linden. *Software Product Line Engineering: Foundations, Principles, and Techniques*. Springer-Verlag Berlin Heidelberg, Berlin, Heidelberg, 2005.

[209] A. Pretschner, M. Broy, I. H. Kruger, and T. Stauner. Software engineering for automotive systems: A roadmap. In *Future of Software Engineering (FOSE '07)*, pages 55–71. IEEE, 2007.

[210] A. Pretschner, C. Salzmann, B. SChätz, and T. Staudner. *Fourth International Workshop on Software Engineering for Automotive Systems (SEAS 2007): Proceedings, ICSE 2007 workshops : [20-26 May 2007, Minneapolis ICSE 2007*. IEEE, [Piscataway, N.J.], 2007.

[211] M. Raatikainen, K. Rautiainen, V. Myllärniemi, and T. Männistö. Integrating product family modeling with development management in agile methods. In Y. Dubinsky, editor, *Proceedings of the 1st international workshop on Software development governance*, page 17. ACM, 2008.

[212] J. Ritchie, editor. *Qualitative research practice: A guide for social science students and researchers*. Sage, Los Angeles, Calif., repr edition, 2011.

[213] J. M. Robarts. Practical considerations for distributed agile projects. In G. Melnik, editor, *Conference Agile, 2008*, pages 327–332. IEEE Computer Soc, 2008.

[214] H. Robinson and H. Sharp. Collaboration, communication and co-ordination in agile software development practice. In I. Mistrík, J. Grundy, A. Hoek, and J. Whitehead, editors, *Collaborative Software Engineering*, pages 93–108. Springer Berlin Heidelberg, 2010.

[215] C. Rothermel. *Referenz- und Bewertungsmodell für Scrum-Projekte im Automobilbereich unter Beachtung der Anforderungen der funktionalen Sicherheit nach ISO 26262*. PhD thesis, Universität Ulm in, Ulm, 28.11.2016.

[216] P. Runeson and M. Höst. Guidelines for conducting and reporting case study research in software engineering. *Empirical Software Engineering*, 14(2):131–164, 2009.

[217] S. Sabar. *Software Process Improvement and Lifecycle Models in Automotive Industry*. PhD thesis, Linköping University, Department of Computer and Information Science, 2011.

[218] J. Saldaña. *The coding manual for qualitative researchers*. Sage, Los Angeles, 2009.

[219] A. J. Santos and V. J. Lucena. Scrumpl - software product line engineering with scrum. In *International Conference on Evaluation of Novel Approaches to Software Engineering*, pages 239–244.

[220] J. Schäuffele and T. Zurawka. *Automotive Software Engineering*. ATZ / MTZ-Fachbuch. Springer Fachmedien, Wiesbaden, 2010.

[221] A. Schloßer, J. Schnitzler, T. Sentis, and J. Richenhagen. Agile processes in automotive industry – efficiency and quality in software development. In M. Bargende, H.-C. Reuss, and J. Wiedemann, editors, *16. Internationales Stuttgarter Symposium*, Proceedings, pages 489–503. Springer Fachmedien Wiesbaden, 2016.

[222] K. Schmid and I. John. Developing, validating and evolving an approach to product line benefit and risk assessment. In *EUROMICRO*, pages 272–283. IEEE Computer Society, 2002.

[223] J.-H. Schneberger, T. Luedeke, and M. Vielhaber. Agile transformation and correlation of customer-specific requirements and system-inherent characteristics - an automotive example. *Procedia CIRP*, 70:78–83, 2018.

[224] K. Schwaber. *Agile project management with Scrum*. Microsoft professional. Microsoft Press, Redmond, Wash., 2004.

[225] K. Schwaber and J. Sutherland. The scrum guide, 2001.

[226] C. B. Seaman. Qualitative methods in empirical studies of software engineering. *IEEE Transactions on Software Engineering*, 25(4):557–572, 1999.

[227] F. Selleri Silva, F. S. F. Soares, A. L. Peres, I. M. d. Azevedo, A. P. L. Vasconcelos, F. K. Kamei, and S. R. d. L. Meira. Using cmmi together with agile software development: A systematic review. *Information and Software Technology*, 58:20–43, 2015.

[228] K. Sethi, Y. Cai, S. Wong, A. Garcia, and C. Sant'Anna. From retrospect to prospect: Assessing modularity and stability from software architecture. In *2009 Joint Working IEEE/IFIP Conference on Software Architecture European Conference on Software Architecture*, pages 269–272, 2009.

[229] H. Sharp and T. Hall, editors. *Agile Processes, in Software Engineering, and Extreme Programming*. Lecture Notes in Business Information Processing. Springer International Publishing, Cham, 2016.

[230] M. Shen, W. Yang, G. Rong, and D. Shao. Applying agile methods to embedded software development: A systematic review. In *2012 2nd International Workshop on Software Engineering for Embedded Systems (SEES)*, pages 30–36.

[231] W. A. Shewhart. *Statistical Method from the Viewpoint of Quality Control*. Dover Books on Mathematics. Dover Publications, Newburyport, 2012.

[232] S. Shlaer and S. J. Mellor. *Object-oriented systems analysis: Modeling the world in data*. Yourdon Press computing series. Yourdon Pr, Englewood Cliffs, N.J., 1988.

[233] J. Shrinivasavadhani and V. Panicker. Remote mentoring a distributed agile team. In G. Melnik, editor, *Conference Agile, 2008*, pages 322–326. IEEE Computer Soc, 2008.

[234] A. Sidky. A structured approach to adopting agile practices [electronic resource]: The agile adoption framework. 2007.

[235] M. B. Snapp and D. Dagefoerde. The accidental agilists: One team's journey from waterfall to agile. In G. Melnik, editor, *Conference Agile, 2008*, pages 171–175. IEEE Computer Soc, 2008.

[236] F. Stallinger and R. Neumann. From software to software system products: An add-on process reference model for enhancing iso/iec 12207 with product management and system-level reuse. In *2012 38th Euromicro Conference on Software Engineering and Advanced Applications*, pages 307–314. IEEE, 2012.

[237] M. Staron. Automotive software development. In *Automotive Software Architectures: An Introduction*, pages 51–79. Springer International Publishing, 2017.

[238] E. Stelzmann, C. Kreiner, G. Spork, R. Messnarz, and F. Koenig. Agility meets systems engineering: A catalogue of success factors from industry practice. In A. Riel, R. V. O'Connor, S. Tichkiewitch, and R. Messnarz, editors, *Systems, Software and Services Process Improvement*, volume 99 of *Communications in Computer and Information Science*, pages 245–256. Springer Berlin Heidelberg, 2010.

[239] K.-J. Stol, P. Ralph, and B. Fitzgerald. Grounded theory in software engineering research. In L. Dillon, W. Visser, and L. Williams, editors, *Proceedings of the 38th International Conference on Software Engineering*, pages 120–131, 2016.

[240] K. Sureshchandra and J. Shrinivasavadhani. Moving from waterfall to agile. In G. Melnik, editor, *Conference Agile, 2008*, pages 97–101. IEEE Computer Soc, 2008.

[241] J. Taiber and J. D. McGregor. Efficient engineering of safety-critical, software-intensive systems. In *2014 International Conference on Connected Vehicles and Expo (ICCVE)*, pages 836–841.

[242] R. Y. Takahira, L. R. Laraia, F. A. Dias, S. Y. Abraham, P. T. S. Nascimento, and A. S. Camargo. Scrum and embedded software development for the automotive industry. In *Proceedings of PICMET'14 Conference: Portland International Center for Management of Engineering and Technology; Infrastructure and Service Integration*, pages 2664–2672, 2014.

[243] S. C. P. Team. *Cmmi for development v1.3: Improving processes for developing better products and services.* Lulu Com, [Place of publication not identified], 2011.

[244] S. Theobald and P. Diebold. Interface problems of agile in a non-agile environment. In J. Garbajosa, X. Wang, and A. Aguiar, editors, *Agile Processes in Software Engineering and Extreme Programming*, pages 123–130. Springer International Publishing, 2018.

[245] S. Thiel, M. A. Babar, G. Botterweck, and L. O'Brien. Software product lines in automotive systems engineering. *SAE International Journal of Passenger Cars - Electronic and Electrical Systems*, 1(1):531–543, 2009.

[246] D. Thomas. Cellphone addiction and academic stress among university students in thailand. *INTERNATIONAL FORUM JOURNAL*, 19(2):80–96, url = http://ojs.aiias.edu/index.php/ojs/article/view/187, 2017.

[247] K. Tian. Adding more agility to software product line methods: A feasibility study on its customization using agile practices. *International Journal of Knowledge and Systems Science*, 5(4):17–34, 2014.

[248] K. Tian and K. Cooper. Agile and software product line methods: Are they so different?, 2006.

[249] C. Tischer, A. Muller, M. Ketterer, and L. Geyer. Why does it take that long? establishing product lines in the automotive domain. In *11th International Software Product Line Conference, 2007*, pages 269–274. IEEE Computer Society, 2007.

[250] M. Trei, S. Maro, J.-P. Steghöfer, and T. Peikenkamp. An iso 26262 compliant design flow and tool for automotive multicore systems. In P. Abrahamsson, A. Jedlitschka, A. Nguyen Duc, M. Felderer, S. Amasaki, and T. Mikkonen, editors, *Product-Focused Software Process Improvement: 17th International Conference, PROFES 2016, Trondheim, Norway, November 22-24, 2016, Proceedings*, pages 163–180. Springer International Publishing, 2016.

[251] P. Trinidad, D. Benavides, A. Durán, A. Ruiz-Cortés, and M. Toro. Automated error analysis for the agilization of feature modeling. *Journal of Systems and Software*, 81(6):883–896, 2008.

[252] P. Trinidad, D. Benavides, A. Ruiz-Cortés, S. Segura, and M. Toro, editors. *Explanations for Agile Feature Models*, Baltimore, MD, 2006.

[253] O. Turetken, I. Stojanov, and J. J. M. Trienekens. Assessing the adoption level of scaled agile development: A maturity model for scaled agile framework. *Journal of Software: Evolution and Process*, 29(6):e1796, 2017.

[254] D. Turk, R. France, and B. Rumpe. Limitations of agile software processes. In *In Proceedings of the Third International Conference on Extreme Programming and Flexible Processes in Software Engineering (XP2002*, pages 43–46. Springer-Verlag, 2002.

[255] S. Urli, M. Blay-Fornarino, P. Collet, and S. Mosser. Using composite feature models to support agile software product line evolution. In Unknown, editor, *Proceedings of the 6th International Workshop on Models and Evolution*, pages 21–26. ACM, 2012.

[256] V. K. Vaishnavi and J. W. Kuechler. *Design Science Research Methods and Patterns: Innovating Information and Communication Technology*. Auerbach Publications, Boston, MA, USA, 1st edition, 2007.

[257] V. K. Vaishnavi and W. Kuechler. *Design science research methods and patterns: Innovating information and communication technology*. CRC Press LLC, Boca Raton, second edition edition, 2015.

[258] R. Valade. The big projects always fail: Taking an enterprise agile. In *Agile 2008 Conference*, pages 148–153.

[259] F. van der Linden, K. Schmid, and E. Rommes. *Software Product Lines in Action*. Springer Berlin Heidelberg, Berlin, Heidelberg, 2007.

[260] VDA QMC Working Group 13 / Automotive SIG. Automotive spice process assessment / reference model, 01.11.2017.

[261] VDA QMC Working Group 13 / Automotive SIG. Automotive spice process assessment / reference model, 2015-07-16.

[262] E. Wallmüller. *SPI - Software Process Improvement mit CMMI, PSP/TSP und ISO 15504*. Carl Hanser Fachbuchverlag, s.l., 1. aufl. edition, 2007.

[263] D. M. Weiss and C. T. R. Lai. *Software product-line engineering: A family-based software development process*. Addison-Wesley, Reading Mass. u.a., 1. print edition, 1999.

[264] K. D. Wentzel. Software reuse—facts and myths. In *Proceedings of the 16th International Conference on Software Engineering*, ICSE '94, pages 267–268. IEEE Computer Society Press, 1994.

[265] C. Wohlin, M. Höst, and K. Henningsson. Empirical research methods in software engineering. In R. Conradi and A. I. Wang, editors, *Empirical Methods and Studies in Software Engineering: Experiences from ESERNET*, pages 7–23. Springer Berlin Heidelberg, 2003.

[266] C. Wohlin, P. Runeson, M. Höst, M. C. Ohlsson, B. Regnell, and A. Wesslén. *Experimentation in software engineering*. Springer, Berlin, 2012.

[267] L. Wozniak and P. Clements. How automotive engineering is taking product line engineering to the extreme. In D. C. Schmidt, editor, *Proceedings of the 19th International Conference on Software Product Line*, pages 327–336. ACM, 2015.

[268] R. K. Yin. *Case study research: Design and methods*, volume 5 of *Applied social research methods series*. Sage, Los Angeles, 4. ed. edition, 2009.

[269] K. Yoshimura, D. Ganesan, and D. Muthig. Defining a strategy to introduce a software product line using existing embedded systems, 2006.

[270] K. Yoshimura, J. Shimabukuro, T. Ohara, C. Okamoto, Y. Atarashi, S. Koizumi, S. Watanabe, and K. Funakoshi. Key activities for introducing software product lines into multiple divisions: Experience at hitachi. In *2011 15th International Software Product Line Conference*, pages 261–266. IEEE, 2011.

[271] C. Young and H. Terashima. How did we adapt agile processes to our distributed development? In G. Melnik, editor, *Conference Agile, 2008*, pages 304–309. IEEE Computer Soc, 2008.

ASPLA Model Assessment Results

This appendix provides the improvement potential and recommendation list for the conducted assessments by Developer 1 and Developer 2.

A.1   Recommendation List for Developer 1

The ASPLA Model recommends to improve Honeycomb 3 (Agile Software Development), Honeycomb 6 (Test Strategy) and Honeycomb 7 (Communication) with a high priority.

Table A.1: Recommendation list for Developer 1

ProcO_03.06	The purchase department shall provide an agile payment strategy.
ProcO_03.06	The payment strategy should be able to be changed, according to the developers' team needs.
ProcO_03.06	The payment strategy shall provide the suppliers the ability to work in an agile way.
ProcO_03.06	The payment strategy shall be adjustable.
ProcO_03.06	The development process shall stay within set development budget.
ProcO_03.06	The purchase department shall provide working contract arrangements for the collaboration with suppliers.
ProcO_03.07	The sprint-length shall be adjustable.
ProcO_03.07	The sprint length should be able to be changed, according to the developers' team needs.
ProcO_03.07	New roles shall be implemented to verify a smooth agile development.
ProcO_03.07	Agile methods and practices shall not stipulated.
ProcO_03.07	Employees shall be trained in agile practices and methods.
ProcO_03.07	Employees shall be empowered to take decisions, solve problems, and develop innovative solutions.
ProcO_03.07	Agile coaches shall advise people to rethink and change the way they go about development.

continued on the next page

ProcO_03.03	The development process shall be capable to react on changes in the market situation.
ProcO_03.03	The release cycle shall be shortened to take new requirements into account.
ProcO_03.03	The development shall address market needs.
ProcO_03.03	Late requirements shall be addressed in the next sprint.
ProcO_06.05	A trace from software units to test cases shall be defined.
ProcO_06.05	A trace from test cases to test results shall be established.
ProcO_06.01	The software shall always be tested.
ProcO_06.01	The test strategy shall fulfill the requirements of ISO 26262.
ProcO_06.01	All software variants should be tested.
ProcO_06.04	The test strategy shall be adjustable to safety requirements.
ProcO_06.04	Each test case shall provide the maximum runtime for the test case.
ProcO_06.04	The test case selection shall be automated.
ProcO_06.04	Test cases that verify safety regulations shall be prioritized.
ProcO_06.04	The test strategy shall be adjustable to safety requirements.
ProcO_07.03	Feedback channel for developer from automated tests shall be implemented.
ProcO_07.03	Customer feedback shall be included into the development.
ProcO_07.09	Direct customer feedback into the development process shall be established.
ProcO_07.04	Managers and higher Management Levels shall receive a summary about the next sprint.
ProcO_07.04	The sprint summary shall be an output of the sprint planning meeting.
ProcO_07.04	Managers and higher Management Levels shall grant access to the backlogs.
ProcO_07.04	The process and progress shall be visible to all participants.

A.2 Recommendation List for Developer 2

The ASPLA Model recommends to improve Honeycomb 3 (Agile Software Development), Honeycomb 4 (Continuous X) and Honeycomb 6 (Test Strategy) with a high priority.

Table A.2: Recommendation list for Developer 2

ProcO_03.06	The purchase department shall provide an agile payment strategy.
ProcO_03.06	The payment strategy should be able to be changed, according to the developers' team needs.
ProcO_03.06	The payment strategy shall provide the suppliers the ability to work in an agile way.
ProcO_03.06	The payment strategy shall be adjustable.
ProcO_03.06	The development process shall stay within set development budget.
ProcO_03.06	The purchase department shall provide working contract arrangements for the collaboration with suppliers.
ProcO_03.03	The development process shall be capable to react on changes in the market situation.
ProcO_03.03	The release cycle shall be shortened to take new requirements into account.
ProcO_03.03	The development shall address market needs.
ProcO_03.03	Late requirements shall be addressed in the next sprint.
ProcO_03.07	The sprint-length shall be adjustable.
ProcO_03.07	The sprint length should be able to be changed, according to the developers' team needs.
ProcO_03.07	New roles shall be implemented to verify a smooth agile development.
ProcO_03.07	Agile methods and practices shall not stipulated.
ProcO_03.07	Employees shall be trained in agile practices and methods.
ProcO_03.07	Employees shall be empowered to take decisions, solve problems, and develop innovative solutions.
ProcO_03.07	Agile coaches shall advise people to rethink and change the way they go about development.
ProcO_04.03	Software test shall be continuously executed and automated.
ProcO_04.03	Software tests shall be automated.
ProcO_04.03	Test shall be continuously executed.
ProcO_04.03	The agile project has to ensure that the process purposes of all 3 software testing processes (SWE.4, SWE.5 and SWE.6) are fulfilled by the defined activities in project Sprints.
ProdO_04.02	Continuous verification tasks shall be automated.
ProdO_04.02	Software items shall be capable to undergo highly automated verification tasks.
ProcO_04.02	Continuous Integration shall be implemented.
ProcO_04.02	Virtual Integration shall be implemented.

continued on the next page

ProcO_04.02	Models for different software variants and hardware versions for the virtual integration shall be provided.
ProcO_04.02	Virtual integration shall not replace real integration into a car.
ProcO_04.02	Continuous Integration (CI) shall be the backbone of the testing process.
ProcO_06.02	The test strategy shall be adjustable to available time.
ProcO_06.02	The selection of tests cases shall use the maximum available time.
ProcO_06.06	Software integration test shall be summarized and communicated to all affected parties.
ProcO_06.06	The possibility to communicate the test results shall be established.
ProcO_06.05	A trace from software units to test cases shall be defined.
ProcO_06.05	A trace from test cases to test results shall be established.

Data Collection in Workshops

This chapter highlights the data collection and gives information about the workshops. Information for the interview study can be found in Section 3.2.

B.1 Workshop 1: Agile Transformation with Arie van Bennekum

The workshop was part of the data collection for the publication [106]. The publication aims at retaining and preserving the basics of agile based on the personal experiences and opinions of the originators of the manifesto for agile software development. The publication was co-authored by Jil Klünder from the University of Hanover.

In order to collect first-hand data about the basics of agile, the researchers chose two different ways to get in touch with the original contributors. First, the author of this thesis searched for email addresses on the private blogs and homepages. Second, the author signed up for a recruiter membership on LinkedIn[1]. With the recruiter profile, it was possible to get in contact with the original contributors and to send them a questionnaire via LinkedIn.

Arie van Bennekum invited the researchers to a Skype™ call to discuss the basics of agile and current directions of the agile movement face-to-face. After the call, Arie van Bennekum invited the Researcher for a 1-day workshop to discuss the origins and future directions of the manifesto in detail. He furthermore suggested, to discuss the future of the agile movement in general. He organized a workshop to discuss these topics in detail.

The workshop took place in October 2017 in Rotterdam, Netherlands. The workshop was separated in two sessions of 2,5 hours each. In the first session, the researchers presented the results from the survey and discussed the findings with Arie van Bennekum. In the second session, Arie van Bennekum presented his view on the future of the agile movement and the importance of agile transformation. Due to the ongoing discussion on agile transformation in large companies in the workshop, the author of this thesis extended the workshop with Arie van Bennekum by an additional day. The second workshop day

---

[1]https://www.linkedin.com/

mediated the experience of agile transformation in large companies with more than 70.000 employees. Therefore the author visited two large companies[2], located in the Netherlands and discussed impediments and success stories with the agile transformation coaches.

B.2   Workshop 2: Daimler AG - Agile Development In-house

In October 2016, a Daimler AG internal workshop was conducted to uncover the challenges and opportunities of combining software product lines and agile software development, identify potential solution ideas and encourage discussion. In 4 hours, 60 participants discussed the area of tension between systematic reuse and agile software development. At the beginning of the workshop, invited external experts were presenting their view on the topic. The workshop topic was addressed by means of the state of the art represented in current research and the state of the practice in IT companies.

B.3   Workshop 3: Daimler AG - Agile Open Space

These workshops started in 2015 as a series of workshops to figure out, how much agile experience is already present in-house at Daimler AG. The workshops are organized by the cross-functional team, called the agile core team and aim at resolving the impediments in daily business. Furthermore the workshops help to establish the agile mindset and to spread the word for an agile way of working.

B.4   Workshop 4: Automated Testing of Software Variants

An expert workshop with three employees from Daimler AG and 4 employees of a manufacturer[3] of large diesel engines took place in March 2017. Developers from system development, process development and methodological development took part in the workshop. The main point of discussion was to figure out, how to address challenges in automated testing and test coverage for a large number of software variants. In the five-hour workshop the participants discussed possible solution approaches, such as the application of Continuous Integration, the advantages and disadvantages of automated testing compared to manual testing, and the implementation and installation of virtual testing against engine models. In addition, test case selection algorithms especially and the capability of principles of evolutionary computing were discussed.

---

[2] The company names are anonymous due to data policy and companies in-house knowledge.
[3] The company name is anonymous due to data policy.

B.5 Workshop 5: Agile Practices and Software Product Lines

Two workshops were held at the "Fraunhofer Institute for Experimental Software Engineering" (IESE) in Kaiserslautern, Germany. Industrial participation was given by two participants working at the Daimler AG. Furthermore, four participants from the departments of embedded systems engineering and process engineering from the Fraunhofer IESE participated in the workshop. Each participant was invited to participate in the workshop due to their experience. The invited participants led to a combination of experience of automotive software development, agile practices, software product lines ,and software engineering in general.

The first workshop took place in September 2017. This one day workshop was divided into two sessions of 3 hours each. In the first session, each of the six participants gave a short presentation about their experience on the combination of software product lines and agile development methods. The author of this thesis presented a first version of the ASPLA Model and his thoughts on assessment models for agile software product line engineering.

The second session was a discussion round to identify common ground, to interconnect the knowledge of the participants and link agile practices and software product line techniques together. Within the workshop, the "Business (B), Architecture (A), Process (P) and Organization (O) (BAPO)" Model was identified as the basis for a discussion to evaluate agile principles according to the major concerns of software product line engineering [158]. The end of the session was the identification of topics for discussion in the follow-up meeting.

The follow-up workshop took place in January 2018 with 4 participants from the first workshop. It consists of two sessions of 3 hours each. In the first session, the product line engineering principles and their importance for supporting the agile way of working according to the BAPO Model, were presented and discussed. In the second session, the results were presented to an independent researcher. The subsequent discussion provided feedback to the categorization. The summarized results are published in in [113].

Appendix **C**

Identified Challenges

This chapter presents the identified challenges for a combination of agile software development and software product lines in the automotive domain. These challenges are presented according to their assigned category: (1) organizational challenges for distributed development, (2) challenges related to the coordination of the software product line, (3) challenges in adopting agile elements within the development process, (4) and challenges regarding automotive specific constraints. Explanatory notes on the table structure for the challenges are presented in Table C.1.

Table C.1: Explanatory notes on the table structure for the identified challenges

<ID>	<Description of identified challenge>		
Related ↑	<Relation to higher level challenge>	Related ↓	<Relation to lower level challenge>
Source	<Initial Source>; <Additional Source(s)>		

C.1 Organizational Challenges

Table C.2: Organizational challenges

[135800]	The existing hierarchy is addicted to the old paradigms and is changing slowly.		
Related ↑	-	Related ↓	[135798], [135843], [136220]
Source	Interview Study (cf. Section 3.2)		
[135798]	Existing hierarchy does not want to give up any responsibilities.		
Related ↑	[135800]	Related ↓	[135336], [135930]

continued on the next page.

175

Source	Interview Study (cf. Section 3.2)		
[135930]	Analyze and prioritize of new required features is too slow.		
Related ↑	[135798]	Related ↓	[135347]
Source	Interview Study (cf. Section 3.2)		
[135843]	The Management does not want to give up any responsibility.		
Related ↑	[135800]	Related ↓	[135340]
Source	Interview Study (cf. Section 3.2)		
[136220]	It is challenging to change large organizations.		
Related ↑	[135800]	Related ↓	[136366]
Source	Literature Review: [50], Additional Literature: [235, 74, 149, 217, 249, 1, 9, 31]		
[135816]	Purchase department is interfering an agile collaboration with suppliers.		
Related ↑	-	Related ↓	[135361]
Source	Interview Study (cf. Section 3.2)		
[135845]	It is challenging to schedule the development process.		
Related ↑	-	Related ↓	[135792], [135863]
Source	Interview Study (cf. Section 3.2)		
[135792]	It is challenging to synchronize the development teams.		
Related ↑	[135845]	Related ↓	[135323], [147768]
Source	Interview Study (cf. Section 3.2)		
[135863]	It is challenging to coordinate agile development.		
Related ↑	[135845]	Related ↓	-
Source	Interview Study (cf. Section 3.2)		
[135867]	It is challenging to manage the collaboration of agile and non-agile development teams within the organization.		
Related ↑	-	Related ↓	[135857], [135861], [135869], [136222]
Source	Interview Study (cf. Section 3.2)		
[135857]	The automotive software development is dependent on technical systems.		
Related ↑	[135867]	Related ↓	[135454], [135865]
Source	Interview Study (cf. Section 3.2)		
[135865]	The development of different sub-systems shall be synchronized.		
Related ↑	[135857]	Related ↓	[135458]
Source	Interview Study (cf. Section 3.2)		
[135861]	The automotive software development is dependent on other developments domains like hardware and mechanical.		
Related ↑	[135867]	Related ↓	[135454], [135458]
Source	Interview Study (cf. Section 3.2)		
[135869]	It is challenging to set up a common interfaces between departments.		
Related ↑	[135867]	Related ↓	[136246]

continued on the next page.

Source	Interview Study (cf. Section 3.2)		
[136246]	It is difficult to determine, which parts of the software development process are able to become more agile.		
Related ↑	[135869]	Related ↓	-
Source	Literature Review: [61]		
[136222]	It is challenging to manage different development cycle-times for related development systems (e.g. hardware or mechanics).		
Related ↑	[135867]	Related ↓	[135321]
Source	Literature Review: [61]		
[147050]	Traditional communication procedures are hindering a collaboration.		
Related ↑	-	Related ↓	[135824], [135830], [135835], [135839], [135847], [136261], [136269]
Source	Interview Study (cf. Section 3.2)		
[135824]	No or little face-to-face conversation.		
Related ↑	[147050]	Related ↓	[138247]
Source	Interview Study (cf. Section 3.2)		
[135830]	The process to maintain and scope the common software parts requires a lot of communication between all participants.		
Related ↑	[147050]	Related ↓	[135649]
Source	Interview Study (cf. Section 3.2)		
[135835]	Slow communication channels slowing down the development.		
Related ↑	[147050]	Related ↓	[135647]
Source	Interview Study (cf. Section 3.2)		
[135839]	The communication is only a top-down communication.		
Related ↑	[147050]	Related ↓	[135647]
Source	Interview Study (cf. Section 3.2)		
[135847]	It is unclear for the developers what they should report in case they are working in an agile development.		
Related ↑	[147050]	Related ↓	[136224], [136283]
Source	Interview Study (cf. Section 3.2)		
[136224]	Long-term predictability is hard to achieve.		
Related ↑	[135847]	Related ↓	[138249]
Source	Literature Review: [61]; Interview Study (cf. Section 3.2)		
[135849]	It is unclear for the managers how the agile software product line could be planned.		
Related ↑	[136224]	Related ↓	[138249], [138251]
Source	Interview Study (cf. Section 3.2)		
[136283]	A long-term predictability is hard to achieve with short-term agility.		
Related ↑	[135847]	Related ↓	[138249]

continued on the next page.

Source	Literature Review: [61]; Interview Study (cf. Section 3.2)		
[136261]	Intra- and inter-organizational communication practices are hard to establish and maintain.		
Related ↑	[147050]	Related ↓	[136263],[136265], [136267]
Source	Literature Review: [172]		
[136263]	A mismatch of adequate communication mechanisms can sometimes hinder the communication.		
Related ↑	[136261]	Related ↓	-
Source	Literature Review: [172]		
[136265]	It is challenging to establish a good communication within development teams.		
Related ↑	[136261]	Related ↓	-
Source	Literature Review: [172], Additional Literature: [238, 233]		
[136267]	It is challenging to establish a good communication between business units.		
Related ↑	[136261]	Related ↓	-
Source	Literature Review: [172], Additional Literature: [238, 233]		
[136269]	A lot of communication overhead to maintain the collaboration.		
Related ↑	[136261]	Related ↓	-
Source	Literature Review: [172]		
[135794]	It is challenging to synchronize distributed development teams.		
Related ↑	-	Related ↓	[138241], [147844]
Source	Interview Study (cf. Section 3.2)		
[135804]	The collaboration with suppliers is challenging.		
Related ↑	-	Related ↓	[135349], [135814]
Source	Interview Study (cf. Section 3.2)		
[135814]	The collaboration of co-located teams with suppliers is challenging.		
Related ↑	[135804]	Related ↓	[135355]
Source	Interview Study (cf. Section 3.2)		
[135820]	The distribution of the development team leads to challenges in the team communication.		
Related ↑	-	Related ↓	[135855], [136230]
Source	Interview Study (cf. Section 3.2)		
[135855]	It is challenging to maintain the automotive software development of a worldwide distributed development with a lot of dependencies.		
Related ↑	[135820]	Related ↓	[135822], [135826], [135812], [135806]
Source	Interview Study (cf. Section 3.2)		
[136230]	Communication overheads and problems caused by outsourcing and attitudinal (cultural) incompatibilities.		
Related ↑	[135820]	Related ↓	[135808]

continued on the next page.

Source	Literature Review [172]; Interview Study (cf. Section 3.2), Additional Literature: [271]		
[135822]	Different time-zones of worldwide distributed development teams.		
Related ↑	[135855]	Related ↓	[138243]
Source	Interview Study (cf. Section 3.2)		
[135826]	Mistakes in translation of development relevant documents.		
Related ↑	[135855]	Related ↓	[135399]
Source	Interview Study (cf. Section 3.2)		
[135826]	Working in co-located teams are hard to manage.		
Related ↑	[135855]	Related ↓	-
Source	Interview Study (cf. Section 3.2)		
[135806]	Motivation to collaborate in a worldwide team is hard to maintain high.		
Related ↑	[135855]	Related ↓	-
Source	Interview Study (cf. Section 3.2)		
[135808]	It is challenging to bring together different cultures in one development team.		
Related ↑	[136230]	Related ↓	[136172], [135810]
Source	Interview Study (cf. Section 3.2)		
[135810]	It is challenging to bring together different mindsets in one development team.		
Related ↑	[135808]	Related ↓	[136174]
Source	Interview Study (cf. Section 3.2)		

C.2 Software Product Line Challenges

Table C.3: Software product line challenges

[135837]	It is challenging to plan and maintain the software product line.		
Related ↑	-	Related ↓	[135510], [147178]
Source	Interview Study (cf. Section 3.2)		
[135796]	It is challenging to plan and coordinate the tasks for the software product line.		
Related ↑	[135837]	Related ↓	[135851], [136165]
Source	Interview Study (cf. Section 3.2)		
[135851]	It is unclear for the managers how features are scoped.		
Related ↑	[135796]	Related ↓	-
Source	Interview Study (cf. Section 3.2)		
[135914]	It is challenging to maintain a high modularity of the software components.		

continued on the next page.

Related ↑	-	Related ↓	[135916], [135918]
Source	Interview Study (cf. Section 3.2)		
[135916]	**It is challenging to setup and maintain a suitable software architecture.**		
Related ↑	[135914]	Related ↓	[135565], [135920], [147687], [147685], [147683]
Source	Interview Study (cf. Section 3.2)		
[135918]	**It is challenging to maintain and refactor a good shaped software architecture.**		
Related ↑	[135914]	Related ↓	[136257],[136259]
Source	Interview Study (cf. Section 3.2)		
[135920]	**It is challenging to integrate not foreseen features into the software.**		
Related ↑	[135916]	Related ↓	[135563]
Source	Interview Study (cf. Section 3.2)		
[136259]	**It is challenging to avoid the erosion of the software architecture.**		
Related ↑	[135918]	Related ↓	[135571]
Source	Literature Review: [86, 40, 23]		
[136257]	**It is necessary to find the right trade-off between the management of architecture evolution and refactoring without sacrificing the principles of agility.**		
Related ↑	[135918]	Related ↓	[138245], [147721]
Source	Literature Review: [178]		
[136238]	**It is challenging to set up a reuse strategy that complements the principles of agile development and foster software reuse.**		
Related ↑	-	Related ↓	[135787], [135924], [136226], [136380]
Source	Literature Review: [78, 45]; Additional Literature: [51, 25]		
[135787]	**It is challenging to avoid the decomposition of the software product line during the development.**		
Related ↑	[136238]	Related ↓	[135571]
Source	Interview Study (cf. Section 3.2)		
[135924]	**It is challenging to freeze the functionality for different variants of the software product line while implementing in an agile environment.**		
Related ↑	[136238]	Related ↓	-
Source	Interview Study (cf. Section 3.2)		
[136226]	**It is unclear how to manage software reuse and agile development.**		
Related ↑	[136238]	Related ↓	[135954], [147124]
Source	Literature Review: [78], Interview Study (cf. Section 3.2)		
[136380]	**Missing awareness for software reuse.**		

continued on the next page.

Related ↑	[136238]	Related ↓	[135641], [135643], [135645], [135651], [135653], [135789], [147756], [147719], [147723]
Source	Literature Review: [172]		
[135789]	It is challenging to manage common software parts which become stunted.		
Related ↑	[136380]	Related ↓	[136170]
Source	Interview Study (cf. Section 3.2)		

C.3 Agile Software Development Challenges

Table C.4: Agile software development challenges

[136218]	It is challenging to address the competitive pressure from the market.		
Related ↑	-	Related ↓	[136362]
Source	Literature Review: [140, 184, 115, 116]		
[136242]	It is challenging to deliver high-quality software within estimated costs at a fast pace.		
Related ↑	-	Related ↓	[136371]
Source	Literature Review: [160]		
[136244]	It is challenging to shorten the time to market.		
Related ↑	-	Related ↓	[135908], [136234], [136281]
Source	Literature Review: [247, 140, 10]; Additional Literature:[270, 116, 189, 138, 62]		
[135908]	The cost of delay for software features is neglected.		
Related ↑	[136244]	Related ↓	[136187], [318223]
Source	Interview Study (cf. Section 3.2)		
[136234]	It is challenging in the automotive domain to shorten development cycles.		
Related ↑	[136244]	Related ↓	[136348]
Source	Literature Review: [116, 115, 63]; Interview Study (cf. Section 3.2)		
[136281]	A long feedback loop with customers and management is hindering agile development in short iterations.		
Related ↑	[136244]	Related ↓	[135373], [147840]
Source	Literature Review: [61], Additional Literature: [229]		
[136248]	It is unclear which agile practices can be used to speed up the development.		
Related ↑	[136244]	Related ↓	[147124]
Source	Literature Review: [61, 59, 194], Additional Literature: [147, 68, 4]		
[138221]	The development is not fully focused on the customer needs.		
Related ↑	-	Related ↓	[136216], [136240], [136251], [136277]
Source	Interview Study (cf. Section 3.2), Additional Literature: [115, 173]		

continued on the next page.

[136216]	It is challenging to manage market uncertainties.		
Related ↑	[138221]	Related ↓	[136358], [138211], [138213]
Source	Literature Review: [116, 115]		

[136240]	It is challenging to deliver high-quality software time.		
Related ↑	[138221]	Related ↓	[138219], [138217], [147802], [147810], [147808], [147804]
Source	Literature Review: [93]		

[136251]	Different variants might address different customer needs that must be satisfied.		
Related ↑	[138221]	Related ↓	[138215], [138217]
Source	Literature Review: [245]		

[136277]	It is challenging to avoid the production of waste, such as functionality that potentially never gets shipped to a customer.		
Related ↑	[138221]	Related ↓	[136373], [138207], [138209]
Source	Literature Review: [142]		

C.4 Automotive Specific Challenges

Table C.5: Automotive specific challenges

[135902]	Hardware restrictions must be taken into account for software development.		
Related ↑	-	Related ↓	[135861], [135904], [135906], [135922]
Source	Interview Study (cf. Section 3.2)		
[135861]	The automotive software development must consider other developments domains, such as hardware and mechanical.		
Related ↑	[135902]	Related ↓	[138231]
Source	Interview Study (cf. Section 3.2)		
[135904]	The cost pressure of hardware components must be considered.		
Related ↑	[135902]	Related ↓	[135910]
Source	Interview Study (cf. Section 3.2)		
[135906]	It is challenging to address all existing hardware variants within the software.		
Related ↑	[135902]	Related ↓	[136180]
Source	Interview Study (cf. Section 3.2)		
[135922]	It is challenging to relate all changes in software with the selected hardware target.		
Related ↑	[135902]	Related ↓	[136184]
Source	Interview Study (cf. Section 3.2)		
[135910]	Often the smallest possible hardware is selected to meet the requirements whereas this does not mean that there is a reduction of quality or functionality.		
Related ↑	[135904]	Related ↓	[135912]
Source	Interview Study (cf. Section 3.2)		
[135912]	It is challenging to manage and select the compilation of different variants of software to fit on the corresponding hardware.		
Related ↑	[135910]	Related ↓	[136182]
Source	Interview Study (cf. Section 3.2)		
[140550]	It is unclear how each software variants can be tested on real hardware in a car.		
Related ↑	-	Related ↓	[135880], [135882], [136255], [136271]
Source	Interview Study (cf. Section 3.2)		
[135880]	It is unclear how far the automation of test could help in the process.		
Related ↑	[140550]	Related ↓	[135429], [135609], [147812]
Source	Interview Study (cf. Section 3.2)		
[135882]	It is unclear how the testing strategy must be adapted in agile development.		

continued on the next page.

Related ↑	[140550]	Related ↓	[135581], [135859], [135875], [135878], [147800]
Source	Interview Study (cf. Section 3.2)		
[136255]	It is a substantial effort to set up tools and to maintain the test environment.		
Related ↑	[140550]	Related ↓	[135433], [135435], [135958]
Source	Literature Review: [140, 79]; Additional Literature: [97]		
[136271]	It is challenging to development in a fast pace and adhere to regulations to comply with the law at the same pace.		
Related ↑	[140550]	Related ↓	[135873], [136273]
Source	Literature Review: [142]; Interview Study (cf. Section 3.2), Additional Literature: [67]		
[147126]	It is challenging to manage system requirements, as they affect software and hardware.		
Related ↑	-	Related ↓	[135926], [135928], [136232]
Source	Interview Study (cf. Section 3.2)		
[135859]	It is challenging to manage all required test and verification steps.		
Related ↑	[135882]	Related ↓	[135676], [147818]
Source	Interview Study (cf. Section 3.2)		
[135875]	It is unclear, how the test strategy to validate the software according to standards is defined.		
Related ↑	[135882]	Related ↓	[135597], [136142], [136279]
Source	Interview Study (cf. Section 3.2)		
[136279]	It is challenging to verify all safety aspects in a fast pace.		
Related ↑	[135875]	Related ↓	[135601], [147691], [147689]
Source	Literature Review: [61, 136, 245]; Interview Study (cf. Section 3.2), Additional Literature: [254, 75, 200]		
[135878]	It is a challenge to scale the test framework to test all variants within the software product line.		
Related ↑	[135882]	Related ↓	[135932], [135934], [136236]
Source	Interview Study (cf. Section 3.2)		
[135932]	It is challenging to validate all variants in a fast pace.		
Related ↑	[135978]	Related ↓	[1355872]
Source	Interview Study (cf. Section 3.2)		
[135934]	It is challenging to validate all variants to work as defined by standards.		
Related ↑	[135978]	Related ↓	[138233]
Source	Interview Study (cf. Section 3.2)		
[136236]	It is challenging to manage the complexity, which is based on the large number of variation points within the product.		
Related ↑	[135978]	Related ↓	[136178]

continued on the next page.

Source	Literature Review: [267], Interview Study (cf. Section 3.2)		
[136178]	Test coverage of a lot of different software variants is hard to keep high.		
Related ↑	[136236]	Related ↓	[135599], [135605]
Source	Interview Study (cf. Section 3.2)		
[135873]	Maintaining the compliance to automotive standards, such as ISO26262 is seen as highly challenging.		
Related ↑	[136271]	Related ↓	[135614], [135884]
Source	Interview Study (cf. Section 3.2)		
[135884]	Certifications tests must be executed, composable certification is far from being legally allowed.		
Related ↑	[135873]	Related ↓	[138235]
Source	Interview Study (cf. Section 3.2)		
[136273]	It is challenging to create documentation (process descriptions and development documentation) in a fast pace.		
Related ↑	[136271]	Related ↓	[135575], [136228]
Source	Literature Review:[142]; Interview Study (cf. Section 3.2), Additional Literature [120, 67, 75]		
[136228]	It is challenging, to use open source software.		
Related ↑	[136273]	Related ↓	[136364]
Source	Literature Review: [250]; Additional Literature: [249]		
[135926]	It is challenging to maintain the development, if requirements are becoming available late in the development process.		
Related ↑	[147126]	Related ↓	[138237]
Source	Interview Study (cf. Section 3.2)		
[135928]	It is challenging to maintain the development, if requirements are incomplete.		
Related ↑	[147126]	Related ↓	[138239]
Source	Interview Study (cf. Section 3.2)		
[136232]	It is challenging to maintain the development if requirements are changing constantly in a fast pace.		
Related ↑	[147126]	Related ↓	[136360]
Source	Literature Review: [17]		
[147882]	Security aspects are a prime goal to satisfy.		
Related ↑		Related ↓	[147693], [147695], [147697]
Source	Interview Study (cf. Section 3.2)		

Appendix D

Identified Recommendations

The tables in Appendix D describe all recommendations given by the ASPLA Model. Each recommendation is assigned to a Base Practice and relates to challenges and additional recommendations. The "Related ↑" and "Related ↓" properties help to trace each recommendation to the corresponding identified challenge. The "Source(s)" category denotes the original source of the recommendations and provides additional literature that support the recommendation. Explanatory notes on the table structure for the recommendations are presented in Table D.1.

Table D.1: Explanatory notes on the table structure for the identified recommendations

<ID>	<Description of identified recommendation>		
Related ↑	<Relation to higher level challenge or recommendation>	Related ↓	<Relation to lower level recommendation>
Source	<Initial Source>; <Additional Source(s)>		

Recommendations for Honeycomb 1: Product Line Architecture

Table D.2: Recommendations for Product Line Architecture

Base Practice: BP_ProcO_01.01			
[135954]	A software product line shall be used to manage the development.		
Related ↑	[136226]	Related ↓	[135403], [136163], [135405], [147214]
Source(s)	Interview Study (cf. Section 3.2); [245]		
[135403]	The development process shall be based on a strategic reuse strategy.		
Related ↑	[135954]	Related ↓	[147212]

continued on the next page

Source(s)	Interview Study (cf. Section 3.2); [245]

[147210]	The reuse approach shall satisfy different market demands.
Related ↑ [138215]	Related ↓ -
Source(s)	Additional Recommendation; [88]

[147212]	The reuse approach shall provide the possibility to maintain different versions and software variants.
Related ↑ [135403]	Related ↓ -
Source(s)	Additional Recommendation; [88]

Base Practice: BP_ProcO_01.02

[147214]	The different reuse strategies shall be merged into one approach valid worldwide.
Related ↑ [145954]	Related ↓ -
Source(s)	Interview Study (cf. Section 3.2)

[147216]	The development of features shall be standardized worldwide.
Related ↑ [135958]	Related ↓ -
Source(s)	Additional Recommendation; [138]

Base Practice: BP_ProcO_01.03

[147667]	The development shall be supported by an appropriate tool chain. This tool chain shall be valid worldwide.
Related ↑ [135408]	Related ↓ -
Source(s)	Literature Review: [250]

[147669]	Unnecessary, in-house quick and dirty solutions and not maintainable software shall not be used.
Related ↑ [135408]	Related ↓ -
Source(s)	Learning Cycle 1

[147671]	The tool chain shall provide interfaces to automate the process.
Related ↑ [135408]	Related ↓ -
Source(s)	Additional Recommendation; Learning Cycle 1, [139, 221, 227]

[147673]	The tool chain shall be as simple as possible, as extensive as necessary.
Related ↑ [135408]	Related ↓ -
Source(s)	Additional Recommendation; Learning Cycle 1

[147679]	The tool chain shall provide the possibility to trace from requirement to software unit.
Related ↑ [135408]	Related ↓ -
Source(s)	Additional Recommendation; [27]

[147681]	The tool chain shall provide the possibility to trace from software unit to the appropriate test cases.

continued on the next page

Related ↑	[135408]	Related ↓	[147822], [147824]
Source(s)	Additional Recommendation; [27]		

[135408]	The tool chain shall be standardized.		
Related ↑	[135958]	Related ↓	[147667], [147673], [147681], [147679], [147671], [147669]
Source(s)	Interview Study (cf. Section 3.2)		

Base Practice: BP_ProcO_01.04

[147683]	The software architecture shall always be reviewed.		
Related ↑	[135916]	Related ↓	-
Source(s)	Additional Recommendation; [83]		

[147685]	Changes in the product line architecture shall always be documented.		
Related ↑	[135916]	Related ↓	-
Source(s)	Additional Recommendation; [124]		

[147687]	The information about changes in the architecture shall be easy accessible for all involved parties.		
Related ↑	[135916]	Related ↓	-
Source(s)	Additional Recommendation; Workshop 1 [Appendix B.1]		

Base Practice: BP_ProcO_01.05

[136163]	The existing software product line shall not be decomposed over time.		
Related ↑	[135954]	Related ↓	[136167]
Source(s)	Interview Study (cf. Section 3.2)		

[138245]	Time frames for architecture refactoring shall be established within the process.		
Related ↑	[136257]	Related ↓	-
Source(s)	Interview Study (cf. Section 3.2)		

[135567]	The software architecture shall be open for refactoring.		
Related ↑	[135565]	Related ↓	-
Source(s)	Interview Study (cf. Section 3.2)		

[135569]	The software architecture shall be open for restructuring.		
Related ↑	[135565]	Related ↓	-
Source(s)	Interview Study (cf. Section 3.2)		

[135571]	Special time frames shall be introduced to the development process to refactor the software architecture.		
Related ↑	[136259]	Related ↓	-
Source(s)	Interview Study (cf. Section 3.2)		

Base Practice: BP_ProcO_01.06

continued on the next page

[135565]	The software architecture shall be modular and capable to insert new features.		
Related ↑	[135916]	Related ↓	[135567], [147701], [147703], [147709], [147705], [147699], [135569]
Source(s)	Interview Study (cf. Section 3.2)		

[147880]	Interfaces between software units shall be standardized.		
Related ↑	[135456]	Related ↓	-
Source(s)	Literature Review: [83]		

[136364]	Open standards shall be used when possible.		
Related ↑	[136228]	Related ↓	-
Source(s)	Interview Study (cf. Section 3.2)		

Base Practice: BP_ProcO_01.07

[135405]	Already certified software components shall be reused.		
Related ↑	[135954]	Related ↓	-
Source(s)	Interview Study (cf. Section 3.2); [27]		

[147691]	An ASIL Level shall be assigned for all features.		
Related ↑	[136279]	Related ↓	-
Source(s)	Additional Recommendation; Review Cycle 1		

[147689]	Documentation for safety relevant features shall always be created.		
Related ↑	[136279]	Related ↓	-
Source(s)	Additional Recommendation; [142]		

Base Practice: BP_ProcO_01.08

[147693]	The development shall always be up to date regarding security features.		
Related ↑	[147882]	Related ↓	-
Source(s)	Additional Recommendation; [27]		

[147695]	Security relevant features shall always be high prior and open for continuous evolution and updates.		
Related ↑	[147882]	Related ↓	-
Source(s)	Additional Recommendation; [202]		

[147697]	Documentation for security relevant features shall always be created.		
Related ↑	[147882]	Related ↓	-
Source(s)	Additional Recommendation; [142]		

Product Attribute: PA_ProdO_01.01

[135563]	The software architecture shall be capable for changes.		
Related ↑	[135920]	Related ↓	-
Source(s)	Interview Study (cf. Section 3.2)		

continued on the next page

[147699]	The software architecture shall be modular, to replace software parts without affecting other parts of the software.		
Related ↑	[135565]	Related ↓	-
Source(s)	Additional Recommendation; [228]		

Product Attribute: PA_ProdO_01.02

[147701]	Monolytic Architectures shall be resolved and replaced by modular architectures.		
Related ↑	[135565]	Related ↓	-
Source(s)	Additional Recommendation; Workshop 2 [Appendix B.2]; [86, 228]		

[147703]	The Architecture shall be capable to manage loosely coupled software units.		
Related ↑	[135565]	Related ↓	-
Source(s)	Additional Recommendation; Workshop 2 [Appendix B.2]; [228]		

Product Attribute: PA_ProdO_01.03

[147705]	The software architecture shall provide the possibility to include fast changing requirements.		
Related ↑	[135565]	Related ↓	-
Source(s)	Additional Recommendation; [202]		

[147707]	The interfaces between software parts shall be standardized.		
Related ↑	[135456]	Related ↓	-
Source(s)	Literature Review: [26]; [157]		

[147709]	The software architecture shall be capable to handle not foreseen features and changing requirements.		
Related ↑	[135565]	Related ↓	-
Source(s)	Additional Recommendation; [202]		

Product Attribute: PA_ProdO_01.04

[136182]	The software shall be capable to handle limited hardware Resource(s).		
Related ↑	[135912]	Related ↓	-
Source(s)	Literature Review: [230]		

[136180]	The software shall be capable to handle different hardware versions.		
Related ↑	[135906]	Related ↓	-
Source(s)	Additional Recommendation; Workshop 2 [Appendix B.2]		

[136184]	The software shall be adjustable to hardware restrictions.		
Related ↑	[135922]	Related ↓	-
Source(s)	Additional Recommendation; Workshop 2 [Appendix B.2]		

Recommendations for Honeycomb 2:
Domain Requirements Engineering

Table D.3: Recommendations for Domain Requirements
Engineering

Base Practice: BP_ProcO_02.01			
[136170]	Synchronization-meetings shall do scoping of common software parts.		
Related ↑	[135789]	Related ↓	-
Source(s)	Interview Study (cf. Section 3.2); [11, 180]		
[147178]	Features for different variants shall be stored in separated backlogs.		
Related ↑	[135837]	Related ↓	-
Source(s)	Interview Study (cf. Section 3.2) (cf. Section 3.2)		
[138239]	Incomplete requirements shall be completed first, before considered for implementation.		
Related ↑	[135928]	Related ↓	-
Source(s)	Interview Study (cf. Section 3.2) (cf. Section 3.2)		

Base Practice: BP_ProcO_02.02			
[147711]	Rapid changes in requirements shall be considered in the scoping meetings.		
Related ↑	[136358]	Related ↓	-
Source(s)	Interview Study (cf. Section 3.2) (cf. Section 3.2)		
[147713]	Changing requirements for features shall result in a reassignment of feature priority.		
Related ↑	[136358]	Related ↓	-
Source(s)	Additional Recommendation; [15]		

Base Practice: BP_ProcO_02.03			
[147715]	"Showstoppers" shall be addressed in an extraordinary meeting.		
Related ↑	[136358]	Related ↓	-
Source(s)	Interview Study (cf. Section 3.2)		
[147717]	"Showstoppers" shall always be addressed first.		
Related ↑	[136358]	Related ↓	-
Source(s)	Additional Recommendation; Workshop 2 [Appendix B.2]		

Base Practice: BP_ProcO_02.04			
[136165]	The low-level hierarchies shall be responsible for the software product line.		
Related ↑	[135796]	Related ↓	-
Source(s)	Interview Study (cf. Section 3.2)		

continued on the next page

[135643]	The responsibility for scoping shall be granted for lower hierarchy-levels.		
Related ↑	[136380]	Related ↓	-
Source(s)	Interview Study (cf. Section 3.2)		

[135641]	Scoping of software functionality shall be part of lower hierarchy-level.		
Related ↑	[136380]	Related ↓	-
Source(s)	Interview Study (cf. Section 3.2)		

[135347]	The developers shall granted more responsibilities.		
Related ↑	[135930]	Related ↓	-
Source(s)	Interview Study (cf. Section 3.2)		

[135338]	The hierarchy level for the approval process of new features shall not exceed three levels.		
Related ↑	[135936]	Related ↓	-
Source(s)	Interview Study (cf. Section 3.2)		

Base Practice: BP_ProcO_02.05

[135651]	Scoping shall cluster functionalities on ECU-Level.		
Related ↑	[136380]	Related ↓	-
Source(s)	Interview Study (cf. Section 3.2)		

[135645]	The scoping shall be in coordination with system-level.		
Related ↑	[136380]	Related ↓	-
Source(s)	Interview Study (cf. Section 3.2)		

[135653]	The scoping shall be in coordination with the used ECUs.		
Related ↑	[136380]	Related ↓	-
Source(s)	Interview Study (cf. Section 3.2)		

Base Practice: BP_ProcO_02.06

[135349]	Suppliers shall be included into the development process.		
Related ↑	[135804]	Related ↓	[135351], [135357]
Source(s)	Interview Study (cf. Section 3.2)		

[135357]	The legal framework shall not hinder the collaboration with a supplier.		
Related ↑	[135349]	Related ↓	[147848], [147850]
Source(s)	Interview Study (cf. Section 3.2); [72]		

[135351]	Suppliers shall participate in the synchronization meetings.		
Related ↑	[135349]	Related ↓	-
Source(s)	Interview Study (cf. Section 3.2); [221]		

Base Practice: BP_ProcO_02.07

[147719]	The similarities in desired software features shall be identified in scoping meetings.		

continued on the next page

Related ↑	[136380]	Related ↓	-
Source(s)	Interview Study (cf. Section 3.2); [11, 180]		

[147721]	A time for refactoring similar features shall be granted.		
Related ↑	[136257]	Related ↓	[147754], [147752]
Source(s)	Additional Recommendation; Workshop 2 [Appendix B.2]		

[136167]	Synchronization meetings shall avoid the software product line from decomposition.		
Related ↑	[136163]	Related ↓	-
Source(s)	Interview Study (cf. Section 3.2)		

Base Practice: BP_ProcO_02.08

[147723]	Potential reuse of software items shall be identified in scoping meetings.		
Related ↑	[136280]	Related ↓	-
Source(s)	InterviewStudy; [11, 180]		

[135456]	Feature from one subsystem shall be able to introduce to other subsystems after synchronization points.		
Related ↑	[135454]	Related ↓	[147880], [147707]
Source(s)	Interview Study (cf. Section 3.2)		

Base Practice: BP_ProcO_02.09

[147752]	Incompatible features shall be refactored to make them compatible with the baseline development.		
Related ↑	[147721]	Related ↓	-
Source(s)	Additional Recommendation; [78, 18, 128, 199]		

[147754]	Time for refactoring to make the features compatible with the software baseline development shall be granted.		
Related ↑	[147721]	Related ↓	[147766]
Source(s)	Additional Recommendation; [78, 18, 128, 199]		

Base Practice: BP_ProcO_02.10

[135510]	Different backlogs shall be implemented for different purpose.		
Related ↑	[135837]	Related ↓	[135383], [135506], [135502], [135559]
Source(s)	Interview Study (cf. Section 3.2)		

[135506]	Items in the backlogs shall be organized according the priority and severity of the item.		
Related ↑	[135510]	Related ↓	[147764], [147760], [147758], [147762]
Source(s)	Interview Study (cf. Section 3.2)		

[135383]	Bugs and ideas shall be inserted into different backlogs.		
Related ↑	[135510]	Related ↓	-

continued on the next page

Source(s)	Interview Study (cf. Section 3.2)

Base Practice: PA_ProdO_02.01

[147756]	Scoping meetings shall identify already implemented features across all software variants.
Related ↑ [136380]	Related ↓ -
Source(s)	Additional Recommendation; Workshop 2 [AppendixB.2]

Base Practice: PA_ProdO_02.02

[135502]	Safety critical software bugs shall be of highest priority.
Related ↑ [135510]	Related ↓ -
Source(s)	Interview Study (cf. Section 3.2)

Base Practice: PA_ProdO_02.03

[147758]	A priority value for software features shall be assigned.
Related ↑ [135506]	Related ↓ -
Source(s)	Interview Study (cf. Section 3.2)

[147762]	A priority value shall help to organize the backlog for development.
Related ↑ [135506]	Related ↓ -
Source(s)	Interview Study (cf. Section 3.2)

Base Practice: PA_ProdO_02.04

[147760]	A severity value for software features shall be assigned.
Related ↑ [135506]	Related ↓ -
Source(s)	Interview Study (cf. Section 3.2)

[147764]	A severity value shall help to organize the backlog for development.
Related ↑ [135506]	Related ↓ -
Source(s)	Interview Study (cf. Section 3.2)

Recommendations for Honeycomb 3:
Agile Software Development

Table D.4:　Recommendations　for　Agile　Software Development

Base Practice: BP_ProcO_03.01			
[138217]	Software releases shall be of high quality.		
Related ↑	[136240]	Related ↓	-
Source(s)	Interview Study (cf. Section 3.2)		
[138219]	Software releases shall be released in the estimated time.		
Related ↑	[136240]	Related ↓	-
Source(s)	Interview Study (cf. Section 3.2)		
[136362]	The development process shall be encouraged to release high quality software in a fast pace.		
Related ↑	[136218]	Related ↓	-
Source(s)	Interview Study (cf. Section 3.2)		
[138223]	Features with good quality shall be included into the software release as early as possible.		
Related ↑	[135908]	Related ↓	-
Source(s)	Interview Study (cf. Section 3.2)		
[136360]	The development process shall be capable to handle fast changing requirements.		
Related ↑	[136232]	Related ↓	-
Source(s)	Interview Study (cf. Section 3.2); [221]		

Base Practice: BP_ProcO_03.02			
[138215]	Customer needs shall be addressed and included in the development for specific markets.		
Related ↑	[136251]	Related ↓	[147210]
Source(s)	Interview Study (cf. Section 3.2)		
[147766]	Market specific features shall be repatriate into the software baseline.		
Related ↑	[147754]	Related ↓	-
Source(s)	Interview Study (cf. Section 3.2); Workshop 2 [Appendix B.2]		

Base Practice: BP_ProcO_03.03			
[136358]	The development process shall be capable to react on changes in the market situation.		
Related ↑	[136216]	Related ↓	[147711], [147713], [147715], [147717]

continued on the next page

Source(s)	Interview Study (cf. Section 3.2)		
[138211]	The release cycle shall be shortened to take new requirements into account.		
Related ↑	[136216]	Related ↓	-
Source(s)	Interview Study (cf. Section 3.2)		
[138213]	The development shall address market needs.		
Related ↑	[136216]	Related ↓	-
Source(s)	Interview Study (cf. Section 3.2)		
[138237]	Late requirements shall be addressed in the next sprint.		
Related ↑	[135926]	Related ↓	-
Source(s)	Interview Study (cf. Section 3.2)		

Base Practice: BP_ProcO_03.04

[135958]	The development process shall be standardized.		
Related ↑	[136255]	Related ↓	[135408], [147216]
Source(s)	Interview Study (cf. Section 3.2)		
[135573]	Documentation shall not be neglected.		
Related ↑	[135575]	Related ↓	-
Source(s)	Interview Study (cf. Section 3.2)		
[135614]	The development shall comply with international standards.		
Related ↑	[135873]	Related ↓	-
Source(s)	Interview Study (cf. Section 3.2)		

Base Practice: BP_ProcO_03.05

[136348]	Four main releases shall be released each year.		
Related ↑	[136234]	Related ↓	[135669], [138225]
Source(s)	Interview Study (cf. Section 3.2)		
[135669]	Software release cycles shall be synchronized.		
Related ↑	[136348]	Related ↓	[135440], [135442], [135444], [135446], [135448], [140554], [147199]
Source(s)	Additional Recommendation; [76, 267, 155]		
[135450]	Software release cycles shall be synchronized with winter test.		
Related ↑	[140554]	Related ↓	-
Source(s)	Additional Recommendation; Workshop 2 [Appendix B.2]		
[135440]	Software release cycles shall be synchronized with hardware development.		
Related ↑	[135669]	Related ↓	-
Source(s)	Additional Recommendation; Workshop 2 [Appendix B.2]		
[135442]	Software release cycles shall be synchronized with mechanical development.		
Related ↑	[135669]	Related ↓	-

continued on the next page

Source(s)	Additional Recommendation; Workshop 2 [Appendix B.2]		
[135444]	Software release cycles shall be synchronized with supplier development.		
Related ↑	[135669]	Related ↓	-
Source(s)	Additional Recommendation; Workshop 2 [Appendix B.2]		
[135446]	Software release cycles shall be synchronized with in-house development.		
Related ↑	[135669]	Related ↓	-
Source(s)	Additional Recommendation; Workshop 2 [Appendix B.2]		
[135448]	Software release cycles shall be synchronized with validation.		
Related ↑	[135669]	Related ↓	-
Source(s)	Additional Recommendation; Workshop 2 [Appendix B.2]		
[135452]	Software release cycles shall be synchronized with summer test.		
Related ↑	[140554]	Related ↓	-
Source(s)	Additional Recommendation; Workshop 2 [Appendix B.2]		
[147768]	Development teams shall be synchronized.		
Related ↑	[135792]	Related ↓	-
Source(s)	Additional Recommendation; [47, 221]		
[147199]	Software release cycles shall be synchronized with the maturity of the overall vehicle, such as A, B, C, D-Samples.		
Related ↑	[135669]	Related ↓	-
Source(s)	Additional Recommendation; Learning Cycle 1		
[135454]	The development of different sub-systems shall be synchronized.		
Related ↑	[135857]	Related ↓	[135456]
Source(s)	Additional Recommendation; Workshop 2 [Appendix B.2]		
[135458]	The development of different systems shall be synchronized.		
Related ↑	[135865]	Related ↓	-
Source(s)	Additional Recommendation; Workshop 2 [Appendix B.2]		
[135323]	The organization shall provide the development team the ability to synchronize the development process.		
Related ↑	[135792]	Related ↓	[135460], [135462], [136521]
Source(s)	Additional Recommendation; Workshop 2 [Appendix B.2]		
[136521]	A synchronization meeting shall be established.		
Related ↑	[135323]	Related ↓	[135315], [135325], [135327], [135329], [135332], [135334]
Source(s)	Additional Recommendation; [47, 221, 155]		
[135315]	The synchronization meetings shall be held in a regular time interval.		
Related ↑	[135315]	Related ↓	-
Source(s)	Additional Recommendation; [155]		
[138231]	The software development shall be synchronized with other departments.		

continued on the next page

Related ↑	[135861]	Related ↓	-
Source(s)	Interview study; [221, 203]		

[135325]	All stakeholders shall attend the synchronization meeting.		
Related ↑	[136521]	Related ↓	-
Source(s)	Additional Recommendation; [155]		

[135327]	The synchronization meeting should be at one location.		
Related ↑	[136521]	Related ↓	-
Source(s)	Additional Recommendation; [225]		

[135332]	The synchronization meeting shall not exceed an 8 hour meeting.		
Related ↑	[136521]	Related ↓	-
Source(s)	Additional Recommendation; [225]		

[135334]	The starting time of the synchronization meeting shall be adjusted to the involved time zones of the participating stakeholders.		
Related ↑	[136521]	Related ↓	-
Source(s)	Additional Recommendation; Workshop 2 [Appendix B.2]		

[135329]	If it is not possible to hold the synchronization meeting at one location, the organization shall provide technical solutions for distributed working.		
Related ↑	[136521]	Related ↓	-
Source(s)	Additional Recommendation; Workshop 3 [Appendix B.3]		

[135460]	Synchronization meetings provide suppliers the ability to synchronize the development with the in-house development.		
Related ↑	[135323]	Related ↓	-
Source(s)	Additional Recommendation; [155]		

[135462]	Synchronization meetings shall provide the stakeholders the possibility to adjust the development.		
Related ↑	[]	Related ↓	-
Source(s)	Additional Recommendation; [155]		

[140554]	Software release cycles shall be synchronized with automotive specific tests, such as summer and winter test.		
Related ↑	[135669]	Related ↓	[135450], [135452]
Source(s)	Interview Study (cf. Section 3.2)		

Base Practice: BP_ProcO_03.06

[135672]	The purchase department shall provide an agile payment strategy.		
Related ↑	[0135361]	Related ↓	[135363], [135365], [135367]
Source(s)	Additional Recommendation; Workshop 3 [Appendix B.3]		

[135367]	The payment strategy should be able to be changed, according to the developers team needs.		
Related ↑	[135672]	Related ↓	-

continued on the next page

Source(s)	Additional Recommendation; Workshop 2 [Appendix B.2]		
[135363]	The payment strategy shall provide the suppliers the ability to work in an agile way.		
Related ↑	[135672]	Related ↓	-
Source(s)	Additional Recommendation; Workshop 2 [Appendix B.2]		
[135365]	The payment strategy shall be adjustable.		
Related ↑	[135672]	Related ↓	-
Source(s)	Additional Recommendation; Workshop 2 [Appendix B.2]		
[136371]	The development process shall stay within set development budget.		
Related ↑	[136242]	Related ↓	-
Source(s)	Additional Recommendation; Workshop 2 [Appendix B.2]		
[135361]	The purchase department shall provide working contract arrangements for the collaboration with suppliers.		
Related ↑	[135816]	Related ↓	[135672]
Source(s)	Additional Recommendation; Workshop 2 [Appendix B.2]		

Base Practice: BP_ProcO_03.07			
[135321]	The sprint-length shall be adjustable.		
Related ↑	[136222]	Related ↓	[135319]
Source(s)	Interview Study (cf. Section 3.2)		
[135319]	The sprint length should be able to be changed, according to the developers team needs.		
Related ↑	[135321]	Related ↓	-
Source(s)	Interview Study (cf. Section 3.2)		
[135340]	New roles shall be implemented to verify a smooth agile development.		
Related ↑	[135843]	Related ↓	[135393]
Source(s)	Additional Recommendation; [20]		
[147124]	Agile methods and practices shall not stipulated.		
Related ↑	[136226]	Related ↓	-
Source(s)	Additional Recommendation; [96]		
[149157]	Employees shall be trained in agile practices and methods.		
Related ↑	[136220]	Related ↓	-
Source(s)	Additional Recommendation; Learning Cycle 1		
[149159]	Employees shall be empowered to take decisions, solve problems, and develop innovative solutions.		
Related ↑	[136220]	Related ↓	-
Source(s)	Additional Recommendation; Learning Cycle 1		

continued on the next page

[149161]	Agile coaches shall advise people to rethink and change the way they go about development.		
Related ↑	[136220]	Related ↓	-
Source(s)	Additional Recommendation; Learning Cycle 1		

Base Practice: BP_ProcO_03.08

[135575]	Software quality reviews shall be implemented.		
Related ↑	[136273]	Related ↓	[135573], [135577]
Source(s)	Additional Recommendation; Workshop 2 [Appendix B.2]; [260]		

[135577]	In-house quality standards shall be respected.		
Related ↑	[135575]	Related ↓	-
Source(s)	Additional Recommendation; Workshop 2 [Appendix B.2]		

Product Attribute: PA_ProdO_03.01

[135377]	The feedback process for customers shall be easy to use.		
Related ↑	[135373]	Related ↓	-
Source(s)	Additional Recommendation; [238]		

[135559]	The process for the end-users to report a failure in software shall be easy understandable.		
Related ↑	[135510]	Related ↓	-
Source(s)	Additional Recommendation; Workshop 1 [Appendix B.1]		

[138207]	Customer feedback shall be used to avoid the development of not accepted functionality.		
Related ↑	[136277]	Related ↓	-
Source(s)	Additional Recommendation; [238]		

[136373]	Each software release shall address a customer need.		
Related ↑	[136277]	Related ↓	-
Source(s)	Additional Recommendation; Workshop 2 [Appendix B.2]		

[138209]	A process shall be established to include customer needs into the requirements for a new release.		
Related ↑	[136277]	Related ↓	-
Source(s)	Additional Recommendation; [82, 244]		

[136187]	The customer shall benefit from faster feature development.		
Related ↑	[135908]	Related ↓	-
Source(s)	Interview Study (cf. Section 3.2)		

[135373]	The customer shall be able to give direct feedback.		
Related ↑	[136281]	Related ↓	[135371], [135377], [147852], [147856], [135385], [135391]
Source(s)	Additional Recommendation; [238]		

continued on the next page

[135371]	The development process shall provide the customer the ability to give feedback.		
Related ↑	[135373]	Related ↓	-
Source(s)	Additional Recommendation; [238]		

[135385]	A feedback platform (Web, App, in the car telematic) shall be implemented.		
Related ↑	[135373]	Related ↓	-
Source(s)	Additional Recommendation; Workshop 3 [Appendix B.3]		

[135391]	Users shall be able to rate the ideas for new software features.		
Related ↑	[135373]	Related ↓	-
Source(s)	Additional Recommendation; Workshop 2 [Appendix B.2]		

[135393]	A new role shall be introduced to handle the features from customers.		
Related ↑	[135340]	Related ↓	-
Source(s)	Additional Recommendation; Workshop 2 [Appendix B.2]		

Recommendations for Honeycomb 4: Continuous X

Table D.5: Recommendations for Continuous X

Base Practice: BP_ProcO_04.01			
[135429]	Test shall be automated.		
Related ↑	[135880]	Related ↓	[147806], [135413], [135607]
Source(s)	Interview Study (cf. Section 3.2); [221, 76, 106]		

[147796]	Feedback channels are established and automated.		
Related ↑	[135647]	Related ↓	-
Source(s)	Additional Recommendation; [106]		

Base Practice: BP_ProcO_04.02			
[135413]	Continuous Integration shall be implemented.		
Related ↑	[135429]	Related ↓	[135415], [135427]
Source(s)	Interview Study (cf. Section 3.2); [77, 136, 141, 241, 27]		

[135415]	Virtual Integration shall be implemented.		
Related ↑	[135413]	Related ↓	[135417], [135419], [135421], [135423]
Source(s)	Additional Recommendation; [63]		

[135417]	Models for different software variants and hardware versions for the virtual integration shall be provided.		
Related ↑	[135415]	Related ↓	-
Source(s)	Interview Study (cf. Section 3.2); [63, 238]		

continued on the next page

[135423]	Virtual integration shall not replace real integration into a car.		
Related ↑	[135415]	Related ↓	-
Source(s)	Additional Recommendation; Workshop 2 [Appendix B.2]		

[135427]	Continuous Integration (CI) shall be the backbone of the testing process.		
Related ↑	[135413]	Related ↓	-
Source(s)	Interview Study (cf. Section 3.2); [241, 63, 221, 243]		

Base Practice: BP_ProcO_04.03

[135609]	Software test shall be continuously executed and automated.		
Related ↑	[135880]	Related ↓	[135413]
Source(s)	Interview Study (cf. Section 3.2); [106, 139]		

[135607]	Software tests shall be automated.		
Related ↑	[135429]	Related ↓	-
Source(s)	Interview Study (cf. Section 3.2); [106]		

[135431]	Test shall be continuously executed.		
Related ↑	[135609]	Related ↓	-
Source(s)	Interview Study (cf. Section 3.2)		

[147800]	The agile project has to ensure that the process purposes of all 3 software testing processes (SWE.4, SWE.5 and SWE.6) are fulfilled by the defined activities in project Sprints.		
Related ↑	[135882]	Related ↓	-
Source(s)	[76]		

Base Practice: BP_ProcO_04.0

[147802]	Software shall be delivered to (internal) customers in a fast pace.		
Related ↑	[136240]	Related ↓	-
Source(s)	Interview Study (cf. Section 3.2)		

[147804]	An infrastructure shall be defined to distribute the software to the internal customers.		
Related ↑	[136240]	Related ↓	-
Source(s)	Additional Recommendation; Workshop 3 [Appendix B.3]		

Base Practice: BP_ProcO_04.05

[147806]	The software shall comply with regulations and tested before the software gets deployed.		
Related ↑	[135429]	Related ↓	-
Source(s)	Interview Study (cf. Section 3.2)		

[147808]	An infrastructure shall be defined to deploy the software to the end customers.		

continued on the next page

Related ↑	[136240]	Related ↓	-
Source(s)	Additional Recommendation; Workshop 3 [Appendix B.3]		

[147810]	Flash over the air shall be established (the process to deliver software to the customer and to update the software on the customers ECUs is secured and tested.)		
Related ↑	[136240]	Related ↓	-
Source(s)	Additional Recommendation; Workshop 2 [Appendix B.2]		

Base Practice: BP_ProcO_04.06

[135411]	The software shall be developed and tested to be always compliant.		
Related ↑	[135581]	Related ↓	-
Source(s)	Interview Study (cf. Section 3.2)		

Product Attribute: PA_ProdO_04.01

[147812]	An integration strategy shall be implemented that ensure that software units and software items are integrated up to a complete integrated software.		
Related ↑	[135880]	Related ↓	[147816], [147814]
Source(s)	Interview Study (cf. Section 3.2)		

[147814]	The environment for integration shall be provided, including synchronization, delivery of software units.		
Related ↑	[147812]	Related ↓	-
Source(s)	Additional Recommendation, Workshop 3 [Appendix B.3]		

[147816]	Integration servers shall be automated.		
Related ↑	[147812]	Related ↓	[147826]
Source(s)	Additional Recommendation, Workshop 3 [Appendix B.3]		

Product Attribute: PA_ProdO_04.02

[147818]	Continuous verification tasks shall be automated.		
Related ↑	[]	Related ↓	-
Source(s)	Interview Study (cf. Section 3.2); [221]		

[147820]	Software items shall be capable to undergo highly automated verification tasks.		
Related ↑	[]	Related ↓	-
Source(s)	Interview Study (cf. Section 3.2); [221]		

Recommendations for Honeycomb 5:
Continuous Model Improvement

Table D.6: Recommendations for Continuous Model Improvement

Base Practice: BP_ProcO_05.02			
[136366]	The integration of a new working model shall be iterative.		
Related ↑	[136220]	Related ↓	[136368]
Source(s)	Additional Recommendation; Workshop 3 [Appendix B.3], [147, 222]		
[136368]	The employees shall granted enough time to get familiar with the new way of working.		
Related ↑	[136366]	Related ↓	-
Source(s)	Additional Recommendation; Workshop 3 [Appendix B.3], [147]		

Recommendations for Honeycomb 6:
Test Strategy

Table D.7: Recommendations for Test Strategy

Base Practice: BP_ProcO_06.01			
[135581]	The software shall always be tested.		
Related ↑	[135882]	Related ↓	[135411], [135603]
Source(s)	Interview Study (cf. Section 3.2)		
[135676]	A test strategy shall be implemented.		
Related ↑	[135859]	Related ↓	[135583], [135589], [147912], [135591]
Source(s)	Interview Study (cf. Section 3.2)		
[136142]	The test strategy shall fulfill the requirements of ISO 26262.		
Related ↑	[135875]	Related ↓	-
Source(s)	Interview Study (cf. Section 3.2)		
[138233]	All software variants should be tested.		
Related ↑	[135934]	Related ↓	-
Source(s)	Literature Review: [171]		

Base Practice: BP_ProcO_06.02			
[135591]	The test strategy shall be adjustable to available time.		
Related ↑	[135676]	Related ↓	[135593], [135595]
Source(s)	Additional Recommendation; Workshop 4 [Appendix B.4]		

continued on the next page

[135593]	The selection of tests cases shall use the maximum available time.		
Related ↑	[135591]	Related ↓	-
Source(s)	Additional Recommendation; Workshop 4 [Appendix B.4]		

Base Practice: BP_ProcO_06.03

[135583]	The test strategy shall be scalable to different test-levels.		
Related ↑	[135676]	Related ↓	[135585]
Source(s)	Interview Study (cf. Section 3.2); [204, 221]		

[135589]	The test strategy shall be adjusted to selected software variants.		
Related ↑	[135676]	Related ↓	-
Source(s)	Additional Recommendation; [171]		

[135587]	Test strategy shall be capable to handle different software variants.		
Related ↑	[135932]	Related ↓	-
Source(s)	Interview Study (cf. Section 3.2)		

[135599]	Test cases shall be variant specific.		
Related ↑	[136178]	Related ↓	-
Source(s)	Interview Study (cf. Section 3.2)		

[135605]	Test strategy shall be scalable for different software variants.		
Related ↑	[135605]	Related ↓	-
Source(s)	Additional Recommendation; [171]		

[135433]	Test equipment shall be scalable for different versions.		
Related ↑	[136255]	Related ↓	-
Source(s)	Additional Recommendation; Workshop 4 [Appendix B.4]		

[135435]	Test equipment shall be at a reasonable price.		
Related ↑	[136255]	Related ↓	-
Source(s)	Additional Recommendation; Workshop 4 [Appendix B.4]		

[138225]	Two software releases should be integrated into real cars.		
Related ↑	[136348]	Related ↓	-
Source(s)	Interview Study (cf. Section 3.2)		

Base Practice: BP_ProcO_06.04

[135603]	Each test case shall provide a priority.		
Related ↑	[135581]	Related ↓	-
Source(s)	Additional Recommendation; Workshop 4 [Appendix B.4]		

[135597]	The test strategy shall be adjustable to safety requirements.		
Related ↑	[135875]	Related ↓	-
Source(s)	Additional Recommendation; Workshop 4 [Appendix B.4]		

[135595]	Each test case shall provide the maximum runtime for the test case.		

continued on the next page

Related ↑	[135591]	Related ↓	-
Source(s)	Additional Recommendation; Workshop 4 [Appendix B.4]		

[147912]	The test case selection shall be automated.		
Related ↑	[135676]	Related ↓	[147832], [147834], [147836]
Source(s)	Additional Recommendation; [148, 204]		

[135601]	Test cases that verify safety regulations shall be prioritized.		
Related ↑	[136279]	Related ↓	-
Source(s)	Additional Recommendation; Workshop 4 [Appendix B.4]		

Base Practice: BP_ProcO_06.05

[147822]	A trace from software units to test cases shall be defined.		
Related ↑	[147681]	Related ↓	-
Source(s)	Additional Recommendation; [27]		

[147824]	A trace from test cases to test results shall be established.		
Related ↑	[147681]	Related ↓	-
Source(s)	Additional Recommendation; [27]		

Base Practice: BP_ProcO_06.06

[147826]	Software integration test shall be summarized and communicated to all affected parties.		
Related ↑	[147816]	Related ↓	-
Source(s)	Additional Recommendation; Workshop 1 [Appendix B.1]		

[147830]	The possibility to communicate the test results shall be established.		
Related ↑	[135647]	Related ↓	-
Source(s)	Additional Recommendation; Workshop 1 [Appendix B.1]		

Product Attribute: PA_ProdO_06.01

[135585]	The applied test-level shall be defined by the development team.		
Related ↑	[135583]	Related ↓	-
Source(s)	Additional Recommendation; Workshop 2 [Appendix B.2]		

[147832]	Every software unit shall have an associated test case.		
Related ↑	[147912]	Related ↓	-
Source(s)	Additional Recommendation; Workshop 4 [Appendix B.4]		

[147834]	Each test case shall describe in detail all necessary test steps.		
Related ↑	[147912]	Related ↓	-
Source(s)	Additional Recommendation; Workshop 4 [Appendix B.4]		

[147836]	Each test case shall provide meta data, such as runtime or hardware requirements to run the test case.		
Related ↑	[147912]	Related ↓	-

continued on the next page

Source(s)	Additional Recommendation; Workshop 4 [Appendix B.4]

Recommendations for Honeycomb 7: Communication

Table D.8: Recommendations for Communication

Base Practice: BP_ProcO_07.01			
[138243]	Meetings shall be aware of different time-zones of the participants.		
Related ↑	[135822]	Related ↓	-
Source(s)	Interview Study (cf. Section 3.2)		

Base Practice: BP_ProcO_07.02			
[138247]	The "OneRoom" Principle shall be exploited.		
Related ↑	[135824]	Related ↓	-
Source(s)	Additional Recommendation; Workshop 1 [Appendix B.1], [139, 72]		
[135647]	Communication channels shall be established.		
Related ↑	[135835]	Related ↓	[147838], [135611], [147830], [147796]
Source(s)	Additional Recommendation; Workshop 1 [Appendix B.1]		
[135355]	Suppliers should be collocated to the development team.		
Related ↑	[135814]	Related ↓	-
Source(s)	Interview Study (cf. Section 3.2)		
[135399]	The common language in development shall be English.		
Related ↑	[135826]	Related ↓	-
Source(s)	Interview Study (cf. Section 3.2)		
[147838]	Good collaboration shall be established and knowledge silos shall be resolved.		
Related ↑	[135647]	Related ↓	[147842]
Source(s)	Additional Recommendation; Workshop 1 [Appendix B.1]; [203]		

Base Practice: BP_ProcO_07.03			
[135611]	Feedback channel for developer from automated tests shall be implemented.		
Related ↑	[135647]	Related ↓	-
Source(s)	Interview Study (cf. Section 3.2)		
[147840]	Customer feedback shall be included into the development.		
Related ↑	[136281]	Related ↓	-
Source(s)	Interview Study (cf. Section 3.2)		

continued on the next page

Base Practice: BP_ProcO_07.04

[138249]	Managers and higher Management Levels shall receive a summary about the next sprint.		
Related ↑	[135849]	Related ↓	[138253]
Source(s)	Additional Recommendation; Workshop 2 [Appendix B.2]		

[138253]	The sprint summary shall be an output of the sprint planning meeting.		
Related ↑	[138249]	Related ↓	-
Source(s)	Additional Recommendation; Workshop 2 [Appendix B.2]		

[138251]	Managers and higher Management Levels shall grant access to the backlogs.		
Related ↑	[135849]	Related ↓	-
Source(s)	Additional Recommendation; Workshop 2 [Appendix B.2]		

[147842]	The process and progress shall be visible to all participants.		
Related ↑	[147838]	Related ↓	-
Source(s)	Additional Recommendation; [214, 227]		

Base Practice: BP_ProcO_07.05

[135649]	Communication channel for scoping shall be established.		
Related ↑	[135830]	Related ↓	-
Source(s)	Interview Study (cf. Section 3.2)		

[147844]	The identification of impediments, dependencies, incompatibilities and similarities of software features shall be a task for the organization as a whole.		
Related ↑	[135794]	Related ↓	[147846]
Source(s)	Additional Recommendation; Workshop 3 [Appendix B.3]		

Base Practice: BP_ProcO_07.0

[136172]	Every team member shall respect the other members in the team.		
Related ↑	[135808]	Related ↓	-
Source(s)	Additional Recommendation; Workshop 1 [Appendix B.1]		

[136174]	Inter-cultural sensitization within the team shall be established.		
Related ↑	[135810]	Related ↓	[136176]
Source(s)	Additional Recommendation; Workshop 3 [Appendix B.3]		

[136176]	Inter-cultural sensitization training shall be offered.		
Related ↑	[136174]	Related ↓	-
Source(s)	Additional Recommendation; Workshop 3 [Appendix B.3]		

Base Practice: BP_ProcO_07.07

[138241]	Synchronization meetings shall be established.		
Related ↑	[138241]	Related ↓	-

continued on the next page

Source(s)	Additional Recommendation; Workshop 2 [Appendix B.2], [47, 221, 155]

[147846]	All involved parties shall be participating actively in the development process.
Related ↑	[147844] Related ↓ -
Source(s)	Additional Recommendation; Workshop 2 [Appendix B.2]

Base Practice: BP_ProcO_07.08

[147848]	The supplier shall be included in to the development process.
Related ↑	[135357] Related ↓ -
Source(s)	Additional Recommendation; [72]

[147850]	The collaboration with the suppliers shall be an open-minded collaboration.
Related ↑	[135357] Related ↓ -
Source(s)	Additional Recommendation; [72]

Base Practice: BP_ProcO_07.09

[147852]	Direct customer feedback into the development process shall be established.
Related ↑	[135373] Related ↓ [147854]
Source(s)	Additional Recommendation; [82, 244, 221, 243]

Base Practice: BP_ProcO_07.10

[147854]	Customer ideas shall be considered.
Related ↑	[147852] Related ↓ -
Source(s)	Additional Recommendation; [82]

[147856]	The customer shall get the possibility to provide ideas and report problems directly.
Related ↑	[135373] Related ↓ -
Source(s)	Additional Recommendation; Workshop 2 [Appendix B.2]

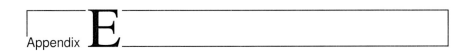

The ASPLA Model

E.1 Honeycomb 1: Product Line Architecture

Table E.1: Product Line Architecture (HC 1)

Purpose:
The purpose of *Product Line Architecture* is to provide a suitable software architecture to enable the implementation of several software variants for different products with a high degree of software reuse.
Process Related Outcomes:
[ProcO_01.01]: A software product line architecture is defined that enables the development of various software variants for different products.
[ProcO_01.02]: The software product line architecture supports a distributed development.
[ProcO_01.03]: The consistency and bidirectional traceability between software requirements, software units and software architecture is supported by a tool chain.
[ProcO_01.04]: The software architecture is agreed and communicated to all affected parties.
[ProcO_01.05]: Time frames to refactor the software architecture are granted on demand within the development process.
[ProcO_01.06]: Standardized interfaces for software units are defined.
[ProcO_01.07]: The software architecture is compliant with safety regulations.
[ProcO_01.08]: The software architecture is compliant with security regulations.
Product Related Outcomes:
[ProdO_01.01]: A high modularity of software components is achieved.
[ProdO_01.02]: The software architecture is open to changes, refactoring is possible.
[ProdO_01.03]: Fast changes in requirements are supported by the software architecture.

continued on the next page

[ProdO_01.04]: Hardware restrictions and limited hardware resources are addressed by the software architecture.

Base Practices:

BP_ProcO_01.01: Define a software product line architecture. Ensure that a software product line is used for development and that the software product line architecture is able to generate various software variants for different products and different markets. *[ProcO_01.01]*

BP_ProcO_01.02: Use only one global software product line. Ensure that only one software product line is used for the worldwide distributed development of a product. *[ProcO_01.02]*

BP_ProcO_01.03: Manage the software product line by means of suitable tools. Ensure traceability and consistency between software requirements, software units and the software architecture by means of suitable tools. *[ProcO_01.03]*

BP_ProcO_01.04: Distribute software product line architecture. Ensure that the worldwide software product line is efficient. Decisions on the software product line architecture are reviewed before they are distributed. Ensure that all involved parties receive the information. *[ProcO_01.04]*

BP_ProcO_01.05: Grant refactoring time. Ensure that additional time frames are provided to conduct the refactoring of the architecture. *[ProcO_01.05]*

BP_ProcO_01.06: Define a standardized interface between software units. Ensure that interfaces are standardized to enable the development to replace software parts easily. *[ProcO_01.06]*

BP_ProcO_01.07: Analyze and consider safety regulations. Ensure that safety regulations are addressed in the software architecture. Ensure that development decisions, addressing the safety regulations are documented to retain the traceability and consistency between software requirements, software units and the software architecture. *[ProcO_01.07]*

BP_ProcO_01.08: Analyze and consider security regulations Ensure that security regulations are addressed in the software architecture. Ensure that development decisions, addressing the security regulations are documented to retain the traceability and consistency between software requirements, software units and the software architecture. *[ProcO_01.08]*

Product Attributes:

PA_ProdO_01.01: The software architecture shall be modular. Ensure that parts of the software can be replaced or reused without affecting other parts of the software, by means of loosely coupling between software units. *[ProdO_01.01]*

PA_ProdO_01.02: The software architecture shall be open to change. Ensure that the software architecture is not a monolithic architecture, by means of a modular architecture structure that is capable to manage loosely coupled software units. *[ProdO_01.02]*

continued on the next page

PA_ProdO_01.03: The software architecture shall provide the possibility to include fast changing requirements. Ensure that the architecture of the software can deal with fast changing requirements, by means of standardized interfaces between software units and a modular architecture. *[ProdO_01.03]*

PA_ProdO_01.04: The software architecture shall be hardware independent. Ensure that the software managed by software product line is working on various hardware versions and that the selected architecture is independent from the selected hardware, by means of a scalable architecture according to the hardware. *[ProdO_01.04]*

Work Products
A_04-02 *Domain Architecture* → [ProcO_01.01]
A_04-04 *Software Architectural Design* → [ProcO_01.01] [ProcO_01.06] [ProdO_01.02] [ProdO_01.03] [ProdO_01.04]
A_04-06 *System Architectural Design* → [ProcO_01.06] [ProdO_01.02] [ProdO_01.04]
A_07-05 *Project Measure* → [ProcO_01.07] [ProcO_01.08]
A_08-17 *Reuse Plan* → [ProcO_01.01] [ProcO_01.02] [ProcO_01.04] [ProdO_01.01]
A_11-05 *Software Unit* → [ProcO_01.04] [ProcO_01.06]
A_13-04 *Communication Record* → [ProcO_01.04]
A_13-22 *Traceability Record* → [ProcO_01.03]
A_14-01 *Change History* → [ProcO_01.03]
A_15-01 *Analysis Report* → [ProcO_01.07] [ProcO_01.08]
A_17-08 *Interface Requirements Specification* → [ProcO_01.06] [ProdO_01.01]
A_19-05 *Reuse Strategy* → [ProcO_01.01] [ProcO_01.02] [ProcO_01.05]

E.2 Honeycomb 2: Domain Requirements Engineering

Table E.2: Domain Requirements Engineering (HC 2)

Purpose:
The purpose of *Domain Requirements Engineering* is to identify the reuse assets that should be developed in a software product line. This includes the identification of products and features that should be part of the product line and the definition of common and variable features.
Process Related Outcomes:
[ProcO_02.01]: An adequate scoping process is established.
[ProcO_02.02]: Rapid changes in requirements are considered and handled by the scoping process.
[ProcO_02.03]: Critical errors of high priority are handled in a privileged way by the scoping process.

continued on the next page

[ProcO_02.04]: Critical but feasible and noncritical features are scoped in a faster pace.

[ProcO_02.05]: Software requirements are assigned to software units in the scoping process.

[ProcO_02.06]: Software parts that are procured from suppliers are identified in the scoping process.

[ProcO_02.07]: Similarities of software features are identified in the scoping process.

[ProcO_02.08]: Common software parts for different products are identified.

[ProcO_02.09]: Incompatibilities between software features are revealed.

[ProcO_02.10]: Features are prioritized and assigned to (market-) specific products.

Product Related Outcomes:

[ProdO_02.01]: A high amount of reusable software elements is achieved.

[ProdO_02.02]: Results and decisions resulting from scoping meetings are stored in backlogs.

[ProdO_02.03]: A priority level is assigned to features.

[ProdO_02.04]: A severity level is assigned to features.

Base Practices:

BP_ProcO_02.01: Set up a scoping meeting. Ensure that scoping meetings are implemented. They are implemented in a recurrent and defined timeframe to prioritize and categorize new required software parts. In the scoping meetings, it is determined, if the feature is part for the common baseline or a product/market specific feature. *[ProcO_02.01]*

BP_ProcO_02.02: Consider rapid changes in requirements in scoping meetings. Ensure that rapid changes in requirements are considered in the scoping meetings each time, even if the original feature was already assigned and prioritized for the development. *[ProcO_02.02]*

BP_ProcO_02.03: Allow situational extraordinary scoping meetings. Ensure that important and necessary features, which could become showstoppers, are scoped in extraordinary scoping meetings and the backlog is adjusted accordingly. *[ProcO_02.03]*

BP_ProcO_02.04: Permit low hierarchy levels to scope features. Ensure that scoping can be conducted on low hierarchy levels and results are published to all involved parties. *[ProcO_02.04]*

BP_ProcO_02.05: Assign required new functionality to the software units. Ensure that required functionality is developed in the most suitable software units and prevent unnecessary double implementation of new functionality. *[ProcO_02.05]*

BP_ProcO_02.06: Identify software units which are supplied and implemented by the supplier. Ensure the identification of software units which is procured by suppliers. *[ProcO_02.06]*

continued on the next page

BP_ProcO_02.07: Identify similarities of desired software features. Ensure that a twofold development of one feature is avoided and grant a time for refactoring to make the similar features compatible with the software baseline development. *[ProcO_02.07]*

BP_ProcO_02.08: Identify software units for potential reuse. Ensure the application of the reuse strategy. *[ProcO_02.08]*

BP_ProcO_02.09: Identify incompatible desired software features. Ensure that incompatible features are resolved and grant a time for refactoring to make the features compatible with the software baseline development. *[ProcO_02.09]*

BP_ProcO_02.10: Prioritize required new software parts. Ensure that for every feature a priority is assigned and a market-specific backlog is defined for the implementation in the next increment. *[ProcO_02.10]*

Product Attributes:

PA_ProcO_02.01: Reusable software units shall be defined. Ensure that software parts which can be reused are identified and required new functionality is first checked against existing functionality to ascertain that the functionality is not implemented already in another software variant, by means of scoping meetings. *[ProdO_02.01]*

PA_ProcO_02.02: New software units shall be prioritized before implementation. Ensure that a priority value is assigned to each feature which identifies the priority for the implementation in the next increment, by means of an ordered list within a backlog. *[ProdO_02.02]*

PA_ProcO_02.03: A priority value for software features shall be assigned. Ensure that the features are rated and a priority value is assigned, by means of assigning the priority value in the requirement specification of the feature. *[ProdO_02.03]*

PA_ProcO_02.04: A severity value for the software feature shall be assigned. Ensure that the features are rated and a severity value is assigned, by means of assigning the severity value in the requirement specification of the feature. *[ProdO_02.04]*

Work Products:

A_02-01 *Commitment/Agreement* → [ProcO_02.06]
A_04-02 *Domain Architecture* → [ProcO_02.05][ProcO_02.06]
A_04-03 *Domain Model* → [ProcO_02.01]
A_04-04 *Software Architectural Design* → [ProcO_02.07] [ProcO_02.08] [ProcO_02.09] [ProcO_02.10]
A_04-06 *System Architectural Design* → [ProcO_02.05]
A_08-12 *Project Plan* → [ProcO_02.01], [ProcO_02.10] [ProdO_02.02]
A_08-17 *Reuse Plan* → [ProdO_02.01] [ProcO_02.08] [ProcO_02.10]
A_08-28 *Change Management Plan* → [ProcO_02.02]
A_09-03 *Reuse Policy* → [ProcO_02.01] [ProcO_02.08] [ProdO_02.01]
A_11-04 *Product Release Package* → [ProdO_02.02]
A_13-04 *Communication Record* → [ProcO_02.01]

continued on the next page

A_13-08 *Baseline* → [ProdO_02.02]
A_13-16 *Change Request* → [ProcO_02.02]
A_14-09 *Work Breakdown Structure* → [ProcO_02.07] [ProcO_02.08] [ProcO_02.09]
A_15-01 *Analysis Report* → [ProdO_02.03] [ProdO_02.04]
A_15-07 *Reuse Evaluation Report* → [ProcO_02.01] [ProdO_02.01]
A_17-03 *Stakeholder Requirement* → [ProcO_02.05]
A_19-05 *Reuse Strategy* → [ProdO_02.01] [ProcO_02.08]

E.3   Honeycomb 3: Agile Software Development

Table E.3: Agile Software Development (HC 3)

Purpose:
The purpose of *Agile Software Development* is to react faster on customer needs and legal constraints to reduce the time to market for innovative feature upon a simultaneous increase of software quality.
Process Related Outcomes:
[ProcO_03.01]: Features are developed in a faster pace and the time to market is reduced upon a simultaneous increase of software quality.
[ProcO_03.02]: Products and features are released as early as possible and the cost of delay for new product and market specific features is reduced.
[ProcO_03.03]: Changes in requirements are included into the development process and are taken into account.
[ProcO_03.04]: Legal constraints are fulfilled by the development process.
[ProcO_03.05]: The agile software development is synchronized with all affected parties.
[ProcO_03.06]: Outsourced agile software development is funded according to the development task.
[ProcO_03.07]: The use of agile practices is not stipulated, context-specific agile practices are used.
[ProcO_03.08]: Knowledge is transferred to other variants in the SPL by retrospectives.
Product Related Outcomes:
[ProdO_03.01]: The software satisfies customer needs and the customer is directly included into the development.
Base Practices:

continued on the next page

BP_ProcO_03.01: **Reduce time to market with a faster feature development.** Ensure that the time from initial idea to first release and time to market is reduced. Further, ensure that the decrease of development time does not result in a decreased software quality. *[ProcO_03.01]*

BP_ProcO_03.02: **Release product and market specific features early.** Ensure that features for specific markets and products are released early and get afterwards repatriate in the software product line. *[ProcO_03.02]*

BP_ProcO_03.03: React on changes during the development. Ensure that late changes in requirements are addressed in an acceptable time. *[ProcO_03.03]*

BP_ProcO_03.04: **Analyze and consider constrains given by the law.** Ensure that legal constraints are fulfilled and required artefacts are created. *[ProcO_03.04]*

BP_ProcO_03.05: Synchronize the agile development with the surrounding processes. Ensure that agile development is synchronized with all affected parties. *[ProcO_03.05]*

BP_ProcO_03.06: Focus on business value. Ensure that agile development is in budget, creates business value and new terms of supplier payments are introduced. *[ProcO_03.06]*

BP_ProcO_03.07: Utilize agile practices whenever applicable. Ensure agile practices are suited for the context they are practiced. *[ProcO_03.07]*

BP_ProcO_03.08: Implement retrospectives and feedback culture. Ensure that knowledge gained in a retrospective of one software variant is transferred to all other software variants. *[ProcO_03.08]*

Product Attributes:

PA_ProdO_03.01: The development shall focus on customer needs. Ensure that customer feedback is integrated into the development of the product, by means of close customer collaboration. *[ProdO_03.01]*

Work Products

A_01-03 *Software item* → [ProcO_03.01]

A_02-01 *Commitment/Agreement* → [ProcO_03.06]

A_03-04 *Customer Satisfaction Data* → [ProdO_03.01]

A_07-01 *Customer Satisfaction Survey* → [ProdO_03.01]

A_07-02 *Field Measure* → [ProdO_03.01]

A_07-05 *Project Measure* → [ProcO_03.07] [ProcO_03.08]

A_08-12 *Project Plan* → [ProcO_03.07]

A_08-28 *Change Management Plan* → [ProcO_03.03]

A_11-05 *Software Unit* → [ProcO_03.05]

A_13-01 *Acceptance Record* → [ProcO_03.07] [ProcO_03.04]

A_13-04 *Communication Record* → [ProcO_03.07] [ProcO_03.08]

A_13-08 *Baseline* → [ProcO_03.07] [ProcO_03.04]

continued on the next page

A_13-17 *Customer Request* → [ProdO_03.01]
A_17-05 *Documentation Requirements* → [ProcO_03.04]

E.4　Honeycomb 4: Continuous X

Table E.4: Continuous X (HC 4)

Purpose:
The purpose of *Continuous X* is to continuously execute tasks which lead to a more stable, compliant and better product.
Process Related Outcomes:
[ProcO_04.01]: The software development process is supported by continuous and automated tasks.
[ProcO_04.02]: Continuous integration is applied and failures in integration are identified earlier in the development process.
[ProcO_04.03]: Continuous software tests are applied and failures in the software are identified earlier in the development process.
[ProcO_04.04]: Continuous delivery to internal customers is applied and supported by the development process.
[ProcO_04.05]: Continuous deployment on real cars is applied and supported by the development process.
[ProcO_04.06]: The software development process ensures that legal constraints are abide by verifying continuous compliance.
Product Related Outcomes:
[ProdO_04.01]: Software units and software items are integrated up to a complete integrated software according to the integration strategy.
[ProdO_04.02]: Software items provide the opportunity to perform verification activities with a high level of automation in regular time intervals.
Base Practices:
BP_ProcO_04.01: Implement supporting tasks. Ensure that supporting and repetitive tasks are included in the development process and an automated feedback is provided. *[ProcO_04.01]*
BP_ProcO_04.02: Set up continuous integration. Ensure that software failures in all software variants are identified in the integration phases due to the use of timed and automated continuous integration. *[ProcO_04.02]*
BP_ProcO_04.03: Apply continuous tests for software. Ensure that software failures are identified by timed and automated software tests. *[ProcO_04.03]*
BP_ProcO_04.04: Set up continuous delivery. Ensure that software is delivered to (internal) customers in a fast pace and the infrastructure to deliver the software is available. *[ProcO_04.03]*

continued on the next page

BP_ProcO_04.05: Set up continuous deployment. Ensure that software is deployable (regarding all legal constraints) to the field and the infrastructure to deploy the software is available. *[ProcO_04.05]*

BP_ProcO_04.06: Set up continuous compliance. Ensure that each software release is (potentially) compliant. *[ProcO_04.06]*

Product Attributes:

PA_ProdO_04.01: An integration strategy shall be implemented. Ensure that software units and software items are integrated up to a complete integrated software according to the integration strategy, by means of integration server and virtual integration. *[ProdO_04.01]*

PA_ProdO_04.02: Continuous verification tasks shall be automated. Ensure that the software units are tested for compliance, by means of software items which are capable to undergo highly automated verification tasks. *[ProdO_04.02]*

Work Products

A_01-03 *Software Item* → [ProdO_04.01]

A_01-50 *Integrated Software Item* → [ProdO_04.01]

A_01-51 *Configuration Datasets* → [ProdO_04.01]

A_08-13 *Quality Plan* → [ProcO_04.02] [ProcO_04.03] [ProcO_04.06]

A_08-28 *Change Management Plan* → [ProdO_04.02]

A_08-50 *Test Specification* → [ProcO_04.02] [ProcO_04.03] [ProdO_04.01]

A_08-52 *Test Plan* → [ProcO_04.02] [ProcO_04.03]

A_11-04 *Product Release Package* → [ProcO_04.04] [ProcO_04.05]

A_13-50 *Test Results* → [ProcO_04.01]

A_17-02 *Build List* → [ProcO_04.02]

A_17-50 *Verification Criteria* → [ProdO_04.02]

A_18-07 *Quality Criteria* → [ProcO_04.03]

A_19-10 *Verification Strategy* → [ProcO_04.06] [ProdO_04.02]

A_19-11 *Validation Strategy* → [ProcO_04.02] [ProcO_04.03]

E.5 Honeycomb 5: Continuous Model Improvement

Table E.5: Continuous Model Improvement (HC 5)

Purpose:
The purpose of the *Continuous Model Improvement* is to continuously reflect on the ASPLA Model and improve the interaction between the assessment result and the suggested improvement for the software development process.
Process Related Outcomes:
[ProcO_05.01]: Suggestions to improve the software development process are proposed by the ASPLA Model.
[ProcO_05.02]: The efficiency of the development process is continuously evaluated.
[ProcO_05.03]: Best practices from the software development process are reduced into the ASPLA Model.
[ProcO_05.04]: The ASPLA Model is reviewed in a regular time frame.
Product Related Outcomes:
<not applicable>
Base Practices:
BP_ProcO_05.01: Propose suggestion to improve the development process. Ensure that suggestions are available according to the evaluation and assessment result given by the ASPLA Model. *[ProcO_05.01]*
BP_ProcO_05.02: Monitor development efficiency. Ensure that metrics are selected to measure the efficiency and the implications on the process when suggestions for improvement are introduced. *[ProcO_05.02]*
BP_ProcO_05.03: Reduce Best Practices. Ensure that best practices from efficient software development processes are reduced into the suggestions given by the ASPLA Model if they are not included so far. *[ProcO_05.03]*
BP_ProcO_05.04: Review the ASPLA Model. Ensure that the ASPLA Model is reviewed in a defined timeframe. *[ProcO_05.04]*
Product Attributes:
<not applicable>
Work Products
A_03-03 *Benchmarking Data* → [ProcO_05.02]
A_03-06 *Process Performance Data* → [ProcO_05.02]
A_07-04 *Process Measure* → [ProcO_05.02]
A_08-13 *Quality Plan* → [ProcO_05.04]
A_08-29 *Improvement Plan* → [ProcO_05.01] [ProcO_05.03] [ProcO_05.04]
A_13-18 *Quality Record* → [ProcO_05.02]
A_15-13 *Assessment/Audit Report* → [ProcO_05.01] [ProcO_05.04]
A_15-16 *Improvement Opportunity* → [ProcO_05.02] [ProcO_05.03]

continued on the next page

A_18-07 *Quality Criteria* → [ProcO_05.02]

E.6 Honeycomb 6: Test Strategy

Table E.6: Test Strategy (HC 6)

Purpose:
The purpose of the *Test Strategy* is to provide an environment to verify the correct behavior and ensure the software quality for various software variants which are developed at a fast pace.
Process Related Outcomes:
[ProcO_06.01]: The requirements coverage for the products and the software variants is ensured by the test strategy within the testing process and legal requirements are fulfilled.
[ProcO_06.02]: The test strategy ensures that failures and bugs in the software units are identified as soon as possible in the development process.
[ProcO_06.03]: A scalable test strategy for different test hierarchies, including software variants, systems and real cars is realized.
[ProcO_06.04]: The individual priority of test cases is determined in a regular time period by the test strategy and suitable test cases are automatically executed.
[ProcO_06.05]: Consistency and bidirectional traceability is established between the software units, the test cases and the test results.
[ProcO_06.06]: Results of the software tests are summarized and communicated to all affected parties.
Product Related Outcomes:
[ProdO_06.01]: For each software unit an associated test case is assigned.
Base Practices:
BP_ProcO_06.01: Set up an appropriate test strategy. Ensure that a sufficient test coverage for all products and software variants is achieved to fulfill legal requirements. *[ProcO_06.01]*
BP_ProcO_06.02: Set up an adaptive test strategy. Ensure that always the best fitting test cases for one software variant are executed at the beginning of a test, as these foster a rapid error detection. *[ProcO_06.02]*
BP_ProcO_06.03: Implement a scalable test strategy. Ensure that the test strategy covers tests for individual software variants as well as tests in the entire systems and in real cars. *[ProcO_06.03]*
BP_ProcO_06.04: Assign test case priority and run suitable tests cases. Ensure that high prior test cases, such as safety related test cases, are automatically selected and executed. *[ProcO_06.04]*

continued on the next page

BP_ProcO_06.05: Maintain traceability. Ensure that a consistent and bidirectional traceability is established between the software units, the test cases and between test cases and test results. *[ProcO_06.05]*

BP_ProcO_06.06: Document test results. Ensure that results of the software integration test are summarized and communicated to all affected parties. [ProcO_06.06]

Product Attributes:

PA_ProdO_06.01: A test case shall be implemented for each software unit. Ensure that all software units, especially critical software units, do have an associated test case, which consists of all test steps in order to be compliant with law, by means of a traceable 1-to-1 mapping between the test cases and the software units. *[ProdO_06.01]*

Work Products

A_08-04 *Configuration Management Plan* → [ProcO_06.05]

A_08-13 *Quality Plan* → [ProcO_06.01] [ProdO_06.01] [ProcO_06.05]

A_08-50 *Test Specification* → [ProcO_06.03] [ProcO_06.04] [ProcO_06.05] [ProcO_06.06] [ProdO_06.01]

A_08-52 *Test Plan* → [ProcO_06.01] [ProcO_06.02] [ProcO_06.03] [ProcO_06.04] [ProcO_06.05] [ProcO_06.06] [ProdO_06.01]

A_11-05 *Software Unit* → [ProdO_06.01]

A_13-04 *Communication Record* → [ProcO_06.05] [ProcO_06.06]

A_13-18 *Quality Record* → [ProcO_06.06]

A_13-22 *Traceability Record* → [ProcO_06.05]

A_13-50 *Test Results* → [ProcO_06.03] [ProcO_06.04] [ProcO_06.06]

A_17-50 *Verification Criteria* → [ProdO_06.01]

A_19-10 *Verification Strategy* → [ProdO_06.01] [ProcO_06.01] [ProcO_06.02] [ProcO_06.03]

A_19-11 *Validation Strategy* → [ProdO_06.01] [ProcO_06.01] [ProcO_06.02] [ProcO_06.03]

E.7 Honeycomb 7: Communication

Table E.7: Communication (HC 7)

Purpose:
The purpose of *Communication* is to support the communication of all participating roles to avoid knowledge silos and react on customer needs in a flexible way.
Process Related Outcomes:
[ProcO_07.01]: All involved parties are participate in the development process directly.
[ProcO_07.02]: Knowledge silos are destructed.
[ProcO_07.03]: Fast feedback channels for faster learning loops are established.
[ProcO_07.04]: The progress of the development is made visible.
[ProcO_07.05]: All involved parties are brought together as good as possible
[ProcO_07.06]: Direct communication channels are established.
[ProcO_07.07]: Vertical commitment in the company is established.
[ProcO_07.08]: Collaboration with supplier is improved.
[ProcO_07.09]: Direct communication with the customer is enhanced.
[ProcO_07.10]: Customer feedback is accessed for new features and ideas.
Product Related Outcomes:
<not applicable>
Base Practices:
BP_ProcO_07.01: Involve all parties affected by the development. Ensure that all involved parties are involved directly in the development process. *[ProcO_07.01]*
BP_ProcO_07.02: Break down knowledge silos. Ensure that the development process is transparent for every participant to avoid knowledge silos. *[ProcO_07.02]*
BP_ProcO_07.03: Establish fast feedback loops. Ensure that fast feedback loops are established to provide a faster learning loop. This includes automatic generated feedback from test systems, feedback from customer, and feedback from all affected parties. *[ProcO_07.03]*
BP_ProcO_07.04: Visualize the process. Ensure that the process and the development progress is visible and easy accessible for all involved parties. *[ProcO_07.04]*
BP_ProcO_07.05: Develop a common understanding for the SPL. Ensure that all affected parties be aware of the development within the software product line. All affected parties are mutually responsible to identify impediments, dependencies, incompatibilities and similarities of software features. *[ProcO_07.05]*

continued on the next page

BP_ProcO_07.06: Overcome hierarchies. Ensure that the communication is not blocked by the hierarchy and every participant can speak to every other directly. *[ProcO_07.06]*

BP_ProcO_07.07: Establish a vertical commitment. Ensure that a vertical commitment is established and all involved parties are involved in the development process. *[ProcO_07.07]*

BP_ProcO_07.08: Trust the supplier. Ensure that a good and open-minded collaboration with the supplier is established and the supplier is included in the process. *[ProcO_07.08]*

BP_ProcO_07.09: Involve the customer. Ensure that a direct customer communication is established. *[ProcO_07.09]*

BP_ProcO_07.10: Consider ideas and desires from customers. Ensure that the customer gets the possibility to enter new innovative features for the software development in an easy way. *[ProcO_07.10]*

Product Attributes:
<not applicable>

Work Products
A_02-01 Commitment/Agreement → [ProcO_07.07] [ProcO_07.08]
A_03-04 Customer Satisfaction Data → [ProcO_07.03] [ProcO_07.09] [ProcO_07.10]
A_07-01 Customer Satisfaction Survey → [ProcO_07.03] [ProcO_07.09] [ProcO_07.10]
A_07-02 Field Measure → [ProcO_07.03] [ProcO_07.09] [ProcO_07.10]
A_11-05 Software Unit → [ProcO_07.01] [ProcO_07.02] [ProcO_07.05] [ProcO_07.06] [ProcO_07.08]
A_13-04 Communication Record → [ProcO_07.02] [ProcO_07.04] [ProcO_07.06] [ProcO_07.07]
A_13-05 Contract Review Record → [ProcO_07.01] [ProcO_07.05] [ProcO_07.08]
A_13-17 Customer Request → [ProcO_07.09] [ProcO_07.10]

E.8 ASPLA Work Products

For each ASPLA Work Product, the characteristic are provided as guidance for the attributes to look for while assessing the development. Work products are defined using the schema:

ASPLA Work Product IDentifier (ASPLA-WP ID). An identifier number for the Work Product which is used to reference the work product.

Work Product identifier (WP ID). An identifier number for the Work Product which is used in the ASPICE model and served for the ASPLA as a basis.

Work Product Name (WPN). Provides a name associated with the Work Product characteristics to identify the type of Work Product. It is likely that organizations call these work products by different names. The name of the Work Product in the organization is not significant.

Work Product Characteristics (WPC). Provides examples of the potential characteristics associated with the Work Product types. [260]

Work products (with the ID XX-00) are sets of characteristics that would be expected to be evident in Work Products of generic types as a result of achievement of an attribute. The generic Work Products form the basis for the classification of specific Work Products defined as process performance indicators [260].

Table E.8: ASPLA Work Products

ASPLA-WP ID: A_01-03 ← **WP ID:** 01-03 Software Item [260]

ASPLA-complement:
- Software item:
  - Test cases for regression test for each software item.
- Documentation:
  - Describes the compatibility to other software variants.
  - Describes the target market.

ASPLA-WP ID: A_01-50 ← **WP ID:** 01-50 Integrated Software [260]
ASPLA-complement: - Provided to verification processes. - Distributed to involved parties automatically.
ASPLA-WP ID: A_01-51 ← **WP ID:** 01-51 Configuration Datasets [260]
continued on the next page

ASPLA-complement:
- Owner/Sponsor are documented.
- Considered for continuous testing.
- Distributed to all involved parties automatically.

ASPLA-WP ID: A_02-01 ← **WP ID:** 2-01 Commitment/Agreement [260]

ASPLA-complement:
- Is adjusted to the agile commitment with incremental software delivery, such as:
  - Smaller iterative commitments.
  - Payment by feature.
  - Payment by time allocation.
- Establishes what the commitment is for and enables an open minded collaboration.
- Includes the agile commitment strategy with the supplier

ASPLA-WP ID: A_03-03← **WP ID:** 03-03 Benchmarking data [260]

ASPLA-complement:
- Introduce Burndown Charts or similar to measure workload and progress.

ASPLA-WP ID: A_03-04 ← **WP ID:** 03-04 Customer satisfaction data [260]

ASPLA-complement:
- A_03-04 is covered by A_07-01

ASPLA-WP ID: A_03-06← **WP ID:** 03-06 Process performance data [260]

ASPLA-complement:
- Survey with developers, to track satisfaction with the work and the process to build new software.

ASPLA-WP ID: A_04-02 ← **WP ID:** 04-02 Domain architecture [260]

ASPLA-WP ID: A_04-03 ← **WP ID:** 04-03 Domain model [260]

ASPLA-complement:
- This WP shall be part of the scoping process on low hierarchy levels.

ASPLA-WP ID: A_04-04 ← **WP ID:** 04-04 Software architectural design [260]

ASPLA-complement:
- The architecture must shall be modular.
- Auxiliary tasks to refactor the architecture are provided.

<out of scope> ← **WP ID:** 04-05 Software detailed design [260]

ASPLA-WP ID: A_04-06 ← **WP ID:** 04-06 System architectural design [260]

<out of scope> ← **WP ID:** 06-01 Customer manual [260]

<out of scope> ← **WP ID:** 06-02 Handling and storage guide [260]

<out of scope> ← **WP ID:** 06-04 Training material [260]

continued on the next page

ASPLA-WP ID: A_07-01 ← **WP ID:** 07-01 Customer satisfaction survey [260]

ASPLA-complement:
- Mechanism to collect data on customer satisfaction:
  - IdeaExchange Forum with rating functionality for features.
  - Direct customer feedback, such as Apps, Web, Forums.
  - App-based feedback
- Easy accessible feedback for customer
- Financial Incentives or Point system/Kudos
Covers: A_03-04; A_07-02; A_07-08

ASPLA-WP ID: A_07-02 is covered by A_07-01 ← **WP ID:** 07-02 Field measure [260]

ASPLA-complement:
- With permission of the customer, trace the car and get infield information.
- Financial Incentives or Point system/Kudos.

<out of scope> ← **WP ID:** 07-03 Personnel performance measure [260]

ASPLA-comment: Transparency of work and a good and pleasant working environment are part of agile. Workload is defined at team level.

ASPLA-WP ID: A_07-04 ← **WP ID:** 07-04 Process measure [260]

ASPLA-WP ID: A_07-05 ← **WP ID:** 07-05 Project measure [260]

ASPLA-complement:
-Use agile methods to verify that goals are reached:
  - DoD
  - Burndown-Charts
Covers: A_07-06; A_07-07

ASPLA-WP ID: A_07-06 is covered by A_07-05 ← **WP ID:** 07-06 Quality measure [260]

ASPLA-WP ID: A_07-07 is covered by A_07-05 ← **WP ID:** 07-07 Risk measure [260]

ASPLA-WP ID: A_07-08 is covered by A_07-01 ← **WP ID:** 07-07 Risk measure [260]

ASPLA-complement:
- With permission of the customer, trace the car and get real life data and information.
- Financial Incentives or Point system/Kudos.

ASPLA-WP ID: A_08-04 ← **WP ID:** 08-04 Configuration Management Plan [260]

ASPLA-WP ID: A_08-12 ← WP ID: 08-12 Project Plan [260]

continued on the next page

ASPLA-complement:
- Backlog management and priority of backlog items shall be established.
- Sprint planning shall be part of the project planning.
Covers: A_08-16

ASPLA-WP ID: A_08-13 ← **WP ID:** 08-13 Quality Plan [260]

ASPLA-complement:
Covers: A_13-19

<out of scope> ← **WP ID:** 08-14 Recovery Plan [260]

ASPLA-WP ID: A_08-16 is covered by A_08-12 ← **WP ID:** 08-16 Release Plan [260]

ASPLA-complement:
- Is the abstraction of the backlog for the development speed.

ASPLA-WP ID: A_08-17 ← **WP ID:** 08-17 Reuse plan [260]

ASPLA-complement:
- Contains variant specific information.
- Defines compatibility.
Covers: A_12-03

ASPLA-WP ID: A_08-18 is covered by A_13-04 ← **WP ID:** 08-18 Review plan [260]

ASPLA-complement:
- Retrospectives and Sprint planning can be seen as continuous reviewing the process. Make Process visible at all time.

<out of scope> ← **WP ID:** 08-19 Risk management plan [260]

<out of scope> ← **WP ID:** 08-20 Risk mitigation plan [260]

ASPLA-WP ID: A_08-26 is covered by A_13-04 ← **WP ID:** 08-26 Documentation Plan [260]

<out of scope> ← **WP ID:** 08-27 Problem Management Plan [260]

ASPLA-WP ID: A_08-28 ← **WP ID:** 08-28 Change Management Plan [260]

ASPLA-complement:
- The development shall be open for changes.

ASPLA-WP ID: A_08-29 ← **WP ID:** 08-29 Improvement Plan [260]

ASPLA-WP ID: A_08-50 ← **WP ID:** 08-50 Test Specification [260]

ASPLA-complement:
- Priority ranking of test cases, e.g. safety critical tests

continued on the next page

<out of scope> ← **WP ID:** 08-51 Technology monitoring plan [260]

ASPLA-WP ID: A_08-52 ← **WP ID:** 08-52 Test plan [260]

ASPLA-WP ID: A_09-03 ← **WP ID:** 09-03 Reuse policy [260]

ASPLA-WP ID: A_11-03 is covered by A_11-04 ← **WP ID:** 11-03 Product release information [260]
ASPLA-complement: - Is generated out from the DoD and the current sprint backlog.

ASPLA-WP ID: A_11-04 ← **WP ID:** 11-04 Product release package [260]
ASPLA-complement: Covers: A_11-03

ASPLA-WP ID: A_11-05 ← **WP ID:** 11-05 Software unit [260]
ASPLA-complement: - Each software unit has an associate Test case

<out of scope> ← **WP ID:** 11-06 System [260]

<out of scope> ← **WP ID:** 11-07 Temporary solution[260]

<out of scope> ← **WP ID:** 12-01 Request for proposal [260]

ASPLA-WP ID: A_12-03 is covered by A_08-17 ← **WP ID:** 12-03 Reuse proposal [260]
ASPLA-complement: - Identifies the intended version where it shall be integrated first.

<out of scope> ← **WP ID:** 12-04 Supplier proposal response [260]
ASPLA-comment: Supplier is working with the team on the solution no predefined proposal is necessary.

ASPLA-WP ID: A_13-01 ← **WP ID:** 13-01 Acceptance Record [260]
ASPLA-complement: - Shall be part of the Definition of Done.

ASPLA-WP ID: A_13-04 ← **WP ID:** 13-04 Communication record [260]
ASPLA-complement: - Visualization of the Process using e.g. Kanban Boards to make the progress visible Covers: A_08-18; A_08-26, A_13-09; A_13-10; A_13-14; A_13-15

ASPLA-WP ID: A_13-05 ← **WP ID:** 13-05 Contract Review record [260]
ASPLA-complement: - One Room Principle and good collaboration with the supplier. - New style of contract is set up with the supplier

continued on the next page

ASPLA-WP ID: A_13-06 is covered by A_13-08 ← **WP ID:** 13-06 Delivery record [260]

ASPLA-complement:
- Backlog contains the record what was released and implemented.

<out of scope> ← **WP ID:** 13-07 Problem record [260]

ASPLA-WP ID: A_13-08 ← **WP ID:** 13-08 Baseline [260]

ASPLA-WP ID: A_13-09 is covered by A_13-04 ← **WP ID:** 13-09 Meeting support record [260]

ASPLA-complement:
- Meeting support is given by the fact that the whole process is visible for every participant., e.g. KanBAN board.

ASPLA-WP ID: A_13-10 is covered by A_13-04 ← **WP ID:** 13-10 Configuration management record [260]

ASPLA-complement:
- The configuration is part of the SPL.

<out of scope> ← **WP ID:** 13-13 Product release approval record [260]

ASPLA-complement:
- Will be done in the sprint planning and contains the sprint backlog. Record shall automatically created.

ASPLA-WP ID: A_13-14 is covered by A_13-04 ← **WP ID:** 13-14 Progress status record [260]

ASPLA-complement:
- The whole process is visible for every participant, e.g. by the use of a KanBAN board.

ASPLA-WP ID: A_13-15 is covered by A_13-04 ← **WP ID:** 13-15 Proposal review record [260]

ASPLA-complement:
- The proposal review record is part of the meeting minutes of the Synchronization meeting with the supplier.

ASPLA-WP ID: A_13-16 ← **WP ID:** 13-16 Change request [260]

ASPLA-complement:
- Will not be present during development, due to the iterative time boxed development it just gets integrated as a new feature.

ASPLA-WP ID: A_13-17 ← **WP ID:** 13-17 Customer request [260]

ASPLA-complement:
- Part of the customer centric development.

continued on the next page

ASPLA-WP ID: A_13-18 ← **WP ID:** 13-18 Quality record [260]

ASPLA-WP ID: A_13-19 is covered by A_08-13 ← **WP ID:** 13-19 Review Record [260]

ASPLA-complement:
- Shall be part of the software development.

<out of scope> ← **WP ID:** 13-20 Risk action request [260]

<out of scope> ← **WP ID:** 13-21 Change Control record [260]

ASPLA-WP ID: A_13-22 ← **WP ID:** 13-22 Traceability record [260]

ASPLA-WP ID: A_13-24 is covered by A_19-11 ← **WP ID:** 13-24 Validation results [260]

ASPLA-WP ID: A_13-25 is covered by A_19-10 ← **WP ID:** 13-25 Verification results [260]

ASPLA-WP ID: A_13-50 ← **WP ID:** 13-50 Test Results[260]

ASPLA-WP ID: A_14-01 ← **WP ID:** 14-01 Change History [260]

ASPLA-complement:
- Shall be supported by the tool.
Covers: A_14-08; A_14-11

<out of scope> ← **WP ID:** 14-02 Corrective Action Register [260]

ASPLA-complement:
- Shall be included in the bug-changelog.

<out of scope> ← **WP ID:** 14-05 Preferred suppliers register [260]

ASPLA-WP ID: A_14-08 is covered by A_14-01 ← **WP ID:** 14-08 Tracking system [260]

ASPLA-complement:
- Shall be supported by a Tool.

ASPLA-WP ID: A_14-09 ← **WP ID:** 14-09 Work breakdown structure [260]

ASPLA-complement:
- Shall be part of the scoping process.

ASPLA-WP ID: A_14-11 is covered by A_14-01 ← **WP ID:** 14-11 Work product list [260]

ASPLA-complement:
- Part of the version control if Work Product is finished and released, it is covered by the DoD of the Sprint, otherwise it is part of the sprint backlog.

<out of scope> ← **WP ID:** 14-50 Stakeholder group list [260]

continued on the next page

ASPLA-complement:
- Customer centric development no prioritizing of stakeholders. Features with the best business value shall be developed and not just because one group was asking for a feature.

ASPLA-WP ID: A_15-01 ← **WP ID:** 15-01 Analysis Report [260]

ASPLA-complement:
- Analysis shall define if features are built in the software baseline or if the feature is market specific.

<out of scope> ← **WP ID:** 15-03 Configuration status report [260]

ASPLA-complement:
- Shall be exported from a version control tool.

<out of scope> ← **WP ID:** 15-05 Evaluation Report [260]

<out of scope> ← **WP ID:** 15-06 Project status report [260]

ASPLA-complement:
- Not necessary, because of sprints length and the results made visible will give information.

ASPLA-WP ID: A_15-07 ← **WP ID:** 15-07 Reuse evaluation report [260]

ASPLA-complement:
- The ASPLA Model focuses on a high reuse amount, therefore, the reuse opportunities shall be identified during scoping process.

ASPLA-WP ID: A_15-08 is covered by A_15-01 ← **WP ID:** 15-08 Risk analysis report [260]

ASPLA-complement:
- If a report is necessary to fulfill the law it shall be created.

<out of scope> ← **WP ID:** 15-09 Risk status report [260]

<out of scope> ← **WP ID:** 15-12 Problem Status Report [260]

ASPLA-WP ID: A_15-13 ← **WP ID:** 15-13 Assessment/audit report [260]

ASPLA-WP ID: A_15-16 ← **WP ID:** 15-16 Improvement Opportunity[260]

<out of scope> ← **WP ID:** 15-18 Process performance report [260]

<out of scope> ← **WP ID:** 15-21 Supplier evaluation report [260]

<out of scope> ← **WP ID:** 16-03 Configuration management system [260]

<out of scope> ← **WP ID:** 16-06 Process repository [260]

ASPLA-WP ID: A_17-02 ← **WP ID:** 17-02 Build list [260]

continued on the next page

ASPLA-complement:
- Shall be automated and supported by a tool.

ASPLA-WP ID: A_17-03 ← **WP ID:** 17-03 Stakeholder requirements [260]
ASPLA-complement:
- Shall be part of the scoping process.

ASPLA-WP ID: A_17-05 ← **WP ID:** 17-05 Documentation requirements [260]
ASPLA-complement:
- Shall be produced if needed to fulfill requirements given by the law.

ASPLA-WP ID: A_17-08 ← **WP ID:** 17-08 Interface requirements specification [260]

ASPLA-WP ID: A_17-11 is covered by A_17-08 ← **WP ID:** 17-11 Software requirements specification [260]

ASPLA-WP ID: A_17-12 is covered by A_19-05 ← **WP ID:** 17-12 System requirements specification [260]

ASPLA-WP ID: A_17-50 ← **WP ID:** 17-50 Verification criteria [260]

<out of scope> ← **WP ID:** 18-01 Acceptance Criteria [260]

<out of scope> ← **WP ID:** 18-06 Product release criteria [260]

ASPLA-WP ID: A_18-07 ← **WP ID:** 18-07 Quality Criteria [260]

<out of scope> ← **WP ID:** 18-50 Supplier qualification criteria [260]

ASPLA-WP ID: A_19-05 ← **WP ID:** 19-05 Reuse Strategy [260]
ASPLA-complement:
Covers: A_17-12

ASPLA-WP ID: A_19-10 ← **WP ID:** 19-10 Verification Strategy [260]
ASPLA-complement:
Covers: A_13-25

ASPLA-WP ID: A_19-11 ← **WP ID:** 19-11 Validation Strategy [260]
ASPLA-complement:
Covers: A_13-24

E.9   Assessment Questions

Table E.9: ASPLA Assessment Questions for Outcomes

BP_ProcO_01.01: Define a software product line architecture.

continued on the next page

Q_001: A systematic approach for software reuse is established.

Q_002: The systematic approach follows the paradigm of a software product line.

Q_003: The systematic reuse approach provide the possibility to generate software for different markets.

Q_004: The systematic reuse approach provide the possibility to generate various software variants.

ProcO_01.02: Use only one software product line.

Q_005: It is ensured that only one systematic reuse approach is defined and established.

Q_006: It is possible to include features from a market into the software for another market.

BP_ProcO_01.03: Manage the software product line by means of suitable tools.

Q_007: An appropriate tool chain supports the development within the software product line.

Q_008: An appropriate tool chain supports the development within the software product line.

Q_009: The tools within the tool chain are maintained and not a "quick and dirty" solution.

Q_010: The tools within the tool chain can be automated, e.g. APIs are available.

Q_011: It is ensured that the tool chain is suitable for the context in which it is used.

Q_012: It is possible to trace from requirement to software unit.

Q_013: It is possible to trace from software unit to the appropriate test cases.

BP_ProcO_01.04: Distribute software product line architecture.

Q_014: Decisions on the software product line architecture are reviewed.

Q_015: Decisions on the software product line architecture are published to all effected parties.

Q_016: Decisions on the software product line architecture are documented.

Q_017: Decisions on the software product line architecture are easy accessible by all affected parties.

BP_ProcO_01.05: Grant refactoring time.

Q_018: The software product line architecture is open for changes.

Q_019: Time to refactor the architecture of the software product line is granted.

BP_ProcO_01.06: Define a standardized interface between software units.

Q_020: Parts of the software can be replaced easily.

Q_021: The reuse strategy standardize interfaces between software units.

BP_ProcO_01.07: Analyze and consider safety regulations.

continued on the next page

Q_022: The software architecture ensures the compliance with safety requirements.

Q_023: All software parts get analyzed and an ASIL Level is assigned.

Q_024: Documentation according to the safety regulations is produced.

BP_ProcO_01.08: Analyze and consider security regulations.

Q_025: The software architecture ensures the compliance with security requirements.

Q_026: Software parts are categorized into security relevant levels and implemented according to the security level.

Q_027: Documentation according to the security regulations is produced.

PA_ProdO_01.01: The software architecture shall be modular.

Q_028: The software architecture is modular.

Q_029: It is possible to replace software parts without affecting other parts of the software.

Q_030: It is possible to reuse software parts.

PA_ProdO_01.02 The software architecture shall be open to change.

Q_031: The architecture of the software is not a monolith.

Q_032: The software architecture is open to change.

PA_ProdO_01.03: The software architecture shall provide the possibility to include fast changing requirements.

Q_033: It is possible to include fast changing requirements into the development.

Q_034: It is ensured that interfaces between software parts are standardized.

Q_035: It is ensured that the architecture is modular and can deal with fast changing requirements.

PA_ProdO_01.04: The software architecture shall be hardware independent.

Q_036: It is possible to change the hardware without big changes in the software.

Q_037: The software architecture is scalable according to the selected hardware.

BP_ProcO_02.01: Set up a scoping meeting.

Q_038: Regular meetings are established, to specify, if the feature is part for the common baseline or a product/market specific feature.

Q_039: It is ensured that the meeting in a recurrent and defined time frame.

Q_040: It is ensured that new features evaluated and clustered.

BP_ProcO_02.02: Consider rapid changes in requirements in scoping meetings.

Q_041: It is ensured that rapid changes in requirements are considered in the scoping meetings each time.

Q_042: It is ensured that a new priority to a requirement can be reassigned.

continued on the next page

BP_ProcO_02.03: Allow situational extraordinary scoping meetings.

Q_043: It is ensured that show-stoppers can be discussed in extraordinary meeting.

Q_044: It is ensured that show-stoppers get a high priority and adjust the backlog accordingly.

BP_ProcO_02.04: Permit low hierarchy levels to scope features.

Q_045: It is ensured that features to be implemented are first authorized by a global agreement.

Q_046: Low hierarchies are allowed to assign the priority of a features to be implemented.

Q_047: Are results of low-hierarchy meetings published to all affected parties.

BP_ProcO_02.05: Assign required new functionality to the software units.

Q_048: It is ensured that features are not implemented redundantly.

Q_049: It is ensured that desired functionality is assigned to the most suitable software units.

BP_ProcO_02.06: Identify software units which are supplied and implemented by the supplier.

Q_050: A process is established to assign development tasks to suppliers.

Q_051: It is ensured that software units which are procured by the suppliers are identified.

BP_ProcO_02.07: Identify similarities of desired software features.

Q_052: It is ensured that a twofold development of one feature is avoided.

Q_053: Time for refactoring, to make the similar features compatible with the software baseline development is granted.

BP_ProcO_02.08: Identify software units for potential reuse.

Q_054: The application of the reuse strategy is ensured.

Q_055: Software for potential reuse is identified.

BP_ProcO_02.09: Identify incompatible desired software features.

Q_056: It is ensured that incompatible features are resolved.

Q_057: A time for refactoring to make the features compatible with the software baseline development is granted.

BP_ProcO_02.10: Prioritize required new software parts.

Q_058: It is ensured that for every feature an implementation priority is assigned.

Q_059: A market-specific backlog is defined for the implementation in the next increment.

PA_ProdO_02.01: Reusable software units shall be defined.

Q_060: It is ensured that software parts which can be reused are identified.

continued on the next page

Q_061: It is ensured that required new functionality is first checked against existing functionality to ascertain that the functionality is not implemented already in another software variant.

PA_ProdO_02.02: New software units shall be prioritized before implementation.
Q_062: It is ensured that a priority value is assigned to each feature which identifies the priority for the implementation in the next increment.
Q_063: A ordered list within a backlog is implemented.

PA_ProdO_02.03: A priority value for software features shall be assigned.
Q_064: It is ensured that features are rated within a meeting.
Q_065: It is ensured that a priority value is assigned to each feature.
Q_066: It is ensured that the priority value is stored in the requirement specification of the feature.

PA_ProdO_02.04: A critically value for the software feature shall be assigned.
Q_067: It is ensured that the features are rated and a critically value is assigned.
Q_068: It is ensured that the critically value is stored in the requirement specification of the feature.

BP_ProcO_03.01: Reduce time to market with a faster feature development.
Q_069: It is ensured that the time from initial idea to first release and time to market is reduced.
Q_070: It is ensured that decrease of development time does not result in a decreased software quality.

BP_ProcO_03.02: Release product and market specific features early.
Q_071: It is possible to release features for specific markets and products early.
Q_072: It is possible to repatriate the implemented features into the software product line.

BP_ProcO_03.03: React on changes during the development.
Q_073: Changes in requirements during development are addressed in an acceptable time.

BP_ProcO_03.04: Analyze and consider constrains given by the law.
Q_074: It is ensured that legal constraints are fulfilled.
Q_075: It is ensured that and required artifacts are created.

BP_ProcO_03.05: Synchronize the agile development with the surrounding processes.
Q_076: A development that uses agile practices is established.

continued on the next page

Q_077: It is ensured that agile development is synchronized with all affected parties.

BP_ProcO_03.06: Focus on business value.
Q_078: It is ensured that agile development is in budget.
Q_079: It is ensured that agile development creates business value.
Q_080: It is ensured that new terms of supplier payments are introduced.

BP_ProcO_03.07: Utilize agile practices whenever applicable.
Q_081: It is ensured that agile practices are suited for the context they are practiced.
Q_269: It is ensured that employees are being trained in agile practices and methods.

BP_ProcO_03.08: Implement retrospectives and feedback culture.
Q_082: It is ensured that knowledge gained in a retrospective of one software variant is transferred to all other software variants.

PA_ProdO_03.01: The development shall focus on customer needs.
Q_083: It is ensured that customer feedback is integrated into the development of the product.
Q_084: A close customer collaboration is established.

BP_ProcO_04.01: Implement supporting tasks.
Q_085: It is ensured that supporting and repetitive tasks are comprised in the development process.
Q_086: It is ensured that automated feedback is provided.

BP_ProcO_04.02: Set up continuous integration.
Q_087: It is ensured that software failures in all software variants are identified in the integration phases.
Q_088: A process for a timed and automated continuous integration is established.

BP_ProcO_04.03: Apply continuous tests for software.
Q_089: It is ensured that software failures are identified by timed and automated software tests.

BP_ProcO_04.04: Set up continuous delivery.
Q_090: It is ensured that software could be delivered to (internal) customers in a fast pace.
Q_091: A infrastructure to deliver the software in a fast pace to customers is available.

BP_ProcO_04.05: Set up continuous deployment.
Q_092: It is ensure that software is deployable (regarding all legal constraints) to the field.
Q_093: As infrastructure to deploy the software is available.

BP_ProcO_04.06: Set up continuous compliance.

continued on the next page

Q_094: It is ensured that each software release is (potentially) compliant.

PA_ProdO_04.01: An integration strategy shall be implemented.
Q_095: It is ensure that software units and software items are integrated up to a complete integrated software.
Q_096: The software integration is done automatically by means of integration server and virtual integration.

PA_ProdO_04.02: Continuous verification tasks shall be automated.
Q_097: It is ensured that the software units are tested for compliance.
Q_098: The software items are design in a way that they are capable to undergo highly automated verification tasks.

BP_ProcO_06.01: Set up an appropriate test strategy.
Q_099 It is ensured that a sufficient test coverage for all products and software variants is achieved to fulfill legal requirements.

BP_ProcO_06.02: Set up an adaptive test strategy.
Q_100: It is ensured that the test strategy is adaptive in case of variants, test critically and available time.
Q_101: It is ensured that always the best fitting test cases for one software variant are executed at the beginning of a test, as these foster a rapid error detection.

BP_ProcO_06.03: Implement a scalable test strategy.
Q_102: It is ensured that the test strategy is scalable.
Q_103: It is ensured that the test strategy covers tests for each individual software variant.
Q_104: It is ensured that the test strategy covers tests in the entire systems and in real cars.

BP_ProcO_06.04: Assign test case priority and run suitable tests cases.
Q_105: It is ensured that a test case priority is assigned to each test case.
Q_106: It is ensured that high prior test cases, such as safety related test cases, are automatically selected and executed.

BP_ProcO_06.05: Maintain traceability.
Q_107: It is ensured that a consistent and bidirectional traceability is established between the software units and the test cases.
Q_108: It is ensured that a consistent and bidirectional traceability is established between test cases and test results.

BP_ProcO_06.06: Document test results.
Q_109: It is ensured that results of the software integration test are summarized and communicated to all affected parties.

continued on the next page

PA_ProdO_06.01: Test case shall be implemented for each software units.

Q_110: It is ensured that each software unit has an unique test case.

Q_111: It is ensured that critical software units do have an associated test case with a high priority.

Q_112: It is ensured that all test cases consist of all test steps in order to be compliant with law.

Q_113: It is ensured that test cases are traceable to the corresponding software unit.

BP_ProcO_07.01: Involve all parties affected by the development.

Q_114: It is ensured that all involved parties are involved directly in the development process.

BP_ProcO_07.02: Break down knowledge silos.

Q_115: It is ensured that the development process is transparent for every participant.

BP_ProcO_07.03: Establish fast feedback loops.

Q_116: It is ensured that fast feedback loops are established to provide a faster learning loop.

Q_117: Automatic generated feedback from test systems are established.

Q_118: Feedback from customer, and feedback from all affected parties are considered.

BP_ProcO_07.04: Visualize the process.

Q_119: It is ensured that the process and the development progress is visible and easy accessible for all involved parties.

BP_ProcO_07.05: Develop a common understanding for the software product line.

Q_120: It is ensured that all affected parties be aware of the development within the software product line.

Q_121: It is ensured that all affected parties are aware of their responsibility to identify impediments, dependencies, incompatibilities and similarities of software features.

BP_ProcO_07.06: Overcome hierarchies.

Q_122: It is ensured that the communication is not blocked by the hierarchy.

Q_123: It is ensured that every participant can speak to every other directly.

BP_ProcO_07.07: Establish a vertical commitment.

Q_124: It is ensured that a vertical commitment is established and all involved parties are involved in the development process:

BP_ProcO_07.08: Trust the supplier.

continued on the next page

Q_125: It is ensured that a good and open-minded collaboration with the supplier is established.

Q_126: It is ensured that supplier is included in the process.

BP_ProcO_07.09: Involve the customer.

Q_127: It is ensured that a direct customer communication is established.

BP_ProcO_07.10: Consider ideas and desires from customers.

Q_128: It is ensured that the customer gets the possibility to enter new innovative features for the software development in an easy way.

Table E.10: ASPLA Assessment Questions for Work Products

Q_129: All necessary Work Product items of "Software item" are available.

Q_130: Do you have a test cases for regression test for each software item?

Q_131: Do you describe and define the compatibility to other software variants?

Q_132: Do you describe and define the compatibility for the target market?

Q_133: All necessary Work Product items of "Integrated Software" are available.

Q_134: A process to provide the integrated software to downstream verification processes is established.

Q_135: A process to distribute the integrated software to involved parties automatically is established.

Q_136: All necessary Work Product items of "Configuration Datasets" are available.

Q_137: It is ensured that Owner/Sponsor are documented.

Q_138: A process that considers the configuration datasets for continuous testing is established.

Q_139: A process to distribute the Configuration Datasets to all involved parties automatically is established.

Q_140: All necessary Work Product items of "Commitment/ Agreement" are available.

Q_141: It is ensured that the commitment with the customer comprises an adjusted agile commitment for incremental software delivery, such as smaller iterative commitments, payment by feature and payment by time allocation.

Q_142: It is ensured that smaller iterative commitments are possible.

Q_143: The commitment ensures an open minded collaboration.

Q_144: An agile commitment strategy with the supplier is ensured.

continued on the next page

Q_145: All necessary Work Product items of "Benchmarking data" are available.

Q_146: Agile elements such as Burndown Charts or DoD are introduced to measure workload and progress.

Q_147: All necessary Work Product items of "Process performance data" are available.

Q_148: It is ensured that surveys with developers are conducted to track satisfaction with the work and the process to build new software.

Q_149: All necessary Work Product items of "Domain architecture" are available.

Q_150: All necessary Work Product items of "Domain model" are available.

Q_151: All necessary Work Product items of "Software architectural design" are available.

Q_152: It is ensured that the software architecture is modular.

Q_153: All necessary Work Product items of "System architectural design" are available.

Q_154: All necessary Work Product items of "Customer satisfaction survey" are available.

Q_155: A mechanism to collect data on customer satisfaction is established.

Q_156: The level of customer satisfaction with products and services is determined.

Q_157: All necessary Work Product items of "Customer satisfaction data are available."

Q_158: A process to record customer data is established.

Q_159: All necessary Work Product items of "Field measure" are available.

Q_160: All necessary Work Product items of "Service level measure" are available.

Q_161: It is possible (with permission of the customer) to trace the car and get real life data and information.

Q_162: Financial Incentives or Point system/Kudos are offered to the customer to measure the system's performance while the car is operational.

Q_163: All necessary Work Product items of "Process measure" are available.

Q_164: Agile practices such as "Definition-of-Done" or "Burndown-Charts" to trace and document the progress are established.

Q_165: All necessary Work Product items of "Project measure" are available.

Q_166: Agile practices such as "Definition-of-Done" or "Burndown-Charts" to verify that goals are reached are established.

Q_167: All necessary Work Product items of "Quality measure" are available.

continued on the next page

Q_168: All necessary Work Product items of "Risk measure" are available.

Q_169: All necessary Work Product items of "Configuration Management Plan" are available.

Q_170: All necessary Work Product items of "Project Plan" are available.
Q_171: Backlogs are established.
Q_172: A priority for implementation is assigned to Backlog items.
Q_173: Backlog items are used for management and sprint planning.

Q_174: All necessary Work Product items of "Release Plan" are available.
Q_175: It is possible to generate the Release Plan out of the backlog for the development sprint.

Q_176: All necessary Work Product items of "Quality Plan" are available.

Q_177: All necessary Work Product items of "Review Record " are available.
Q_178: Reviews are an essential part of the software development and generated for each development sprint.

Q_179: All necessary Work Product items of "Reuse plan" are available.
Q_180: Variant specific information is part of the implementation per software unit.
Q_181: Compatibility between software units and software variants are defined.

Q_182: All necessary Work Product items of "Reuse proposal" are available.
Q_183: It is ensured that a software unit contain the intended version where it shall be integrated first.

Q_184: All necessary Work Product items of "Change Management Plan" are available.
Q_185: The development is open to changes.

Q_186: All necessary Work Product items of "Improvement Plan" are available.

Q_187: All necessary Work Product items of "Test Specification" are available.
Q_188: Each test case has an assigned priority value.
Q_189: Safety critical tests are high prior.

Q_190: All necessary Work Product items of "Test plan" are available.
Q_191: It is possible to rank test cases in the test plan according to the priority level.
Q_192: The test plan selects high prioritized test cases at the beginning of the test process.

Q_193: All necessary Work Product items of "Reuse policy" are available.

continued on the next page

Q_194: All necessary Work Product items of "Product release information" are available.

Q_195: The product release information is generated out from the DoD and the current sprint backlog.

Q_196: All necessary Work Product items of "Product release package" are available.

Q_197: All necessary Work Product items of "Software unit" are available.

Q_198: It is ensured that each software unit has an associate test case.

Q_199: All necessary Work Product items of "Acceptance Record " are available.

Q_200: It is ensured that agile practices such as the "Definition-of-Done" are accepted for an Acceptance Record.

Q_201: All necessary Work Product items of "Communication record" are available.

Q_202: The development is visualized to make the progress visible.

Q_203: The visualization is easy accessible for all involved parties.

Q_204: All necessary Work Product items of "Review plan" are available.

Q_205: The process is continuously reviewed using retrospectives and adjustable sprint planning.

Q_206: The current progress is visible at all time.

Q_207 All necessary Work Product items of "Meeting support record" are available.

Q_208: Meeting support is given by the fact that the whole process is visible for every participant, e.g. KanBAN board.

Q_209 All necessary Work Product items of "Documentation Plan" are available.

Q_210: All necessary Work Product items of "Configuration management record" are available.

Q_211: The configuration is part of the software product line management and supported by suitable tools.

Q_212: All necessary Work Product items of "Progress status record" are available.

Q_213: The whole process is visible for every participant., e.g. KanBAN board.

Q_214 All necessary Work Product items of "Proposal review record" are available.

Q_215: The proposal review record is part of the meeting minutes of the Synchronization meeting with the supplier.

Q_216 All necessary Work Product items of "Contract Review record" are available.

Q_217: The One Room Principle is established and all affected parties are united.

Q_218: A good collaboration with the supplier is established.

continued on the next page

Q_219: A new style of contract is set up with the supplier to bring suppliers into a closer collaboration with the in-house development.

Q_220: All necessary Work Product items of "Baseline" are available.

Q_221: It is ensured that a baseline is created after each sprint.

Q_222: All necessary Work Product items of "Delivery record " are available.

Q_223: The Delivery record can be generated from the Definition-of-Done after each software release.

Q_224: The sprint backlog contains the record what was released and implemented.

Q_225: All necessary Work Product items of "Change request" are available.

Q_226: It is ensured that no change request is present during the development sprint.

Q_227: It is ensured that change requests are introduced as a new feature in the sprint planning.

Q_228 All necessary Work Product items of "Customer request" are available.

Q_229: It is ensured that the customer is included into the development.

Q_230: All necessary Work Product items of "Quality record" are available.

Q_231: All necessary Work Product items of "Traceability record" are available.

Q_232: The traceability is supported by appropriate tools and a record of changes can be generated automatically.

Q_233: All necessary Work Product items of "Test Results" are available.

Q_234: It is ensured that test results are created continuously and failures in the development are report back to the developer.

Q_235: All necessary Work Product items of "Change History" are available.

Q_236: The Change history is supported by appropriate tools and a record of changes can be generated automatically.

Q_237: All necessary Work Product items of "Tracking system" are available.

Q_238: The Tracking system is supported by an appropriate tool.

Q_239: All necessary Work Product items of "Work product list" are available.

Q_240: It is ensured that finished and released work products are part of DoD of the Sprint.

Q_241: It is ensured that unfinished work products are part of the sprint backlog

Q_242 All necessary Work Product items of "Work breakdown structure" are available.

Q_243: It is ensured that the Work breakdown structure is part of the scoping process for the SPL.

Q_244: All necessary Work Product items of "Analysis Report" are available.

continued on the next page

Q_245: It is ensured that the analysis report defines if features are built in the software baseline or for which markets they are developed.

Q_246: All necessary Work Product items of "Risk analysis report" are available.

Q_247: It is ensured that all report which are necessary to fulfill the constraints given by the law are created.

Q_248: All necessary Work Product items of "Reuse evaluation report" are available.

Q_249: It is ensured that the reuse opportunities are identified during scoping process.

Q_250: All necessary Work Product items of "Assessment/audit report" are available.

Q_251: All necessary Work Product items of "Improvement Opportunity" are available.

Q_252: All necessary Work Product items of "Build list" are available.

Q_253: It is ensured that the build process is automated.

Q_254: It is ensured that the build list generated for each software build.

Q_255 All necessary Work Product items of "Stakeholder requirements" are available.

Q_256: It is ensured that Stakeholder requirements are evaluated in scoping meetings.

Q_257: All necessary Work Product items of "Documentation requirements" are available.

Q_258: All necessary Work Product items of "Interface requirements specification" are available.

Q_259: It is ensured that the interfaces between software units are standardized.

Q_260: All necessary Work Product items of "Software requirements specification" are available.

Q_261: All necessary Work Product items of "Verification criteria" are available.

Q_262: All necessary Work Product items of "Quality Criteria" are available.

Q_263: All necessary Work Product items of "Reuse Strategy" are available.

Q_264: All necessary Work Product items of "System requirements specification" are available.

Q_265: All necessary Work Product items of "Verification Strategy" are available.

Q_266: All necessary Work Product items of "Verification results" are available.

Q_267: All necessary Work Product items of "Validation Strategy" are available.

Q_268: All necessary Work Product items of "Validation results" are available.

E.10 The Relationship between the ASPLA Model and Standards

ASPICE: Automotive SPICE process assessment / reference model

ASPICE [260] "does not predefine any concrete life cycle model, method, tool, templates, metrics, [or] proceedings" [76, p. 50]. Hence, "the only valid question would be to ask whether concrete process implementations, following or including agile methods or not, actually satisfy the Automotive SPICE principles" [76, p. 50].

However, the ASPICE Guidelines [76] present recommendations that address planning within an agile environment, the (1) project life cycle, (2) management of requirements, (3) project planning, (4) risk management, (5) the software architecture, (6) software testing, (7) the quality assurance, and the use of (8) pair programming with regard to agile development.

Table E.11: The ASPLA Model compared with the ASPICE guidelines [76]

(1) Planning in agile environment requires that agile project planning is in line with the customer release planning [76].
Addressed in: BP_ProcO_03.05

(2) Project life cycle requires that the project life cycle is appropriate for the context and fits to the project scope, requirements, deliveries, and complexity [76].
Addressed in: BP_ProcO_03.07

(3) Management of project requirements requires a complete and consistent overview of all project requirements [76].
Addressed in: BP_ProcO_01.03, BP_ProcO_07.02, BP_ProcO_07.04, BP_ProcO_07.07

(4) Risk management requires that a risk management for the development project is integrated [76].
Addressed in: BP_ProcO_01.07, BP_ProcO_01.08, PA_ProdO_02.04, BP_ProcO_06.04

(5) Software architecture requires that a traceability between requirements, architecture, design, and integration tests is established [76].
Addressed in: BP_ProcO_01.03, BP_ProcO_01.07, BP_ProcO_01.08, BP_ProcO_06.05, PA_ProdO_06.01

continued on the next page

(6) Software testing requires that "the process purposes of all 3 software testing processes (SWE.4, SWE.5 and SWE.6) are fulfilled by the defined activities in project Sprints" [76, p. 53].

Addressed in: BP_ProcO_06.01, BP_ProcO_06.03

(7) Independent quality assurance requires that work product and process quality assurance is performed without conflicts of interest [76].

Addressed in: BP_ProcO_03.04

(8) Pair programming requires that the programming method does not conflict with code review requirements.

Addressed in: BP_ProcO_03.07

ISO/IEC 26550: Reference model for product line engineering and management

This Section related the ASPLA Model to ISO/IEC 26550 [128], the *reference model for product line engineering and management*. Aspects, as required by the ISO/IEC 26550, [128] are related to Base Practices and Product Attributes. Each aspect shall be addressed within the recommended Honeycomb Attributes.

Domain engineering life cycle

The domain engineering life cycle manage the common product line by identifying, implementing and managing common features of the product[128]. Furthermore, it defines five important aspects.

These aspects comprise methods and tools for domain engineering; (1) product line scoping, (2) domain requirements engineering, (3) domain design, (4) domain realization, and (5) domain verification and validation (cf. Section 2.2.1). Each aspect is further divided into smaller aspects that need to be considered.

Table E.12 the aspects that need to be considered within the domain engineering life cycle and relates them to Base Practices and Product Attributes in the ASPLA Model.

Table E.12: The ASPLA Model compared with the domain engineering life cycle ISO/IEC 26550 [128].

(1) **Product line scoping** defines the common parts of a product line and consists of product scoping, domain scoping and asset scoping [128].	
Product scoping	BP_ProcO_02.01, BP_ProcO_02.04
Domain scoping	BP_ProcO_02.01, BP_ProcO_02.05, BP_ProcO_02.07
Asset scoping	BP_ProcO_02.08, PA_ProdO_02.01

(2) **Domain requirements engineering** includes the identification of products and features that should be part of the product line and the definition of common and variable features [128].	
Elicitation	PA_ProdO_03.01, BP_ProcO_07.09
Analysis	BP_ProcO_02.01, BP_ProcO_02.05, BP_ProcO_02.07
Specification	BP_ProcO_02.01
Verification and validation	BP_ProcO_02.01, BP_ProcO_03.04
Management	BP_ProcO_02.01, BP_ProcO_02.02, BP_ProcO_02.03, BP_ProcO_02.04

continued on the next page

(3) Domain design sets up the product line architecture, which introduces the variability to implement all member products [128].	
Commonality and variability analysis	BP_ProcO_01.01, BP_ProcO_01.06, BP_ProcO_02.01
Design	BP_ProcO_01.01, BP_ProcO_01.04
Verification and validation	BP_ProcO_01.01, BP_ProcO_06.01
Management	BP_ProcO_01.01, BP_ProcO_01.03

(4) Domain realization comprises the implementation of common and variable domain assets [128].	
Identification, evaluation, selection, and integration of commercial off-the-shelf components	BP_ProcO_02.06
Interface realization	BP_ProcO_01.04, BP_ProcO_01.06
Component realization	BP_ProcO_01.04, BP_ProcO_01.06
Verification and validation	BP_ProcO_06.01
Management	BP_ProcO_01.03

(5) Domain verification and validation ensure that domain assets implemented and tested as specified. [128].	
Domain test planning	BP_ProcO_06.01, BP_ProcO_06.03, BP_ProcO_06.05
Domain test design	BP_ProcO_06.01, BP_ProcO_06.03
Domain test execution	BP_ProcO_04.03
Domain test closure and report	BP_ProcO_07.03, BP_ProcO_06.06
Domain test management	BP_ProcO_01.03, BP_ProcO_04.01

Application engineering life cycle

The application engineering life cycle creates customized adjustments and extensions to the common platform [128]. The life cycle introduces four important aspects(cf. Section 2.2.1); (1) application requirements engineering, (2) application design, (3) application realization, and (4) application verification and validation.

Table E.13 summarizes the aspects that need to be considered within the application engineering life cycle and relates them to Base Practices and Product Attributes in the ASPLA Model.

Table E.13: The ASPLA Model compared with the application engineering life cycle ISO/IEC 26550 [128].

(1) **Application requirements engineering** develops customized requirements for application specific implementation [128].	
Elicitation	BP_ProcO_02.08, BP_ProcO_07.09, BP_ProcO_07.10
Analysis	BP_ProcO_02.01, BP_ProcO_02.04, BP_ProcO_02.08, BP_ProcO_02.09
Specification	BP_ProcO_03.02, BP_ProcO_01.07, BP_ProcO_01.08
Verification and validation	BP_ProcO_06.01, BP_ProcO_06.03
Management	BP_ProcO_01.03, BP_ProcO_02.01, BP_ProcO_07.09, BP_ProcO_07.10

(2) **Application design** specifies the application architecture based on the domain architecture, to satisfy customer requirements [128].	
Binding variants of the domain architecture	BP_ProcO_02.01
Application specific architecture design.	BP_ProcO_01.05, PA_ProdO_01.01, PA_ProdO_01.02, PA_ProdO_01.03
Verification and validation	BP_ProcO_06.01
Management	BP_ProcO_01.03, BP_ProcO_01.05, BP_ProcO_07.03

(3) **Application realization** is the implementation of product-specific functionality [128].	
Binding component-level variability	BP_ProcO_02.01
Identification, evaluation, selection, and integration of commercial off-the-shelf components	BP_ProcO_02.05, BP_ProcO_02.06
Interface realization	BP_ProcO_01.06
Component realization	BP_ProcO_02.01 BP_ProcO_02.06
Verification and validation	BP_ProcO_06.01
Management	BP_ProcO_01.03

(4) **Application verification and validation** extends domain verification and validation and ensures that the final product is implemented and work as expected.[128].	
Application test planning	BP_ProcO_06.01, BP_ProcO_06.03, BP_ProcO_06.05
Application test design	BP_ProcO_06.01, BP_ProcO_06.03

continued on the next page

Application test execution	BP_ProcO_04.03
Application test closure and report	BP_ProcO_07.03
Application test management	BP_ProcO_01.03, BP_ProcO_04.01

Organizational management process group

The organizational management processes help to manage the product line., by defining the product line strategy and the overall planning [128]. These processes comprise the (1) organizational-level product line planning, (2) organizational product line-enabling management, and (3) organizational product line management.

Table E.14 summarizes the aspects that need to be considered within the organizational management processes group and relates them to Base Practices and Product Attributes in the ASPLA Model.

Table E.14: The ASPLA Model compared with the organizational management process group ISO/IEC 26550 [128].

(1) **Organizational-level product line planning** defines the set up the product line and tries to optimize business value [128].	
Business opportunity analysis	BP_ProcO_02.04, BP_ProcO_03.06, PA_ProdO_03.01
Customer relationship management	PA_ProdO_03.01, BP_ProcO_07.03, BP_ProcO_07.09, BP_ProcO_07.10
Developing a sourcing strategy	BP_ProcO_02.06, BP_ProcO_07.08
Organizational transition planning	<out of scope>
Organizational operations planning	BP_ProcO_07.01, BP_ProcO_07.02, BP_ProcO_07.04, BP_ProcO_07.05
Organizational product line evolution planning	BP_ProcO_07.05
Value management planning	BP_ProcO_05.02

(2) **Organizational product line-enabling management** helps to establish and evolve a product line [128].	
Structuring the product line organization	<out of scope>
Training and human resource management	<out of scope>
Organizational quality management	BP_ProcO_03.08

continued on the next page

(3) Organizational product line management initiates the transition towards a product line. [128].	
Product line evolution management	BP_ProcO_01.05, PA_ProdO_03.01, BP_ProcO_07.09, BP_ProcO_07.10
Deployment and innovation management	BP_ProcO_05.01, BP_ProcO_05.02
Operations management	BP_ProcO_05.02
Organizational risk management	BP_ProcO_07.01, BP_ProcO_07.02, BP_ProcO_07.05, BP_ProcO_07.06, BP_ProcO_07.07, BP_ProcO_07.08
Organization-level monitoring and control	BP_ProcO_03.06, BP_ProcO_07.04

Technical management process group

The technical management processes help to create and evolve the product line [128]. Therefore, it comprises of (1) process management, (2) variability management, (3) asset management, and (4) support management.

Table E.15 summarizes the aspects that need to be considered within the organizational management processes group and relates them to Base Practices and Product Attributes in the ASPLA Model.

Table E.15: The ASPLA Model compared with the technical management process group ISO/IEC 26550 [128].

(1) Process management deals with the processes of cooperation in cross-functional and inter-organizational teams. [128].	
Applying process enabling processes for product lines	BP_ProcO_05.01
Domain engineering process definition	BP_ProcO_01.02, BP_ProcO_07.05, BP_ProcO_07.07
Application engineering process definition	BP_ProcO_01.01
Definition and application of relationship management processes and supporting information systems	BP_ProcO_02.06
Applying process monitoring and control for product lines	BP_ProcO_05.02
Applying process improvement for product lines	BP_ProcO_05.01

continued on the next page

(2) **Variability management** defines how software variants are differentiated from each other and variability is managed [128].	
Variability modelling	\<out of scope\>
Variability mechanism	\<out of scope\>
Variability binding	\<out of scope\>
Variability documentation	BP_ProcO_03.04
Variability tracing	BP_ProcO_01.03
Variability control and evolution	BP_ProcO_01.03

(3) **Asset management** manages domain assets and application assets [128].	
Asset identification	BP_ProcO_03.02, BP_ProcO_02.07, BP_ProcO_02.08, PA_ProdO_02.01
Asset base implementation	BP_ProcO_02.07, PA_ProdO_02.01
Asset verification and validation	BP_ProcO_06.01
Asset evolution	BP_ProcO_02.07

(4) **Support management** supports other processes and aims at improving the quality of other processes [128].	
Technical quality management	BP_ProcO_05.01, BP_ProcO_03.08
Configuration management	\<out of scope\>
Decision management	BP_ProcO_03.06, BP_ProcO_07.05, BP_ProcO_07.06, BP_ProcO_07.07
Technical risk management	BP_ProcO_07.02, BP_ProcO_07.05
Tool management	BP_ProcO_01.03

Appendix **F**

Literature Reviews

This Appendix contains the detailed overview of the identified literature. Table F.1 contains the identified publications for the literature review 1 described in Section 4.1. The results for the literature review 2 (cf. Section 4.2) is presented in Table F.2.

F.1   Agile Software Product Lines

Table F.1 contains the number of studies according to the publishing date.

Table F.1: Publications by year

Year	Automotive & Agile	Automotive & SPL	Related Research Area
2004			[170, 160]
2005			
2006			[199, 252, 151, 248]
2007			[118, 192]
2008	[258]		[177, 188, 251, 178, 81, 78, 211]
2009		[245]	[10, 80, 193, 17, 171]
2010			[77, 181, 79, 219]
2011	[157]		[18, 33, 44, 50, 90, 52, 207, 156, 11, 23]
2012		[114]	[43, 59, 136, 194, 230, 255, 172, 142]
2013		[60]	[8, 137, 115]
2014	[5, 140, 241, 242]	[46]	[61, 73, 84, 247, 180, 65, 6, 187]
2015	[93, 150]	[267]	[45]
2016	[221, 191, 107]	[40, 250]	
2017	[53, 98, 104, 108, 109]	[94, 195, 86]	
2018	[223]	[111, 112]	[146, 95]

F.2   Assessments for Agile Software Product Lines in the Automotive Domain

Table F.1 contains the number of studies for literature review 2 presented in Section 4.2). The findings are separated according to the publishing date and the direction of the search string (cf. Figure 4.2).

Table F.2: Publication overview, purpose and year

	Direction 1	Direction 2	Direction 3
2002 - 2004			
2005			[158]
2006			[269]
2007			[259]
2008	[176]		
2009			
2010	[243]		[134]
2011			[270]
2012			
2013		[197]	
2014			
2015	[92, 227]	[85]	
2016			
2017	[98, 76, 203]		
2018	[111]	[198]	

Appendix G

Publications

The contribution gained through this thesis are summarized as a monolithic work, however parts of the results have been published and shared with the scientific community based on the following contributions.

- [110] Philipp Hohl, Michael Stupperich, Jürgen Münch, Kurt Schneider: Die Variantenvielfalt agil managen: Agile Software-Produktlinien im Automobilsegment, *In Proc. of ESE'16*, 2016.

- [107] Philipp Hohl, Jürgen Münch, Kurt Schneider, Michael Stupperich: Forces that Prevent Agile Adoption in the Automotive Domain, *In Proc. of PROFES'16*, 2016.

- [109] Philipp Hohl, Jürgen Münch, Michael Stupperich: Forces that Support Agile Adoption in the Automotive Domain, *In GI Edition Proc. of Software Engineering'17*, 2017.

- [144] Jil Klünder, Philipp Hohl, Masud Fazal-Baqaie, Stephan Krusche, Steffen Küpper, Oliver Linssen, Christian R. Prause: HELENA Study: Reasons for Combining Agile and Traditional Software Development Approaches in German Companies, *In Proc. of PROFES'17*, 2017.

- [104] Philipp Hohl, Javad Ghofrani, Jürgen Münch, Michael Stupperich, Kurt Schneider: Searching for common ground - Existing literature on automotive agile software product lines, *In Proc. of ICSSP'17*, 2017.

- [147] Jil Klünder, Anna Schmitt, Philipp Hohl, Kurt Schneider: Fake News: Simply Agile, *In Gesellschaft für Informatik, Projektmanagement und Vorgehensmodelle*, 2017.

- [108] Philipp Hohl, Jürgen Münch, Kurt Schneider, Michael Stupperich: Real-Life Challenges on Agile Software Product Lines in Automotive. *In Proc. of PROFES'17*, 2017.

- [105] Philipp Hohl, Javad Ghofrani, Jürgen Münch, Michael Stupperich, Kurt Schneider: Searching for common ground: Existing literature on automotive agile software product lines, *In GI Edition Proc. of Software Engineering und Software Management'18*, 2018.

- [146] Jil Klünder, Philipp Hohl, Kurt Schneider: Becoming Agile while preserving software product lines - An Agile Transformation Model For Large Companies, *In Proc. of ICSSP'18,* 2018.

- [111] Philipp Hohl, Michael Stupperich, Jürgen Münch, Kurt Schneider: An Assessment Model to Foster the Adoption of Agile Software Product Lines in the Automotive Domain, *In Proc. of ICE/IEEE ITMC'18*, 2018.

- [112] Philipp Hohl, Michael Stupperich, Jürgen Münch, Kurt Schneider: Combining Agile Development and Software Product Lines in Automotive: Challenges and Recommendations, *In Proc. of ICE/IEEE ITMC'18*, 2018.

- [145] Jil Klünder, Philipp Hohl, Stephan Krusche, Pernille Lous, Masud Fazal-Baqaie, Steffen Küpper, Christian R. Prause, Towards a Better Understanding of the Motivation of German Organizations to Apply Certain Development Methods, *In Proc. of PROFES'18*, 2018.

- [113] Philipp Hohl, Sven Theobald, Martin Becker, Michael Stupperich, Jürgen Münch: Mapping Agility to Automotive Software Product Line Concerns, *In Proc. of PROFES'18*, 2018.

- [106] Philipp Hohl, Jil Klünder, Arie van Bennekum, Ryan Lockard, James Gifford, Jürgen Münch, Michael Stupperich, Kurt Schneider: Directions of the "Agile Manifesto" - Views of the Originators -. Journal of Software Engineering Research and Development, 2018.

CV

Personal details

Name	Philipp Nikolaus Hohl
Date of birth	28.03.1988
Place of birth	Ravensburg
Address	Graf-Sternberg-Straße 1, 88214 Ravensburg
Mail	Philipp-Hohl@hohltronics.de
Mobil	0176 / 84887214
Twitter	www.twitter.com/PhilippHohl
LinkedIn	www.linkedin.com/in/philipphohl
Xing	www.xing.com/profile/Philipp_Hohl
Skype	hohl-philipp

Social skills and key qualifications

Communicative skills with the ability to motivate and lead.
Intercultural sensitization and intercultural communication.
Teaching diverse communities

Education

03/2008 – 08/2011	University of Applied Sciences Ravensburg-Weingarten, Bachelor of Engineering, Electrical Engineering and Information Technology
08/2011 – 02/2013	University of Applied Sciences Ravensburg-Weingarten, Master of Engineering, Electrical Engineering

Work Experience

03/2010 – 05/2010	Intern, National Instruments, Munich
06/2010 – 08/2010	Intern, National Instruments, Madrid
03/2011 – 08/2011	Bachelor Thesis at SET GmbH, "Development and Test of a FlexRay Star-Coupler for Fly-by-Wire Applications", (Bachelor of Engineering)
11/2011 – 06/2012	Working student at SET GmbH – Smart embedded Technologies, Department Avionic
08/2012 – 08/2013	Master Thesis at National Instruments, "Channel Quality Information in LTE - Development and Implementation of Algorithms in NI LabVIEW to analyze the Quality of LTE MIMO systems", (Master of Engineering)
04/2013 – 10/2015	Test Engineer and Framework Developer for Test Automation at ifm syntron gmbh, Tettnang
11/2015 – 11/2018	PhD Student in cooperation with Daimler AG, Leibniz Universität Hannover and Hermann Hollerith Zentrum (Reutlingen University), "An Assessment Model to Foster the Adoption of Agile Software Product Lines in the Automotive Domain"
09/2013 –	Lecturer at Hochschule Ravensburg-Weingarten, "System Analysis and Simulation with LabVIEW"

Language and software skills

Language	German (first language), English (fluent), Spanish (basic knowledge), Latin (Latinum)
Software tools	LabVIEW (Certified LabVIEW Developer CLD), [NI Diadem, NI Teststand, MS Office] (Expert), [Pulsonix, Eagle, Jenkins] (Intermediate), [MATLAB, Vector CANape] (Basic)
Programming Languages	LabVIEW (Expert), [Windows Batch Scripting, C, HTML CSS] (Basic)